Contemporary Issues in Leadership

TO TOM

WITH BEST WISHES

Bob Taylor

JULY 94

Contemporary Issues in Leadership

THIRD EDITION

——— □ ———

edited by William E. Rosenbach and Robert L. Taylor

Foreword by Howard T. Prince II

Westview Press

BOULDER □ SAN FRANCISCO □ OXFORD

Copyright © 1993 by Westview Press, Inc.

Published in 1993 in the United States of America by Westview Press, Inc., 5500 Central Avenue, Boulder, Colorado 80301-2877, and in the United Kingdom by Westview Press, 36 Lonsdale Road, Summertown, Oxford OX2 7EW

Library of Congress Cataloging-in-Publication Data
Contemporary issues in leadership / edited by William E. Rosenbach and
Robert L. Taylor ; foreword by Howard T. Prince II—3rd ed.
    p.   cm.
    Includes bibliographical references.
    ISBN 0-8133-1754-1—ISBN 0-8133-1755-X (pbk.)
    1. Leadership.   I. Rosenbach, William E.   II. Taylor, Robert L.
(Robert Lewis), 1939–   .
HM141.C69   1993
303.3'4—dc20   93-1255
                                                                                    CIP

Printed and bound in the United States of America

The paper used in this publication meets the requirements
of the American National Standard for Permanence of Paper
for Printed Library Materials Z39.48-1984.

10   9   8   7   6   5   4   3   2   1

Contents

v

Foreword

Despite harsh criticism of the concept by many social scientists, interest in the study and practice of leadership seems higher than ever. For example, anyone who followed the American presidential campaign in 1992 heard the following words over and over again: vision, change, trust, character, leadership.

Notwithstanding the yearnings of many people for leadership by some strong personality (the great man or woman) in places such as the former Soviet Union as well as in the United States, the gift of freedom and the rise of democracy in so many formerly oppressed countries has called attention perhaps as never before to the need also to take followers into greater account and to think of leadership as more complex than just the role of the leader. President Clinton's often repeated statement during the campaign that "I can't do this alone" and the number of people who responded to Ross Perot's appeals to followers attest to the significance and power of people involved in leadership other than those identified as leaders.

Following the war in Vietnam, the U.S. Army reoriented its leadership theories and leader development systems to empower leaders and followers at all levels in ways that correspond to the realities of modern warfare, just as the Israeli Defense Forces had done since the founding of the modern state of Israel. Corporate leaders such as Jack Welch of General Electric also have recognized the need for patterns of leadership that activate followers in new ways in order to ensure economic competitiveness and the capacity for adaptive changes in response to a global business environment.

Forces such as the establishment of new democracies, the persistence of social injustice, and demands for self-development in the workplace are pressing leaders and leadership scholars to include followers as active participants in the leadership phenomenon. Some, such as Joseph Rost, have gone so far as to call for a "postindustrial" paradigm for leadership that is defined in terms of social change and reciprocal influence among group members such that leaders and followers become almost indistinguishable.

As people of color and women respond to greater opportunity to participate more fully in economic and political life, leaders must deal with increasingly complex and dynamic leadership situations. Some of the newer participants in leadership make strong demands to shape the ends of leadership; they call for social change and greater social and economic justice, for example. Others challenge how leadership is to be exercised by asserting not only greater rights to participate but even new leadership styles and claims of superiority for these new, more interactive styles.

Along with the growing awareness of how followers influence leaders comes the recognition of the need to find ways to think about and practice effective and responsible followership. Paradoxically, unless we recognize and accept our responsibilities as followers in the leadership process, we weaken leadership at the very moment in history when much wider participation in that process has suddenly become possible around the world. Here in America, we will need both effective followership and good leadership to tackle the complex social and economic problems at home even as we also attempt to influence events elsewhere as the lone superpower in the last decade of the century.

In this third edition of *Contemporary Issues in Leadership,* Bill Rosenbach and Bob Taylor have assembled a collection of articles that are rich in their potential for challenging old ways of thinking about leaders and followers. Of the twenty-one articles, only four have appeared in earlier editions and one has been revised from an earlier edition. Some of these pieces are approaching the status of classics and deserve to be included again. The newer selections include articles from popular as well as scholarly treatments of leadership in an effort to make some of the best and most provocative works available in this collection.

One of the potentially most useful articles appears for the first time in this book and adds to the literature on transforming or transformational leadership. In "A New Leadership Paradigm," Marshall Sashkin and Bill Rosenbach trace the development of this concept from James MacGregor Burns through Bernard Bass to their own work on this powerful form of human engagement. In doing so, they also remind us not to dismiss other forms of leadership, labeled transactional by Burns and others. In contrast to Sashkin and Rosenbach, Joseph Rost argues that we need to reconceptualize most of the old ideas and theories of leadership as ways of looking at good management, not leadership. Rost proposes a radical new definition for leadership that some will find stimulating, others inadequate. In one of the four articles carried over from the second edition, John Kotter also tackles the distinction between leaders and managers, as does Abraham Zaleznik in an article the editors had included in the first but not the second edition.

This is a book that will serve both the scholar and the curious reader well. Its four sections are organized around basic questions about leadership as well as contemporary considerations of changes that are shaping the study and practice of leadership. At a time when the number of articles and books is increasing at such a rate that even leadership specialists can hardly keep up, Bill Rosenbach and Bob Taylor have provided an invaluable service by keeping up with the burgeoning work and collecting some of the best for our consideration.

But don't expect to finish this book feeling satisfied that you now understand all about leadership. The best you can hope for is a sense of excitement about the changes in the field around the increasing importance of followers to both the study and the practice of leadership, along with new respect for the difficulty of adequately coming to grips with such a complex human endeavor. You're likely to have more questions than answers after exploring these pages. If that turns out to be the case, then the editors have done their job well.

Howard T. Prince II
Dean, Jepson School of Leadership Studies
University of Richmond

Preface

The study of leadership has continued to change in both content and method. The number of books, articles, and papers on the topic has increased in all of the associated disciplines. These often distinctly different fields of inquiry are providing a multidisciplinary and even, in a few instances, an interdisciplinary analysis of leadership, resulting in a broader and deeper understanding of the concept.

All over the world, the need to understand leadership has heightened. People are joining together to bring about changes, and the quality of their leadership will be critical to their progress toward achieving their shared goals. In today's world, followers are given a much more prominent role than they have traditionally experienced: Leadership is seen as a means to the empowerment of followers. To study leadership apart from the complex interactions leaders have with followers is to miss the most important aspect of leadership.

This edition represents a shift in our thinking that started with the initial volume. Whereas we first merely explored transformational leadership as an interesting new concept, we are now convinced that the research and literature confirms the transformational leadership paradigm as most meaningful in today's diverse and complex world.

Several chapters from the previous edition are repeated here. Three readings that appear in this edition are original pieces that have not been previously published. Some of the articles are time-honored classics, others quite current. We have attempted to present a blend of scholarly and nonacademic pieces that are well written and thought provoking.

There are four parts to the book. Part One explores the concept of leadership and how it differs from management. The chapters in this section examine the personal qualities of leaders and how leaders establish their credibility with followers. Followers and followership are the focus of Part Two, which looks at how followers make leadership possible and explores the implications of empowerment. In Part Three we recognize that diversity enhances rather than constrains leadership effectiveness but also presents unique challenges. Finally, Part Four concludes that shortcomings in our understanding of leadership, unique organizational challenges, and an uncertain future provide leaders with a special opportunity to redefine their role by cocreating and articulating a vision that empowers followers.

We have experienced a feeling of excitement and growth as a result of studying leadership from perspectives unfamiliar to us. We acknowledge that there are many legitimate ways to study leadership but firmly believe that real understanding comes from an interdisciplinary perspective. We have found it to be hard work, occasionally disappointing, but most often challenging and fun.

We are indebted to the authors and publishers of the readings included here as well as to our students, who over the years have asked questions about leadership that we could not adequately answer. This book could not have been completed without the assistance of one of those students, Amy Sozio. We are also grateful for the time and consideration of many of our colleagues who made suggestions for this third edition. Judy Hepler's assistance in preparing the manuscript is appreciated. Finally, the professionals at Westview Press, as always, provided empowering leadership when we needed it.

William E. Rosenbach
Robert L. Taylor

PART ONE

UNDERSTANDING LEADERSHIP

Although the study of leadership is emerging as a legitimate discipline in and of itself, one still finds little agreement on what leadership really is. James McGregor Burns's 1978 remark that leadership is one of the most observed and least understood phenomena on earth is still true. In 1984 he wrote that we know a lot about *leaders* but very little about *leadership,* and that also remains true today. There are almost as many definitions of leadership as there are people who have attempted to define it, so we hesitate to add yet another. However, we believe that if one is to understand leadership, one must understand its essential nature—that is, the process of leaders and followers engaging in reciprocal influence to achieve a shared purpose. Leadership is all about getting people to work together to make things happen that might not otherwise occur or prevent things from happening that ordinarily would take place.

A great deal of energy has been focused on the question of if and how leadership differs from management. There is no consensus on this issue. Management functions such as planning, organizing, and controlling cannot be separated from the influence process of leadership, but the question of whether a leader must also be a good manager (or vice versa) is beside the point. The real issue is whether a group of people can achieve a shared goal with the advice, assistance, and direction of another individual (or group). It means little whether they followed an established procedure or arrived at their destination without design. What makes the difference is that someone helped them create a vision, energized the group to use the available resources for action, and kept the vision alive so that progress could be made toward the desired goal.

The paradoxes of leadership are many. Individuals who possess all of the important characteristics and qualities don't necessarily become leaders, and if they do, their efforts often result in great harm and tragedy to others. Moreover, leaders and followers often find themselves using unethical means to achieve ethical ends and vice versa. The paradoxes of leadership are real and intense, making study of the subject all the more relevant.

Effective leaders come in all statures and from all cultures. Some leaders take charge; others nurture the group so that everyone accepts responsibility. We know leaders who are great orators; we also know those who are quiet and uninspiring with words but effectively lead by example. Some act decisively, others slowly and deliberately. The key is that effective leaders set the stage with their personalities and expectations and present a consistent image.

What leaders do is important, but *how* they do it is of equal concern. Therefore, much leadership research has focused on style. No single style or personality is best for all situations. The more ambiguous and complex the task, the greater the need to have broad participation—a collegial style. Relatively simple tasks can often be dealt with by a leader acting alone—an independent style. Style is related not only to task but also to timing. Participative styles are time consuming; the path to consensus decisions is often long and tedious. When decisions must be made quickly, the leader must act alone on available information and, very often, on intuition.

All successful leaders seem to have a global view. They must thoroughly understand not only the microcosm of the organization but also where the organization stands in the larger perspective. To create a vision of the future, leaders must understand the environment in which the organization exists today and in which it will exist tomorrow. Studying the classics can provide the foundation for such an understanding. Also, leaders serve a variety of people in organizations, and they need to relate to them culturally as well as professionally. Leaders who have studied the arts and humanities often develop a heightened sensitivity to values and feelings. It is not surprising, then, that we often see successful leadership as a passion, a wellspring of emotion—imagine the leader as producer-director, and the metaphor comes alive.

Leaders must synthesize many inputs to find the highest common denominator and determine what the group values. In a productive, successful organization, the leader helps group members to achieve their personal goals as they in turn strive to accomplish organizational goals. How the leader relates to all the members depends upon his or her understanding of human nature. If, as we believe, leadership is based upon confidence, self-knowledge, and introspection, then a thorough grounding in history, literature, the arts, language, and human behavior is appropriate training for leadership.

We believe that everyone has the potential to be a leader. Self-knowledge is a personal endeavor, and all have the opportunity to explore who they are and what they believe. It is not always easy to ask the hard questions: Who am I? What are my strengths and weaknesses? Where am I going? What are my values? These questions should not be asked unless one is ready to accept the answers and deal with them.

We evaluate leaders in terms of their personal effectiveness in achieving shared goals. In addition, leaders are continually involved in self-evaluation: To a leader, making a difference is important. The role that a leader chooses to play (or is expected to play) also relates to his or her effectiveness. The leader may be a communicator who represents the goals and values of the organization to all of its constituencies. Or the leader can choose to focus internally, acting as a buffer against outside influences. The leader can also elect to be a storyteller, primarily inspiring members to work toward a common objective. Many leaders lead by example, working the hardest and making sacrifices to create a positive environment in which all can contribute. Effective leaders know their strengths and weaknesses and act accordingly.

In this book, we will distinguish between two basic types of leadership. *Transactional* leaders recognize the rewards participants want from their work and try to see that they get them in exchange for effort. The leader clarifies the role the follower must play to attain desired outcomes, giving participants the confidence necessary to achieve the goals. At the same time, the leader recognizes what the followers need, clarifying how those needs can be fulfilled in exchange for satisfactory effort and performance.

Transformational leadership involves strong personal identification with the leader; group members join in a shared vision of the future, going beyond self-interest and the pursuit of personal rewards. The transformational leader motivates followers to perform beyond expectations by creating an awareness of the importance of designated outcomes, defining and inculcating shared values and beliefs among all members, influencing followers to transcend their own self-interest, and elevating participant motivations to the higher orders of self-esteem and self-actualization. Transformational leaders enable followers to develop a mental picture of the vision and transform purpose into action.

Leadership Perspectives

"Reflections on Leadership" by Thomas E. Cronin (Chapter 1) analyzes the issues associated with trying to define leadership. He questions whether we can teach leadership and raises several important points for discussion. First, Cronin suggests that we cannot understand leadership without understanding followership (a point we explore in depth in Part Two). Second, he contends that leaders may be dispersed throughout society and that we may be able to find them by looking in logical, practical ways. He concludes with a set of leadership qualities, bringing into perspective the questions raised by students of leadership.

In "What Leaders Really Do" (Chapter 2), John P. Kotter argues that leadership is different from management but not for the reasons most people think. Leadership isn't mystical and mysterious, nor is it necessarily better than management or a replacement for it. Rather, leadership and management are distinct and complementary systems of action: Management is about coping with complexity; leadership is about coping with change. Kotter maintains that most organizations are overmanaged and underled. However, he also warns that strong leadership with weak management is no better, and sometimes actually worse, than the reverse. The challenge for organizations is to combine strong leadership with strong management and use each to balance the other.

In Chapter 3 we present Abraham Zaleznik's classic 1977 *Harvard Business Review* article, "Managers and Leaders: Are They Different?" along with a 1992 "Retrospective Commentary." Zaleznik posits that a bureaucratic society that breeds managers may restrict the emergence of young leaders, who need mentors and emotional interaction to develop. According to Zaleznik, managers and leaders differ in personality, attitudes toward goals, conceptions of work, relationships with others, and sense of self. He concludes that if organizations work at it, they can develop leaders as well as managers.

James M. Kouzes and Barry Z. Posner note that successful leadership depends more on followers' perceptions of the leader than on the leader's own perception in "The Credibility Factor: What People Expect of Leaders" (Chapter 4). Honesty, competence, vision, and inspiration, they say, are four characteristics that determine a leader's credibility. The authors note that credibility is earned over time but always remains fragile. Five fundamental actions help build credibility: knowing one's followers, standing up for one's beliefs, speaking with passion, leading by example, and conquering oneself. Kouzes and Posner affirm that self-confidence comes from two sources: knowledge and integrity.

In "Power and Leadership in Organizations" (Chapter 5), Edwin P. Hollander and Lynn R. Offermann examine the growing interest among researchers in the role of followers. The historical development of this trend is examined, along with current applications aimed at greater follower involvement. The authors discuss problems and prospects of empowering followers, along with challenges to be met.

In Chapter 6, "A New Leadership Paradigm," Marshall Sashkin and William E. Rosenbach propose that there has been a "paradigm shift" in leadership theory and practice. They review the evolution of the concept of transformational leadership and examine three empirically derived models. They describe Bernard Bass's Transactional/Transformational Leadership Theory and his Multifactor Leadership Questionnaire, Kouzes and Posner's model of transformational leadership and their Leadership Practices Inventory, and Sashkin's Visionary Leadership Theory and his

Leader Behavior Questionnaire. They also discuss four apparent paradoxes of leadership that are really not paradoxes at all if viewed from the perspective of transformational leadership. The chapter concludes with a discussion of some of the criticism of the concept of transformational leadership.

1

Reflections on Leadership

THOMAS E. CRONIN

Introduction

Leadership is one of the most widely talked about subjects and at the same time one of the most elusive and puzzling. Americans often yearn for great, transcending leadership for their communities, companies, the military, unions, universities, sports teams, and for the nation. However, we have an almost love-hate ambivalence about power wielders. And we especially dislike anyone who tries to boss us around. Yes, we admire the Washingtons and Churchills, but Hitler and Al Capone were leaders too—and that points up a fundamental problem. Leadership can be exercised in the service of noble, liberating, enriching ends, but it can also serve to manipulate, mislead and repress.

"One of the most universal cravings of our time," writes James MacGregor Burns, "is a hunger for compelling and creative leadership." But exactly what is creative leadership? A *Wall Street Journal* cartoon had two men talking about leadership. Finally, one turned to the other in exasperation and said: "Yes, we need leadership, but we also need someone to tell us what to do." That is to say, leadership for most people most of the time is a rather hazy, distant and even confusing abstraction. Hence, thinking about or defining leadership is a kind of intellectual leadership challenge in itself.

What follows are some thoughts about leadership and education for leadership. These thoughts and ideas are highly personal and hardly scientific. As I shall suggest below, almost anything that can be said about leadership can be contradicted with counter examples. Moreover, the whole subject is riddled with paradoxes. My ideas here are the product of my studies of political leadership and my own participation in politics

Another version of this chapter appeared in *Presidential Studies Quarterly*, 14:1 (Winter 1984). Copyright © 1983 by Thomas E. Cronin. Printed by permission of author.

from the town meeting level to the White House staff. Some of my ideas come from helping to advise universities and foundations and the Houston-based American Leadership Forum on how best to go about encouraging leadership development. Finally, my thoughts have also been influenced in a variety of ways by numerous conversations with five especially insightful writers on leadership—Warren Bennis, James MacGregor Burns, David Campbell, Harlan Cleveland and John W. Gardner.

Teaching Leadership

Can we teach people to become leaders? Can we teach leadership? People are divided on these questions. It was once widely held that "leaders are born and not made," but that view is less widely held today. We also used to hear about "natural leaders" but nowadays most leaders have learned their leadership ability rather than inherited it. Still there is much mystery to the whole matter. In any event, many people think colleges and universities should steer clear of the whole subject. What follows is a set of reasons why our institutions of higher learning generally are "bashful about teaching leadership." These reasons may overstate the case, but they are the objections that serious people often raise.

First, many people still believe that leaders are born and not made. Or that leadership is somehow almost accidental or at least that most leaders emerge from circumstances and normally do not create them. In any event, it is usually added, most people, most of the time, are not now and never will be leaders.

Second, American cultural values hold that leadership is an elitist and thus anti-American phenomenon. Plato and Machiavelli and other grand theorists might urge upon their contemporaries the need for selecting out and training a select few for top leadership roles. But this runs against the American grain. We like to think that anyone can become a top leader here. Hence, no special training should be given to some special select few.

Third is the complaint that leadership training would more than likely be preoccupied with skills, techniques, and the *means* of getting things done. But leadership for what? A focus on *means* divorced from *ends* makes people—especially intellectuals—ill at ease. They hardly want to be in the business of training future Joe McCarthys or Hitlers or Idi Amins.

Fourth, leadership study strikes many as an explicitly vocational topic. It's a practical and applied matter—better learned in summer jobs, in internships or on the playing fields. You learn it on the job. You learn it from gaining experience, from making mistakes and learning from these. And you should learn it from mentors.

Fifth, leadership often involves an element of manipulation or devious-ness, if not outright ruthlessness. Some consider it as virtually the same as learning about jungle-fighting or acquiring "the killer instinct." It's just not "clean" enough a subject matter for many people to embrace. Plus, "leaders" like Stalin and Hitler gave "leadership" a bad name. If they were leaders, then spare us of their clones or imitators.

Sixth, leadership in the most robust sense of the term is such an ecu-menical and intellectually all-encompassing subject that it frightens not only the timid but even the most well educated of persons. To teach lead-ership is an act of arrogance. That is, it is to suggest one understands far more than even a well-educated person can understand—history, ethics, philosophy, classics, politics, biography, psychology, management, sociol-ogy, law, etc. ... and [is] steeped deeply as well in the "real world."

Seventh, colleges and universities are increasingly organized in highly specialized divisions and departments all geared to train specialists. While the mission of the college may be to educate "the educated person" and society's future leaders, in fact the incentive system is geared to train-ing specialists. Society today rewards the expert or the super specialist—the data processors, the pilots, the financial whiz, the heart surgeon, the special team punt returners, and so on. Leaders, however, have to learn to become generalists and usually have to do so well after they have left our colleges, graduate schools and professional schools.

Eighth, leadership strikes many people (and with some justification) as an elusive, hazy and almost mysterious commodity. Now you see it, now you don't. So much of leadership is intangible, you can't possibly define all the parts. A person may be an outstanding leader here, but fail there. Trait theory has been thoroughly debunked. In fact, leadership is highly situational and contextual. A special chemistry develops between leaders and followers and it is usually context specific. Followers often do more to determine the leadership they will get than can any teacher. Hence, why not teach people to be substantively bright and well-read and let things just take their natural course.

Ninth, virtually anything that can be said about leadership can be de-nied or disproven. Leadership studies, to the extent they exist, are unsci-entific. Countless paradoxes and contradictions litter every manuscript on leadership. Thus, we yearn for leadership, but yearn equally to be free and left alone. We admire risk-taking, entrepreneurial leadership, but we roundly criticize excessive risk-taking as bullheadedness or plain stupid. We want leaders who are highly self-confident and who are perhaps in-curably optimistic—yet we also dislike hubris and often yearn for at least a little self-doubt (e.g., Creon in *Antigone*). Leaders have to be almost singleminded in their drive and commitment but too much of that makes a person rigid, driven and unacceptable. We want leaders to be good listeners and represent their constituents, yet in the words of Walter Lippmann, effective leadership often consists of giving the people not what they want but what they will learn to want. How in the world, then, can you be rigorous and precise in teaching leadership?

Tenth, leadership at its best comes close to creativity. And how do you teach creativity? We are increasingly made aware of the fact that much of creative thinking calls upon unconscious thinking, dreaming and even fantasy. Some fascinating work is being done on intuition and the nonrational—but it is hardly a topic with which traditional disciplines in traditional colleges are comfortable.

Relationships

A few other initial observations need to be made about leadership. Chief among these is that the study of leadership needs inevitably to be linked or merged with the study of followership. We cannot really study leaders in isolation from followers, constituents or group members. The leader is very much a product of the group, and very much shaped by its aspirations, values and human resources. The more we learn about leadership, the more the leader-follower linkage is understood and reaffirmed. A leader has to resonate with followers. Part of being an effective leader is having excellent ideas, or a clear sense of direction, a sense of mission. But such ideas or vision are useless unless the would-be leader can communicate them and get them accepted by followers. A two-way engagement or two-way interaction is constantly going on. When it ceases, leaders become lost, out of touch, imperial or worse.

The question of leaders linked with followers raises the question of the transferability of leadership. Can an effective leader in one situation transfer this capacity, this skill, this style—to another setting? The record is mixed indeed. Certain persons have been effective in diverse settings. George Washington and Dwight Eisenhower come to mind. Jack Kemp and Bill Bradley, two well-known and respected members of Congress, were previously successful professional athletes. Scores of business leaders have been effective in the public sector and vice versa. Scores of military leaders have become effective in business or politics. Some in both. However, there are countless examples of those who have not met with success when they have tried to transfer their leadership abilities from one setting to a distinctively different setting. Sometimes this failure arises because the new group's goals or needs are so different from the previous organization. Sometimes it is because the leadership needs are different. Thus, the leadership needs of a military officer leading a platoon up a hill in battle may well be very different from the leadership requirements of someone asked to change sexist attitudes and practices in a large corporation or racist and ethnic hatred in an inner city. The leadership required of a candidate for office is often markedly different from that required of a campaign manager. Leadership required in founding a company may be exceedingly different from that required in the company's second generation.

Another confusing aspect about leadership is that leadership and management are often talked about as if they were the same. While it is true that an effective manager is often an effective leader and leadership requires, among other things, many of the skills of an effective manager, there are differences. Leaders are the people who infuse vision into an organization or a society. At their best, they are preoccupied with values and the longer range needs and aspirations of their followers. Managers are concerned with doing things *the right way.* Leaders are more concerned with identifying and then getting themselves and their organizations focused on *doing the right thing.* John Quincy Adams, Herbert Hoover and Jimmy Carter were often good, sometimes excellent, managers. Before coming to the White House, they were all recognized for being effective achievers. As businessmen, diplomats, governors or cabinet members, they excelled. As presidential leaders, they were found wanting. None was invited back for a second term. While none was considered an outright failure, each seemed to fail in providing the vision needed for the times. They were unable to lift the public's spirit and get the nation moving in new, more desirable directions.

As this brief digression suggests, being a leader is not the same thing as being holder of a high office. An effective leader is someone concerned with far more than the mechanics of office. While a good manager is concerned, and justifiably so, with efficiency, with keeping things going, with the routines and standard operating procedures, and with reaffirming ongoing systems, the creative leader acts as an inventor, risk taker and generalist entrepreneur—ever asking or searching for what is right, where are we headed, and keenly sensing new directions, new possibilities and welcoming change. We need all the talented managers we can get, but we also need creative leaders. Ironically, too, an effective leader is not very effective for long unless he or she can recruit managers to help make things work over the long run.

Characteristics

One of the most important things to be said about leadership is that it is commonly very dispersed throughout a society. Our leadership needs vary enormously. Many of the great breakthroughs occur because of people well in advance of their time who are willing to agitate for change and suggest fresh new approaches that are, as yet, unacceptable to majority opinion. Many of the leadership needs of a nation are met by persons who do not hold high office and who often don't look or even act as leaders. Which brings us to the question of defining leadership. Agreement on a definition is difficult to achieve. But for the purposes at hand, leaders are people who perceive what is needed and what is right and know how to mobilize people and resources to accomplish mutual goals.

Leaders are individuals who can help create options and opportunities—who can help clarify problems and choices, who can build morale and coalitions, who can inspire others and provide a vision of the possibilities and promise of a better organization, or a better community. Leaders have those indispensable qualities of contagious self-confidence, unwarranted optimism and incurable idealism that allow them to attract and mobilize others to undertake demanding tasks these people never dreamed they could undertake. In short, leaders empower and help liberate others. They enhance the possibilities for freedom—both for people and organizations. They engage with followers in such a way so that many of the followers become leaders in their own right.

As implied above, many of the significant breakthroughs in both the public and private sectors of this nation have been made by people who saw all the complexities ahead of them, but so believed in themselves and their purposes that they refused to be overwhelmed and paralyzed by doubts. They were willing to invent new rules and gamble on the future.

Good leaders, almost always, have been get-it-all-together, broken-field runners. They have been generalists. Tomorrow's leaders will very likely have begun life as trained specialists. Our society particularly rewards the specialist. John W. Gardner puts it well:

> All too often, on the long road up, young leaders become "servants of what is rather than shapers of what might be." In the long process of learning how the system works, they are rewarded for playing within the intricate structure of existing rules. By the time they reach the top, they are very likely to be trained prisoners of the structure. This is not all bad; every vital system re-affirms itself. But no system can stay vital for long unless some of its leaders remain sufficiently independent to help it to change and grow.

Only as creative generalists can these would-be leaders cope with the multiple highly organized groups—each fighting for special treatment, each armed with its own narrow definition of the public interest, often to the point of paralyzing *any* significant action.

Overcoming fears, especially fears of stepping beyond the boundaries of one's tribe, is a special need for the leader. A leader's task, as a renewer of organizational goals and aspirations, is to illuminate goals, to help reperceive one's own and one's organization's resources and strengths, to speak to people on what's only dimly in their minds. The effective creative leader is one who can give voice and form so that people say, "Ah, yes—that's what I too have been feeling."

Note too, however, that leaders are always aware of and at least partly shaped by the higher wants and aspirations and common purposes of their followers and constituents. Leaders consult and listen just as they educate and attempt to renew the goals of an organization. They know how "to squint with their ears." Civic leaders often emerge as we are able to agree upon goals. One analyst has suggested that it is no good for us to just go looking for leaders. We must first rediscover our own goals and values. If we are to have the leaders we need, we will first have to agree upon priorities. In one sense, if we wish to have leaders to follow, we will often have to show them the way.

In looking for leadership and in organizational affiliations—people are looking for *significance, competence, affirmation, and fairness.* To join an organization, an individual has to give up some aspect of his or her uniqueness, some part of his or her soul. Thus, there is a price in affiliating and in following. The leader serves as a strength and an attraction in the organization—but psychologically there is also a *repulsion* to the leader—in part because of the dependence on the leader. John Steinbeck said of American presidents that the people believe that "they were ours and we exercise the right to destroy them." Effective leaders must know how to absorb these hostilities, however latent they may be.

The leader also must be ever sensitive to the distinction between *power* and *authority.* Power is the strength or raw force to exercise control or coerce someone to do something, while authority is power that is *accepted* as legitimate by subordinates. The whole question of leadership raises countless issues about participation and the acceptance of power in superior-subordinate relationships. How much participation or involvement is needed, is desirable? What is the impact of participation on effectiveness? How best for the leader to earn moral and social acceptance for his or her authority? America generally prizes participation in all kinds of organizations, especially civic and political life. Yet, we must realize too that a part of us yearns for charismatic leadership. Ironically, savior figures and charismatic leaders often, indeed almost always, create distance and not participation.

One of the most difficult tasks for those who would measure and evaluate leadership is the task of trying to look at the elements that make up leadership. One way to look at these elements is to suggest that a leader has various *skills,* also has or exercises a distinctive *style* and, still more elusive, has various *qualities* that may be pronounced. By skill, I mean the capacity to do something well. Something that is learnable and can be improved, such as speaking or negotiating or planning. Most leaders need to have *technical skills* (such as writing well); *human relations skills,* the capacity to supervise, inspire, build coalitions and so on; and also what might be called *conceptual* skills—the capacity to play with ideas, shrewdly seek advice and forge grand strategy. Skills can be examined. Skills can be taught. And skills plainly make up an important part of leadership capability. Skills alone, however, cannot guarantee leadership success.

A person's leadership style may also be critical to effectiveness. Style refers to how a person relates to people, to tasks and to challenges. A person's style is usually a very personal and distinctive feature of his or her personality and character. A style may be democratic or autocratic, centralized or decentralized, empathetic or detached, extroverted or introverted, assertive or passive, engaged or remote. This hardly exhausts the diverse possibilities—but is meant to be suggestive. Different styles may work equally well in different situations. However, there is often a proper fit between the needs of an organization and the needed leadership style. A fair amount of research has been done in this area—but much more remains to be learned.

A person's *behavioral style* refers to one's way of relating to other people—to peers, subordinates, rivals, bosses, advisers, the press. A person's *psychological style* refers to one's way of handling stress, tensions, challenges to the ego, internal conflicts. Considerable work needs to be done in these areas—particularly if we are to learn how best to prepare people for shaping their leadership styles to diverse leadership situations and needs. But it is a challenge worth accepting.

James MacGregor Burns, in his book *Leadership,* offers us yet one additional distinction worth thinking about. Ultimately, Burns says, there are two overriding kinds of social and political leadership: *transactional* and *transformational leadership.* The transactional leader engages in an exchange, usually for self-interest and with short-term interests in mind. It is, in essence, a bargain situation: "I'll vote for your bill if you vote for mine." Or "You do me a favor and I will shortly return it." Most pragmatic officeholders practice transactional leadership most of the time. It is commonly a practical necessity. It is the general way people do business and get their jobs done—and stay in office. The transforming or transcending leader is the person who, as briefly noted earlier, so engages with followers as to bring them to a heightened political and social consciousness and activity, and in the process converts many of those followers into leaders in their own right. The transforming leader, with a focus on the higher aspirations and longer range, is also a teacher, mentor and educator—pointing out the possibilities and the hopes and the often only dimly understood dreams of a people—and getting them to undertake the preparation and the job needed to attain these goals.

Of course, not everyone can be a leader. And rarely can any one leader provide an organization's entire range of leadership needs. Upon closer inspection, most firms and most societies have all kinds of leaders and these diverse leaders, in turn, are usually highly dependent for their success on the leadership performed by other leaders. Some leaders are excellent at creating or inventing new structures. Others are great task leaders—helping to energize groups at problem solving. Others are excellent social (or affective) leaders, helping to build morale and renew the spirit of an organization or a people. These leaders are often indispensable in providing what might be called the human glue that holds groups together.

Further, the most lasting and pervasive leadership of all is often intangible and noninstitutional. It is the leadership fostered by ideas embodied in social, political or artistic movements, in books, in documents, in speeches, and in the memory of great lives greatly lived. Intellectual or idea leadership at its best is provided by those—often not in high political or corporate office—who can clarify values and the implications of such values for policy. The point here is that leadership is not only dispersed and diverse, but interdependent. Leaders need leaders as much as followers need leaders. This may sound confusing but it is part of the truth about the leadership puzzle.

Leadership Qualities

In the second half of this essay, I will raise, in a more general way, some of the qualities I believe are central to leadership. Everyone has his or her own list of leadership qualities. I will not be able to discuss all of mine, but permit me to offer my list and then describe a few of the more important ones in a bit more detail.

Leadership Qualities—A Tentative List
- Self-knowledge/self-confidence
- Vision, ability to infuse important, transcending values into an enterprise
- Intelligence, wisdom, judgment
- Learning/renewal
- Worldmindedness/a sense of history and breadth
- Coalition building/social architecture
- Morale building/motivation
- Stamina, energy, tenacity, courage, enthusiasm
- Character, integrity/intellectual honesty
- Risk-taking/entrepreneurship
- An ability to communicate, persuade/listen
- Understanding the nature of power and authority

- An ability to concentrate on achieving goals and results
- A sense of humor, perspective, flexibility

Leadership consists of a spiral upwards, a spiral of self-improvement, self-knowledge and seizing and creating opportunities so that a person can make things happen that would not otherwise have occurred. Just as there can be a spiral upwards, there can be a spiral downwards—characterized by failure, depression, self-defeat, self-doubt, and paralyzing fatalism.

If asked to point to key qualities of successful leadership, I would suggest [the following].

Leaders Are People Who Know Who They Are and Know Where They Are Going

"What a man thinks about himself," Thoreau wrote, "that is what determines, or rather indicates, his fate." One of the most paralyzing of mental illnesses is wrong perception of self. This leads to poor choosing and poor choosing leads to a fouled-up life. In one sense, the trouble with many people is not what they don't know, it is what they do know, but it is misinformed or misinformation.

Leaders must be self-reliant individuals with great tenacity and stamina. The world is moved by people who are enthusiastic. Optimism and high motivations count for a lot. They can lift organizations. Most people are forever waiting around for somebody to light a fire under them. They are people who have not learned the valuable lesson that ultimately you are the one who is responsible for you. You don't blame others. You don't blame circumstances. You simply take charge and help move the enterprise forward.

I am sure many of you have been puzzled, as I have been, about why so many talented friends of ours have leveled off earlier than needs to be the case. What is it that prevents people from becoming the best they could be? Often it is a lack of education, a physical handicap or a disease such as alcoholism. Very often, however, it is because people have not been able to gain control over their lives. Various things nibble away at their capacity for self-realization or what Abraham Maslow called self-actualization. Family problems, inadequate financial planning, and poor health or mental health problems are key factors that damage self-esteem. Plainly, it is difficult to handle life, not to mention leadership responsibilities, if people feel they do not control their own lives. This emotional feeling of helplessness inevitably leads people to believe they aren't capable, they can't do the job. It also inhibits risk-taking and just about all the qualities associated with creativity and leadership.

Picture a scale from, at one end, an attitude of "I don't control anything and I feel like the bird in a badminton game"—to the other end of the scale where there is an attitude of "I'm in charge." Either extreme may be pathological, but plainly the higher up, relatively, toward the "I'm in charge" end of the scale, the more one is able to handle the challenges of transforming or creative leadership.

Thus, the single biggest factor is motivating or liberating would-be leaders in their attitude toward themselves and toward their responsibilities to others.

Leaders also have to understand the situations they find themselves in. As observed in *Alice in Wonderland*, before we decide where we are going, we first have to decide where we are right now. After this comes commitment to something larger and longer term than just our own egos. People can achieve meaning in their lives only when they can give as well as take from their society. Failure to set priorities and develop significant personal purposes undermines nearly any capacity for leadership. "When a man does not know what harbor he is making for, no wind is the right wind."

Leaders Set Priorities and Mobilize Energies

Too many people become overwhelmed with trivia, with constant close encounters of a third rate. Leaders have always to focus on the major problems of the day, and on the higher aspirations and needs of their followers. Leadership divorced from important transcending purpose becomes manipulation, deception and, in the extreme, is not leadership at all, but repression and tyranny.

The effective modern leader has to be able to live in an age of uncertainty. Priorities have to be set and decisions have to be made even though all the information is not in—this will surely be even more true in the future than it has been in the past. The information revolution has tremendously enlarged both the opportunities and the frustrations for leaders. Knowing what you don't know becomes as important as knowing what you do know. A willingness to experiment and explore possible strategies even in the face of uncertainty may become a more pronounced characteristic of the creative leader.

The creative priority setter learns both to encourage and to question his or her intuitive tendencies. Oliver Wendell Holmes, Jr., said that "to have doubted one's own first principles is the mark of a civilized man" and so it continues to be. The ability to look at things differently, and reach out for more and better advice, is crucial. The ability to admit error and learn from mistakes is also vitally important.

Leaders need to have considerable self-confidence, but they also must have a dose of self-doubt. Leaders must learn how to communicate the need for advice and help, how to become creative listeners, how to empathize, and understand. In Sophocles' compelling play, *Antigone*, the tragic hero, King Creon, hears his son's advice but imprudently rejects it or perhaps does not even hear it. But it, Haemon's, is advice any leader should take into account:

> Let not your first thought be your only thought. Think if there cannot be some other way. Surely, to think your own the only wisdom, and yours the only word, the only will, betrays a shallow spirit, an empty heart. It is no weakness for the wisest man to learn when he is wrong, know when to yield. ...
>
> So, father, pause and put aside your anger. I think, for what my young opinion's worth, that good as it is to have infallible wisdom, since this is rarely found, the next best thing is to be willing to listen to wise advice.

Leaders need to be able to discover their own strengths and the strengths of those with whom they work. They have to learn how to share and to delegate. They have to be able to make people believe they are important, that they are or can be winners. People yearn to think that what they are doing is something useful, something important. The transforming or creative leader knows how to nourish conviction and morale within an organization.

Good leaders know how to serve as morale-builders and renewers of purpose, able to get people to rededicate themselves to long-cherished but sometimes dimly understood values. Motivation is sometimes as much as 40 to 50 percent of the leadership enterprise. You can do very little alone with just faith and determination, yet you can do next to nothing without them. Organizations of all kinds need constantly to rediscover or renew their faith, direction, and sense of purpose.

Leaders Have to Provide the Risk-Taking, Entrepreneurial
Imagination for Their Organizations and Communities

Leaders are able to see things in a different and fresh context. Warren Bennis suggests that creative leadership requires the capacity to recontextualize a situation. Willis Harmon suggests a leader is one who reperceives situations and challenges and comes up with new approaches, insights and solutions.

A third-grade class begins and the teacher says: "Class, take out your pencils and paper and draw a picture of anything you can think of." Students begin to draw balls, trees, automobiles, and so forth. Teacher asks Sally, in the second row: "What are you drawing?" Sally says, "I'm drawing a picture of God." Teacher says: "But no one has ever seen God; we don't know what he looks like." An undaunted Sally responds: "Well, they sure will when I get through!"

This little story illustrates the sometimes irrational self-confidence and "failure is impossible" factor that motivates the galvanizing leader. The founding revolutionaries in America, Susan Anthony, Martin Luther King, Jr., Saul Alinsky and countless others had the vision of a better and newer society and they, in effect, said, "They'll know a better or more just society when we get through."

Mark Twain once said, "a man is viewed as a crackpot until his idea succeeds." We need a hospitable environment for the dissenter and the creative individual. We need to avoid killing the spark of individuality that allows creativity to flourish. We kill it with rules, red tape, procedures, standard operating restrictions and countless admonitions "not to rock the boat."

Creativity is the ability to recombine things. To see a radio here and a clock there and put them together. Hence, the clockradio. Open-mindedness is crucial. Too many organizations are organized with structures to solve problems that no longer exist. Vested interest grows up in every human institution. People all too often become prisoners of their procedures.

Psychologist David Campbell points out that history records a long list of innovations that come from outside the "expert" organization. (See also John Jewkes, *The Sources of Invention.*) The automobile was not invented by the transportation experts of that era, the railroaders. The airplane was not invented by automobile experts. Polaroid film was not invented by Kodak. Handheld pocket calculators were not invented by IBM, digital watches were not invented by watchmakers. Apple computers and herbal tea are yet two more examples. The list is endless and the moral is vivid.

Leaders get organizations interested in what they are going to become, not what they have been. Creative leadership requires also not being afraid to fail. An essential aspect of creative leadership is curiosity. The best way to have inventive ideas is to have lots of ideas, and to have an organization that welcomes fresh ideas—whatever their merit. As any scientist knows, the art of research requires countless experimentation and failure before you get the results you want, or sometimes the unexpected result that constitutes the true breakthrough.

Leaders recognize the utility of dreaming, fantasy and unconscious thinking. One advocate of creative thinking writes,

> Production of dramatically new ideas by a process of purely conscious calculation rarely seems to occur. Unconscious thinking, thinking which you are unaware of, is a major contribution to the production of new ideas. ...

Leaders Need to Have a Sense of Humor and a Sense of Proportion

Leaders take their work seriously, but do not take themselves too seriously. Humor relieves strain and enables people to relax and see things in a slightly different or fresh light. Effective leaders usually can tell a joke, take a joke, and tell a good story. They also usually know the art of telling parables. Lincoln, FDR and JFK come quickly to mind, while Hoover, Nixon and Carter were humorless men. Adlai Stevenson put it this way: "If I couldn't laugh, I couldn't live—especially in politics."

In this same light, leaders need to be able to share the credit. Leadership sometimes consists of emphasizing the dignity of others and of keeping one's own sense of importance from becoming inflated. Dwight Eisenhower had a slogan he tried to live by which went as follows: "There's no telling how much one can accomplish so long as one doesn't need to get all the credit for it."

Thus, leaders need to have a sense of proportion and a sense of detachment. They must avoid being workaholics and recognize that they will have to be followers in most of the enterprises of life and leaders only a small fraction of the time. Emerson put it well when he tried to answer the question, "What is Success?"

> To laugh often and love much, to win the respect of intelligent persons and the affection of children; to appreciate beauty; to find the best in others; to give one's self; to leave the world a lot better whether by a healthy child, a garden patch, or a redeemed social condition; to have played and laughed with enthusiasm and sung with exaltation, to know even one life has breathed easier because you have lived—that is to have succeeded.

Humor, proportion and also *compassion*. A person able to understand emotions and passion and at least on occasion to express one's self with passion and conviction. Enthusiasm, hope, vitality and energy are crucial to radiating confidence.

Leaders Have to Be Skilled Mediators and Negotiators, But They Also Have to Be Able to Stir Things Up and Encourage Healthy and Desired Conflict

An old Peanuts cartoon has a dejected Charlie Brown coming off a softball field as the game concludes. In exasperation he whines, "How can we lose when we are so sincere?" Sincerity and purity of heart are not enough to succeed in challenging leadership jobs.

The strength of leaders often lies in their tenacity, in knowing how to deal with competing factions, knowing when to compromise, when to amplify conflict, and when to move an organization or a community away from paralyzing divisiveness and toward a vision of the common good.

Most citizens avoid conflict and find conflicts of any kind painful. The truly effective leader welcomes several kinds of conflict and views conflict as an opportunity for change or revitalization.

Stirring things up is often a prerequisite for social and economic break-through. Women's rights, black rights, consumer protection, tax reform movements and even our election campaigns are occasions for division and conflict. They are a reality the leader has to learn to accept, under-stand and turn to his advantage. Harry Truman said:

> A President who's any damn good at all makes enemies, makes a lot of ene-mies. I even made a few myself when I was in the White House, and I wouldn't be without them.

George Bernard Shaw and others have put it only slightly differently. Rea-sonable people, they observe, adjust themselves to reality and cope with what they find. Unreasonable people dream dreams of a different, a bet-ter, world and try to adapt the world to themselves. This discontent or un-reasonableness is often the first step in the progress of a person as well as for a community or nation.

But be aware that "stirrer uppers" and conflict-amplifiers are often threatening in any organization or society. In the kingdom of the blind, the one-eyed man is king. This may well be, as the proverb has it. But in the kingdom of the one-eyed person, the two-eyed person is looked upon with considerable suspicion and may even be considered downright dan-gerous.

Thus, it takes courage and guts as well as imagination and stamina to be the two-eyed person in a one-eyed world. Harlan Cleveland points out that just about every leader has had the experience of being in an office surrounded by experts. The sum of the meeting will be, "Let's do nothing cautiously." The leader is the one who has to say, "Let's take the first step." He or she is the functional equivalent of the first bird off the tele-phone wire, or what Texans call the "bell cow." The experts always have an excuse. They are like the losing tennis player whose motto is: "It's not whether you win or lose, it's how you place the blame."

An Effective Leader Must Have Integrity

This has been suggested earlier in several implicit ways, but it is perhaps the most central of leadership qualities. A leader must be able to see peo-ple in all of their relationships, in the wholeness of their lives and not just as a means to getting a job done, as a means for enhanced productivity.

Some may call it character, others would call it authenticity, compas-sion or empathy. Whatever we call it, character and integrity are much easier kept than recovered. People can see through a phony. People can readily tell whether a person has respect for others. Respect and responsi-bility generally migrate to those who are fair, compassionate and care about values, beliefs and feelings of others. People who cannot rise above their prejudices usually fail. People who permit a shell to be built up around their heart will not long be able to exercise creative leadership. Michael Maccoby captures this concern.

> The exercise of the heart is that of experiencing, thinking critically, willing, and acting, so as to overcome egocentrism and to share passion with other people ... and to respond to their needs with the help one can give. ... It requires discipline, learning to concentrate, to think critically, and to communicate. The goal, a developed heart, implies integrity, a spiritual center, a sense of "I" not motivated by greed or fear, but by love of life, adventure and fellow feelings.

A leader's integrity requires also that he or she not be captured by peer pressures, protocol, mindless traditions or conventional rules. The truly effective leader is able to see above and beyond normal constraints and discern proper and desirable ends. The leader also possesses a sense of history and a concern for posterity. This ability, an exceptional capacity to disregard external pressures, is the ability that separates leaders from followers.

The Leader Has to Have Brains and Breadth

In the future, even more so than in the past, only the really bright individuals will be leaders.

Harlan Cleveland highlights this quality well when he writes:

> It used to be that a leader was a two-fisted businessman who chopped up the jobs that needed to be done, then left everyone alone and roared at them if they didn't work right. ...
> Loud commands worked if one person knew all things, but because of the way we [now] make decisions, through committees, a person charging around with a loud voice is just in the way.

Today's leaders must widen their perspectives and lengthen the focal point of their thinking. Leaders today have to learn how to thread or weave together disparate parts and move beyond analytical to integrative thinking. This will require well-read, well-traveled persons who can rise above their specialties and their professions. It will require as well persons who are not afraid of politics, but who rather view the art of politics as the art of bringing about the difficult and the desirable.

American Leadership

The creative political leader must work in a tension-filled world between unity and dissent, majority rule and minority rights and countless other contradictions. Tocqueville said of us, "These Americans yearn for leadership, but they also want to be left alone and free." The political leader is always trying to reconcile this and other paradoxes—but the important point is to be able to live with the paradoxes and dilemmas. And beyond this, the political leader must also be able to create, and preserve, a sense of community and shared heritage, the civic bond that ties us—disparate and feisty, rugged individualists—together.

Effective leaders of today and tomorrow also know how to vary their styles of leadership depending on the maturity of their subordinates. They involve their peers and their subordinates in their responsibility networks. They must be good educators and good communicators. They also have to have that spark of emotion or passion that can excite others to join them in the enterprise.

Most effective leaders will also be effective communicators: good writers, good speakers and good conversationalists. A few noted scientists may get by with mumbling, but they are the exception. For so much of leadership consists nowadays in persuading and informing that someone who cannot communicate well, cannot succeed. To paraphrase George Orwell, "If people cannot communicate well, they cannot think well, and if they cannot think well, others will do their thinking for them."

America is especially good at training experts, specialists and managers. We have plenty of these specialist leaders, but they are almost always one-segment leaders. We are in special need of educating multi-segment leaders. Persons who have a global perspective and understand that the once tidy lines between domestic and international, and public and private, are irretrievably blurred. Indispensable to a leader is a sense of breadth, the intellectual capacity to handle complex mental tasks, to see relationships between apparently unrelated objects, to see patterns in incomplete information, to draw accurate conclusions from inchoate data.

Vision is the ability to see all sides of an issue and to eliminate biases. Vision and breadth of knowledge put one in a strategic position—preventing the leader from falling into the traps that short-sightedness, mindless parochialism often set for people.

None of these qualities can guarantee creative leadership, but they can, when encouraged, provide a greater likelihood of it. We need all the leadership we can get—in and out of government. The vitality of nongovernmental America lies in our ability to educate and nourish more citizen-leaders. Those of us who expect to reap the blessings of freedom and liberty must undergo the fatigues of supporting them and provide the leadership to sustain them.

Learning About Leadership

Permit me to return again to the question of whether leadership can be learned, and possibly taught. My own belief is that students cannot usually be taught to be leaders. But students, and anyone else for that matter, can profitably be exposed to leadership, discussions of leadership skills and styles, and leadership strategies and theories. Individuals can learn in their own minds the strengths as well as limitations of leadership. People can learn about the paradoxes and contradictions and ironies of leadership, which, however puzzling, are central to appreciating the diversity and the dilemmas of problem-solving and getting organizations and nations to function.

Learning about leadership means recognizing bad leadership as well as good. Learning about leadership means understanding the critical linkage of ends and means. Learning about leadership also involves the study of the special chemistry that develops between leaders and followers, not only the chemistry that existed between Americans and Lincoln, but also between Mao and the Chinese peasants, between Lenin and the Bolsheviks, between Martin Luther King, Jr., and civil rights activists, between Jean Monnet and those who dreamed of a European Economic Community.

Students can learn to discern and define situations and contexts within which leadership has flourished. Students can learn about the fallibility of the trait theory. Students can learn about the contextual problems of leadership, of why and when leadership is sometimes transferable, and sometimes not. Students can learn about the crucial role that advisors and supporters play in the leadership equation. Students can also learn about countless problem-solving strategies and theories, and participate in role playing exercises that sharpen their own skills in such undertakings.

Students of leadership can learn widely from reading biographies about both the best and the worst leaders. Plutarch's *Lives* would be a good place to start. Much can be learned from mentors and from intern-participant observing. Much can also be learned about leadership by getting away from one's own culture and examining how leaders in other circumstances go about the task of motivating and mobilizing others. Countless learning opportunities exist that can sharpen a student's skills as a speaker, debater, negotiator, problem clarifier and planner. Such skills should not be minimized. Nor should anyone underestimate the importance of history, economics, logic, and a series of related substantive fields that help provide the breadth and the perspective indispensable to societal leadership.

Above all, students of leadership can make an appointment with themselves and begin to appreciate their own strengths and deficiencies. Personal mastery is important. So too the ability to use one's intuition, and to enrich one's creative impulses. John Gardner suggests, "It's what you learn after you know it all that really counts." Would-be leaders learn to manage their time more wisely. Would-be leaders learn that self-pity and resentment are like toxic substances. Would-be leaders learn the old truth that most people are not for or against you but rather preoccupied with themselves. Would-be leaders learn to break out of their comfortable imprisonments; they learn to cast aside dull routines and habits that enslave most of us. Would-be leaders learn how to become truly sharing and caring people—in their families, in their professions and in their communities. And would-be leaders constantly learn too that they have more to give than they have ever given, no matter how much they have given.

Let me conclude by paraphrasing from John Adams:

We must study politics [and leadership] and war [and peace] that our sons [and daughters] have the liberty to study mathematics and philosophy, geography, natural history and naval architecture, navigation, commerce, and agriculture, in order to give their children the right to study painting, poetry, music, architecture, statuary, tapestry, and porcelain.

2

What Leaders Really Do

JOHN P. KOTTER

Leadership is different from management, but not for the reasons most people think. Leadership isn't mystical and mysterious. It has nothing to do with having "charisma" or other exotic personality traits. It is not the province of a chosen few. Nor is leadership necessarily better than management or a replacement for it.

Rather, leadership and management are two distinctive and complementary systems of action. Each has its own function and characteristic activities. Both are necessary for success in an increasingly complex and volatile business environment.

Most U.S. corporations today are overmanaged and underled. They need to develop their capacity to exercise leadership. Successful corporations don't wait for leaders to come along. They actively seek out people with leadership potential and expose them to career experiences designed to develop that potential. Indeed, with careful selection, nurturing, and encouragement, dozens of people can play important leadership roles in a business organization.

But while improving their ability to lead, companies should remember that strong leadership with weak management is no better, and is sometimes actually worse, than the reverse. The real challenge is to combine strong leadership and strong management and use each to balance the other.

Of course, not everyone can be good at both leading and managing. Some people have the capacity to become excellent managers but not strong leaders. Others have great leadership potential but, for a variety of reasons, have great difficulty becoming strong managers. Smart companies value both kinds of people and work hard to make them a part of the team.

But when it comes to preparing people for executive jobs, such companies rightly ignore the recent literature that says people cannot manage *and* lead. They try to develop leader-managers. Once companies understand the fundamental difference between leadership and management, they can begin to groom their top people to provide both.

The Difference Between
Management and Leadership

Management is about coping with complexity. Its practices and procedures are largely a response to one of the most significant developments of the twentieth century: the emergence of large organizations. Without good management, complex enterprises tend to become chaotic in ways that threaten their very existence. Good management brings a degree of order and consistency to key dimensions like the quality and profitability of products.

Leadership, by contrast, is about coping with change. Part of the reason it has become so important in recent years is that the business world has become more competitive and more volatile. Faster technological change, greater international competition, the deregulation of markets, overcapacity in capital-intensive industries, an unstable oil cartel, raiders with junk bonds, and the changing demographics of the work force are among the many factors that have contributed to this shift. The net result is that doing what was done yesterday, or doing it 5% better, is no longer a formula for success. Major changes are more and more necessary to survive and compete effectively in this new environment. More change always demands more leadership.

Consider a simple military analogy: a peacetime army can usually survive with good administration and management up and down the hierarchy, coupled with good leadership concentrated at the very top. A wartime army, however, needs competent leadership at all levels. No one yet has figured out how to manage people effectively into battle; they must be *led*.

These different functions—coping with complexity and coping with change—shape the characteristic activities of management and leadership. Each system of action involves deciding what needs to be done, creating networks of people and relationships that can accomplish an agenda, and then trying to ensure that those people actually do the job. But each accomplishes these three tasks in different ways.

Companies manage complexity first by *planning and budgeting*—setting targets or goals for the future (typically for the next month or year), estab-

lishing detailed steps for achieving those targets, and then allocating resources to accomplish those plans. By contrast, leading an organization to
constructive change begins by *setting a direction*—developing a vision of
the future (often the distant future) along with strategies for producing
the changes needed to achieve that vision.

Management develops the capacity to achieve its plan by *organizing and
staffing*—creating an organizational structure and set of jobs for accomplishing plan requirements, staffing the jobs with qualified individuals,
communicating the plan to those people, delegating responsibility for carrying out the plan, and devising systems to monitor implementation. The
equivalent leadership activity, however, is *aligning people.* This means
communicating the new direction to those who can create coalitions that
understand the vision and are committed to its achievement.

Finally, management ensures plan accomplishment by *controlling and
problem solving*—monitoring results versus the plan in some detail, both
formally and informally, by means of reports, meetings, and other tools;
identifying deviations; and then planning and organizing to solve the
problems. But for leadership, achieving a vision requires *motivating and inspiring*—keeping people moving in the right direction, despite major obstacles to change, by appealing to basic but often untapped human needs,
values, and emotions.

A closer examination of each of these activities will help clarify the
skills leaders need.

Setting a Direction vs.
Planning and Budgeting

Since the function of leadership is to produce change, setting the direction
of that change is fundamental to leadership.

Setting direction is never the same as planning or even long-term planning, although people often confuse the two. Planning is a management
process, deductive in nature and designed to produce orderly results, not
change. Setting a direction is more inductive. Leaders gather a broad
range of data and look for patterns, relationships, and linkages that help
explain things. What's more, the direction-setting aspect of leadership
does not produce plans; it creates vision and strategies. These describe a
business, technology, or corporate culture in terms of what it should become over the long term and articulate a feasible way of achieving this
goal.

Most discussions of vision have a tendency to degenerate into the mystical. The implication is that a vision is something mysterious that mere
mortals, even talented ones, could never hope to have. But developing
good business direction isn't magic. It is a tough, sometimes exhausting

process of gathering and analyzing information. People who articulate such visions aren't magicians but broad-based strategic thinkers who are willing to take risks.

Nor do visions and strategies have to be brilliantly innovative; in fact, some of the best are not. Effective business visions regularly have an almost mundane quality, usually consisting of ideas that are already well known. The particular combination or patterning of the ideas may be new, but sometimes even that is not the case.

For example, when CEO Jan Carlzon articulated his vision to make Scandinavian Airline Systems (SAS) the best airline in the world for the frequent business traveler, he was not saying anything that everyone in the airline industry didn't already know. Business travelers fly more consistently than other market segments and are generally willing to pay higher fares. Thus, focusing on business customers offers an airline the possibility of high margins, steady business, and considerable growth. But in an industry known more for bureaucracy than vision, no company had ever put these simple ideas together and dedicated itself to implementing them. SAS did, and it worked.

What's crucial about a vision is not its originality but how well it serves the interests of important constituencies—customers, stockholders, employees—and how easily it can be translated into a realistic competitive strategy. Bad visions tend to ignore the legitimate needs and rights of important constituencies—favoring, say, employees over customers or stockholders. Or they are strategically unsound. When a company that has never been better than a weak competitor in an industry suddenly starts talking about becoming number one, that is a pipe dream, not a vision.

One of the most frequent mistakes that overmanaged and underled corporations make is to embrace "long-term planning" as a panacea for their lack of direction and inability to adapt to an increasingly competitive and dynamic business environment. But such an approach misinterprets the nature of direction setting and can never work.

Long-term planning is always time consuming. Whenever something unexpected happens, plans have to be redone. In a dynamic business environment, the unexpected often becomes the norm, and long-term planning can become an extraordinarily burdensome activity. This is why most successful corporations limit the time frame of their planning activities. Indeed, some even consider "long-term planning" a contradiction in terms.

In a company without direction, even short-term planning can become a black hole capable of absorbing an infinite amount of time and energy. With no vision and strategy to provide constraints around the planning process or to guide it, every eventuality deserves a plan. Under these circumstances, contingency planning can go on forever, draining time and attention from far more essential activities, yet without ever providing the clear sense of direction that a company desperately needs. After awhile, managers inevitably become cynical about all this, and the planning process can degenerate into a highly politicized game.

Planning works best not as a substitute for direction setting but as a complement to it. A competent planning process serves as a useful reality check on direction-setting activities. Likewise, a competent direction-setting process provides a focus in which planning can then be realistically carried out. It helps clarify what kind of planning is essential and what kind is irrelevant.

Aligning People vs. Organizing and Staffing

A central feature of modern organizations is interdependence, where no one has complete autonomy, where most employees are tied to many others by their work, technology, management systems, and hierarchy. These linkages present a special challenge when organizations attempt to change. Unless many individuals line up and move together in the same direction, people will tend to fall all over one another. To executives who are overeducated in management and undereducated in leadership, the idea of getting people moving in the same direction appears to be an organizational problem. What executives need to do, however, is not organize people but align them.

Managers "organize" to create human systems that can implement plans as precisely and efficiently as possible. Typically, this requires a number of potentially complex decisions. A company must choose a structure of jobs and reporting relationships, staff it with individuals suited to the jobs, provide training for those who need it, communicate plans to the work force, and decide how much authority to delegate and to whom. Economic incentives also need to be constructed to accomplish the plan, as well as systems to monitor its implementation. These organizational judgments are much like architectural decisions. It's a question of fit within a particular context.

Aligning is different. It is more of a communications challenge than a design problem. First, aligning invariably involves talking to many more individuals than organizing does. The target population can involve not only a manager's subordinates but also bosses, peers, staff in other parts of the organization, as well as suppliers, governmental officials, or even customers. Anyone who can help implement the vision and strategies or who can block implementation is relevant.

Trying to get people to comprehend a vision of an alternative future is also a communications challenge of a completely different magnitude from organizing them to fulfill a short-term plan. It's much like the difference between a football quarterback attempting to describe to his team the next two or three plays versus his trying to explain to them a totally new approach to the game to be used in the second half of the season.

Whether delivered with many words or a few carefully chosen symbols, such messages are not necessarily accepted just because they are understood. Another big challenge in leadership efforts is credibility—getting people to believe the message. Many things contribute to credibility: the track record of the person delivering the message, the content of the message itself, the communicator's reputation for integrity and trustworthiness, and the consistency between words and deeds.

Finally, aligning leads to empowerment in a way that organizing rarely does. One of the reasons some organizations have difficulty adjusting to rapid changes in markets or technology is that so many people in those companies feel relatively powerless. They have learned from experience that even if they correctly perceive important external changes and then initiate appropriate actions, they are vulnerable to someone higher up who does not like what they have done. Reprimands can take many different forms: "That's against policy" or "We can't afford it" or "Shut up and do as you're told."

Alignment helps overcome this problem by empowering people in at least two ways. First, when a clear sense of direction has been communicated throughout an organization, lower-level employees can initiate actions without the same degree of vulnerability. As long as their behavior is consistent with the vision, superiors will have more difficulty reprimanding them. Second, because everyone is aiming at the same target, the probability is less that one person's initiative will be stalled when it comes into conflict with someone else's.

Motivating People vs. Controlling and Problem Solving

Since change is the function of leadership, being able to generate highly energized behavior is important for coping with the inevitable barriers to change. Just as direction setting identifies an appropriate path for movement and just as effective alignment gets people moving down that path, successful motivation ensures that they will have the energy to overcome obstacles.

According to the logic of management, control mechanisms compare system behavior with the plan and take action when a deviation is detected. In a well-managed factory, for example, this means the planning process establishes sensible quality targets, the organizing process builds an organization that can achieve those targets, and a control process makes sure that quality lapses are spotted immediately, not in 30 or 60 days, and corrected.

For some of the same reasons that control is so central to management, highly motivated or inspired behavior is almost irrelevant. Managerial processes must be as close as possible to fail-safe and risk-free. That means they cannot be dependent on the unusual or hard to obtain. The whole purpose of systems and structures is to help normal people who behave in normal ways to complete routine jobs successfully, day after day. It's not exciting or glamorous. But that's management.

Leadership is different. Achieving grand visions always requires an occasional burst of energy. Motivation and inspiration energize people, not by pushing them in the right direction as control mechanisms do but by satisfying basic human needs for achievement, a sense of belonging, recognition, self-esteem, a feeling of control over one's life, and the ability to live up to one's ideals. Such feelings touch us deeply and elicit a powerful response.

Good leaders motivate people in a variety of ways. First, they always articulate the organization's vision in a manner that stresses the values of the audience they are addressing. This makes the work important to those individuals. Leaders also regularly involve people in deciding how to achieve the organization's vision (or the part most relevant to a particular individual). This gives people a sense of control. Another important motivational technique is to support employee efforts to realize the vision by providing coaching, feedback, and role modeling, thereby helping people grow professionally and enhancing their self-esteem. Finally, good leaders recognize and reward success, which not only gives people a sense of accomplishment but also makes them feel like they belong to an organization that cares about them. When all this is done, the work itself becomes intrinsically motivating.

The more that change characterizes the business environment, the more that leaders must motivate people to provide leadership as well. When this works, it tends to reproduce leadership across the entire organization, with people occupying multiple leadership roles throughout the hierarchy. This is highly valuable, because coping with change in any complex business demands initiatives from a multitude of people. Nothing less will work.

Of course, leadership from many sources does not necessarily converge. To the contrary, it can easily conflict. For multiple leadership roles to work together, people's actions must be carefully coordinated by mechanisms that differ from those coordinating traditional management roles.

Strong networks of informal relationships—the kind found in companies with healthy cultures—help coordinate leadership activities in much the same way that formal structure coordinates managerial activities. The key difference is that informal networks can deal with the greater demands for coordination associated with nonroutine activities and change. The multitude of communication channels and the trust among the individuals connected by those channels allow for an ongoing process of accommodation and adaptation. When conflicts arise among roles, those same relationships help resolve the conflicts. Perhaps most important, this process of dialogue and accommodation can produce visions that are linked and compatible instead of remote and competitive. All this requires a great deal more communication than is needed to coordinate managerial roles, but unlike formal structure, strong informal networks can handle it.

Of course, informal relations of some sort exist in all corporations. But too often these networks are either very weak—some people are well connected but most are not—or they are highly fragmented—a strong network exists inside the marketing group and inside R&D but not across the two departments. Such networks do not support multiple leadership initiatives well. In fact, extensive informal networks are so important that if they do not exist, creating them has to be the focus of activity early in a major leadership initiative.

Creating a Culture of Leadership

Despite the increasing importance of leadership to business success, the on-the-job experiences of most people actually seem to undermine the development of attributes needed for leadership. Nevertheless, some companies have consistently demonstrated an ability to develop people into outstanding leader-managers. Recruiting people with leadership potential is only the first step. Equally important is managing their career patterns. Individuals who are effective in large leadership roles often share a number of career experiences.

Perhaps the most typical and most important is significant challenge early in a career. Leaders almost always have had opportunities during their twenties and thirties to actually try to lead, to take a risk, and to learn from both triumphs and failures. Such learning seems essential in developing a wide range of leadership skills and perspectives. It also teaches people something about both the difficulty of leadership and its potential for producing change.

Later in their careers, something equally important happens that has to do with broadening. People who provide effective leadership in important jobs always have a chance, before they get into those jobs, to grow beyond the narrow base that characterizes most managerial careers. This is usually the result of lateral career moves or of early promotions to unusually broad job assignments. Sometimes other vehicles help, like special task-force assignments or a lengthy general management course. Whatever the case, the breadth of knowledge developed in this way seems to be helpful in all aspects of leadership. So does the network of relationships that is often acquired both inside and outside the company. When enough people get opportunities like this, the relationships that are built also help create the strong informal networks needed to support multiple leadership initiatives.

Corporations that do a better-than-average job of developing leaders put an emphasis on creating challenging opportunities for relatively young employees. In many businesses, decentralization is the key. By definition, it pushes responsibility lower in an organization and in the process creates more challenging jobs at lower levels. Johnson & Johnson, 3M, Hewlett-Packard, General Electric, and many other well-known companies have used that approach quite successfully. Some of those same companies also create as many small units as possible so there are a lot of challenging lower level general management jobs available.

Sometimes these businesses develop additional challenging opportunities by stressing growth through new products or services. Over the years, 3M has had a policy that at least 25% of its revenue should come from products introduced within the last five years. That encourages small new ventures, which in turn offer hundreds of opportunities to test and stretch young people with leadership potential.

Such practices can, almost by themselves, prepare people for small- and medium-sized leadership jobs. But developing people for important leadership positions requires more work on the part of senior executives, often over a long period of time. That work begins with efforts to spot people with great leadership potential early in their careers and to identify what will be needed to stretch and develop them.

Again, there is nothing magic about this process. The methods successful companies use are surprisingly straightforward. They go out of their way to make young employees and people at lower levels in their organizations visible to senior management. Senior managers then judge for themselves who has potential and what the development needs of those people are. Executives also discuss their tentative conclusions among themselves to draw more accurate judgments.

Armed with a clear sense of who has considerable leadership potential and what skills they need to develop, executives in these companies then spend time planning for that development. Sometimes that is done as part of a formal succession planning or high-potential development process; often it is more informal. In either case, the key ingredient appears to be an intelligent assessment of what feasible development opportunities fit each candidate's needs.

To encourage managers to participate in these activities, well-led businesses tend to recognize and reward people who successfully develop leaders. This is rarely done as part of a formal compensation or bonus formula, simply because it is so difficult to measure such achievements with precision. But it does become a factor in decisions about promotion, especially to the most senior levels, and that seems to make a big difference. When told that future promotions will depend to some degree on their ability to nurture leaders, even people who say that leadership cannot be developed somehow find ways to do it.

Such strategies help create a corporate culture where people value strong leadership and strive to create it. Just as we need more people to provide leadership in the complex organizations that dominate our world today, we also need more people to develop the cultures that will create that leadership. Institutionalizing a leadership-centered culture is the ultimate act of leadership.

3

Managers and Leaders:
Are They Different?

ABRAHAM ZALEZNIK

Most societies, and that includes business organizations, are caught between two conflicting needs: one for managers to maintain the balance of
operations, and one for leaders to create new approaches and imagine
new areas to explore. One might well ask why there is a conflict. Cannot
both managers and leaders exist in the same society, or even better, cannot
one person be both a manager and a leader? The author of this article does
not say that is impossible but suggests that because leaders and managers
are basically different types of people, the conditions favorable to the
growth of one may be inimical to the other. Exploring the world views of
managers and leaders, the author illustrates, using Alfred P. Sloan and
Edwin Land among others as examples, that managers and leaders have
different attitudes toward their goals, careers, relations with others, and
themselves. And tracing their different lines of development, the author
shows how leaders are of a psychologically different type than managers;
their development depends on their forming a one-to-one relationship
with a mentor.

What is the ideal way to develop leadership? Every society provides its
own answers, defines its deepest concerns about the purposes, distribu-
tions, and uses of power. Business has contributed its answer to the leadership question by evolving a new breed called the manager. Simultaneously, business has established a new power ethic that favors collective
over individual leadership, the cult of the group over that of personality.
While ensuring the competence, control, and the balance of power relations among groups with the potential for rivalry, managerial leadership

unfortunately does not necessarily ensure imagination, creativity, or ethical behavior in guiding the destinies of corporate enterprises.

Leadership inevitably requires using power to influence the thoughts and actions of other people. Power in the hands of an individual entails human risks: first, the risk of equating power with the ability to get immediate results; second, the risk of ignoring the many different ways people can legitimately accumulate power; and third, the risk of losing self-control in the desire for power. The need to hedge these risks accounts in part for the development of collective leadership and the managerial ethic. Consequently, an inherent conservatism dominates the culture of large organizations. In *The Second American Revolution,* John D. Rockefeller, 3rd. describes the conservatism of organizations: "An organization is a system, with a logic of its own, and all the weight of tradition and inertia. The deck is stacked in favor of the tried and proven way of doing things and against the taking of risks and striking out in new directions."[1]

Out of this conservatism and inertia organizations provide succession to power through the development of managers rather than individual leaders. And the irony of the managerial ethic is that it fosters a bureaucratic culture in business, supposedly the last bastion protecting us from the encroachments and controls of bureaucracy in government and education. Perhaps the risks associated with power in the hands of an individual may be necessary ones for business to take if organizations are to break free of their inertia and bureaucratic conservatism.

Manager Vs. Leader Personality

Theodore Levitt has described the essential features of a managerial culture with its emphasis on rationality and control:

> Management consists of the rational assessment of a situation and the systematic selection of goals and purposes (what is to be done?); the systematic development of strategies to achieve these goals; the marshalling of the required resources; the rational design, organization, direction, and control of the activities required to attain the selected purposes; and, finally, the motivating and rewarding of people to do the work.[2]

In other words, whether his or her energies are directed toward goals, resources, organization structures, or people, a manager is a problem solver. The manager asks himself, "What problems have to be solved, and what are the best ways to achieve results so that people will continue to contribute to this organization?" In this conception, leadership is a practical effort to direct affairs; and to fulfill his task, a manager requires that many people operate at different levels of status and responsibility. Our democratic society is, in fact, unique in having solved the problem of providing well-trained managers for business. The same solution stands ready to be applied to government, education, health care, and other institutions. It takes neither genius nor heroism to be a manager, but rather persistence, tough-mindedness, hard work, intelligence, analytical ability and, perhaps most important, tolerance and good will.

Another conception, however, attaches almost mystical beliefs to what leadership is and assumes that only great people are worthy of the drama of power and politics. Here, leadership is a psychodrama in which, as a precondition for control of a political structure, a lonely person must gain control of him- or herself. Such an expectation of leadership contrasts sharply with the mundane, practical, and yet important conception that leadership is really managing work that other people do.

Two questions come to mind. Is this mystique of leadership merely a holdover from our collective childhood of dependency and our longing for good and heroic parents? Or, is there a basic truth lurking behind the need for leaders that no matter how competent managers are, their leadership stagnates because of their limitations in visualizing purposes and generating value in work? Without this imaginative capacity and the ability to communicate, managers, driven by their narrow purposes, perpetuate group conflicts instead of reforming them into broader desires and goals.

If indeed problems demand greatness, then, judging by past performance, the selection and development of leaders leave a great deal to chance. There are no known ways to train "great" leaders. Furthermore, beyond what we leave to chance, there is a deeper issue in the relationship between the need for competent managers and the longing for great leaders.

What it takes to ensure the supply of people who will assume practical responsibility may inhibit the development of great leaders. Conversely, the presence of great leaders may undermine the development of managers who become very anxious in the relative disorder that leaders seem to generate. The antagonism in aim (to have many competent managers as well as great leaders) often remains obscure in stable and well-developed societies. But the antagonism surfaces during periods of stress and change, as it did in the Western countries during both the Great Depression and World War II. The tension also appears in the struggle for power between theorists and professional managers in revolutionary societies.

It is easy enough to dismiss the dilemma I pose (of training managers while we may need new leaders or leaders at the expense of managers) by saying that the need is for people who can be *both* managers and leaders. The truth of the matter as I see it, however, is that just as a managerial culture is different from the entrepreneurial culture that develops when leaders appear in organizations, managers and leaders are very different kinds of people. They differ in motivation, personal history, and in how they think and act.

A technologically oriented and economically successful society tends to depreciate the need for great leaders. Such societies hold a deep and abiding faith in rational methods of solving problems, including problems of value, economics, and justice. Once rational methods of solving problems are broken down into elements, organized, and taught as skills, then society's faith in technique over personal qualities in leadership remains the guiding conception for a democratic society contemplating its leadership requirements. But there are times when tinkering and trial and error prove inadequate to the emerging problems of selecting goals, allocating resources, and distributing wealth and opportunity. During such times, the democratic society needs to find leaders who use themselves as the instruments of learning and acting, instead of managers who use their accumulation of collective experience to get where they are going.

The most impressive spokesman, as well as exemplar of the managerial viewpoint, was Alfred P. Sloan, Jr. who, along with Pierre du Pont, designed the modern corporate structure. Reflecting on what makes one management successful while another fails, Sloan suggested that "good management rests on a reconciliation of centralization and decentralization, or 'decentralization with coordinated control'."[3]

Sloan's conception of management, as well as his practice, developed by trial and error, and by the accumulation of experience. Sloan wrote: "There is no hard and fast rule for sorting out the various responsibilities and the best way to assign them. The balance which is struck ... varies according to what is being decided, the circumstances of the time, past experience, and the temperaments and skills of the executive involved."[4]

In other words, in much the same way that the inventors of the late nineteenth century tried, failed, and fitted until they hit on a product or method, managers who innovate in developing organizations are "tinkerers." They do not have a grand design or experience the intuitive flash of insight that, borrowing from modern science, we have come to call the "breakthrough."

Managers and leaders differ fundamentally in their world views. The dimensions for assessing these differences include managers' and leaders' orientations toward their goals, their work, their human relations, and their selves.

Attitudes Toward Goals

Managers tend to adopt impersonal, if not passive, attitudes toward goals. Managerial goals arise out of necessities rather than desires, and therefore, are deeply embedded in the history and culture of the organization.

Frederic G. Donner, chairman and chief executive officer of General Motors from 1958 to 1967, expressed this impersonal and passive attitude toward goals in defining GM's position on product development:

> To meet the challenge of the marketplace, we must recognize changes in customer needs and desires far enough ahead to have the right products in the right places at the right time and in the right quantity.
>
> We must balance trends in preference against the many compromises that are necessary to make a final product that is both reliable and good looking, that performs well and that sells at a competitive price in the necessary volume. We must design, not just the cars we would like to build, but more importantly, the cars that our customers want to buy.[5]

Nowhere in this formulation of how a product comes into being is there a notion that consumer tastes and preferences arise in part as a result of what manufacturers do. In reality, through product design, advertising, and promotion, consumers learn to like what they then say they need. Few would argue that people who enjoy taking snapshots *need* a camera that also develops pictures. But in response to novelty, convenience, a shorter interval between acting (taking a snap) and gaining pleasure (seeing the shot), the Polaroid camera succeeded in the marketplace. But it is inconceivable that Edwin Land responded to impressions of consumer need. Instead, he translated a technology (polarization of light) into a product, which proliferated and stimulated consumers' desires.

The example of Polaroid and Land suggests how leaders think about goals. They are active instead of reactive, shaping ideas instead of responding to them. Leaders adopt a personal and active attitude toward goals. The influence a leader exerts in altering moods, evoking images and expectations, and in establishing specific desires and objectives determines the direction a business takes. The net result of this influence is to change the way people think about what is desirable, possible, and necessary.

Conceptions of Work

What do managers and leaders do? What is the nature of their respective work? Leaders and managers differ in their conceptions. Managers tend to view work as an enabling process involving some combination of people and ideas interacting to establish strategies and make decisions. Managers help the process along by a range of skills, including calculating the interests in opposition, staging and timing the surfacing of controversial issues, and reducing tensions. In this enabling process, managers appear flexible in the use of tactics: they negotiate and bargain, on the one hand, and use rewards and punishments, and other forms of coercion, on the other. Machiavelli wrote for managers and not necessarily for leaders.

Alfred Sloan illustrated how this enabling process works in situations of conflict. The time was the early 1920s when the Ford Motor Co. still dominated the automobile industry using, as did General Motors, the conventional water-cooled engine. With the full backing of Pierre du Pont, Charles Kettering dedicated himself to the design of an air-cooled engine, which, if successful, would have been a great technical and market coup for GM. Kettering believed in his product, but the manufacturing division heads at GM remained skeptical and later opposed the new design on two grounds: first, that it was technically unreliable, and second, that the corporation was putting all its eggs in one basket by investing in a new product instead of attending to the current marketing situation.

In the summer of 1923 after a series of false starts and after its decision to recall the copper-cooled Chevrolets from dealers and customers, GM management reorganized and finally scrapped the project. When it dawned on Kettering that the company had rejected the engine, he was deeply discouraged and wrote to Sloan that without the "organized resistance" against the project it would succeed and that unless the project were saved, he would leave the company.

Alfred Sloan was all too aware of the fact that Kettering was unhappy and indeed intended to leave General Motors. Sloan was also aware of the fact that, while the manufacturing divisions strongly opposed the new engine, Pierre du Pont supported Kettering. Furthermore, Sloan had himself gone on record in a letter to Kettering less than two years earlier expressing full confidence in him. The problem Sloan now had was to make his decision stick, keep Kettering in the organization (he was much too valuable to lose), avoid alienating du Pont, and encourage the division heads to move speedily in developing product lines using conventional water-cooled engines.

The actions that Sloan took in the face of this conflict reveal much about how managers work. First, he tried to reassure Kettering by presenting the problem in a very ambiguous fashion, suggesting that he and the Executive Committee sided with Kettering, but that it would not be practical to force the divisions to do what they were opposed to. He presented the problem as being a question of the people, not the product. Second, he proposed to reorganize around the problem by consolidating all functions in a new division that would be responsible for the design, production, and marketing of the new car. This solution, however, appeared as ambiguous as his efforts to placate and keep Kettering in General Motors. Sloan wrote: "My plan was to create an independent pilot operation under the sole jurisdiction of Mr. Kettering, a kind of copper-cooled-car division. Mr. Kettering would designate his own chief engineer and his production staff to solve the technical problems of manufacture."[6]

While Sloan did not discuss the practical value of this solution, which included saddling an inventor with management responsibility, he in effect used this plan to limit his conflict with Pierre du Pont.

In effect, the managerial solution that Sloan arranged and pressed for adoption limited the options available to others. The structural solution narrowed choices, even limiting emotional reactions to the point where the key people could do nothing but go along, and even allowed Sloan to say in his memorandum to du Pont, "We have discussed the matter with Mr. Kettering at some length this morning and he agrees with us absolutely on every point we made. He appears to receive the suggestion enthusiastically and has every confidence that it can be put across along these lines."[7]

Having placated people who opposed his views by developing a structural solution that appeared to give something but in reality only limited options, Sloan could then authorize the car division's general manager, with whom he basically agreed, to move quickly in designing water-cooled cars for the immediate market demand. Years later Sloan wrote, evidently with tongue in cheek, "The copper-cooled car never came up again in a big way. It just died out, I don't know why."[8]

In order to get people to accept solutions to problems, managers need to coordinate and balance continually. Interestingly enough, this managerial work has much in common with what diplomats and mediators do, with Henry Kissinger apparently an outstanding practitioner. The manager aims at shifting balances of power toward solutions acceptable as a compromise among conflicting values.

What about leaders, what do they do? Where managers act to limit choices, leaders work in the opposite direction, to develop fresh approaches to long-standing problems and to open issues for new options. Stanley and Inge Hoffmann, the political scientists, liken the leader's work to that of the artist. But unlike most artists, the leader himself is an integral part of the aesthetic product. One cannot look at a leader's art without looking at the artist. On Charles de Gaulle as a political artist, they wrote: "And each of his major political acts, however tortuous the means or the details, has been whole, indivisible and unmistakably his own, like an artistic act."[9]

The closest one can get to a product apart from the artist is the ideas that occupy, indeed at times obsess, the leader's mental life. To be effective, however, the leader needs to project his ideas into images that excite people, and only then develop choices that give the projected images substance. Consequently, leaders create excitement in work.

John F. Kennedy's brief presidency shows both the strengths and weaknesses connected with the excitement leaders generate in their work. In his inaugural address he said, "Let every nation know, whether it wishes us well or ill, that we shall pay any price, bear any burden, meet any hardship, support any friend, oppose any foe, in order to assure the survival and the success of liberty.''

This much-quoted statement forced people to react beyond immediate concerns and to identify with Kennedy and with important shared ideals. But upon closer scrutiny the statement must be seen as absurd because it promises a position which if in fact adopted, as in the Viet Nam War, could produce disastrous results. Yet unless expectations are aroused and mobilized, with all the dangers of frustration inherent in heightened desire, new thinking and new choices can never come to light.

Leaders work from high-risk positions, indeed often are temperamentally disposed to seek out risk and danger, especially where opportunity and reward appear high. From my observations, why one individual seeks risks while another approaches problems conservatively depends more on his or her personality and less on conscious choice. For some, especially those who become managers, the instinct for survival dominates their need for risk, and their ability to tolerate mundane, practical work assists their survival. The same cannot be said for leaders who sometimes react to mundane work as to an affliction.

Relations with Others

Managers prefer to work with people; they avoid solitary activity because it makes them anxious. Several years ago, I directed studies on the psychological aspects of career. The need to seek out others with whom to work and collaborate seemed to stand out as important characteristics of managers. When asked, for example, to write imaginative stories in response to a picture showing a single figure (a boy contemplating a violin, or a man silhouetted in a state of reflection), managers populated their stories with people. The following is an example of a manager's imaginative story about the young boy contemplating a violin:

> Mom and Dad insisted that junior take music lessons so that someday he can become a concert musician. His instrument was ordered and had just arrived. Junior is weighing the alternatives of playing football with the other kids or playing with the squeak box. He can't understand how his parents could think a violin is better than a touchdown.
>
> After four months of practicing the violin, junior has had more than enough, Daddy is going out of his mind, and Mommy is willing to give in reluctantly to the men's wishes. Football season is now over, but a good third baseman will take the field next spring.[10]

This story illustrates two themes that clarify managerial attitudes toward human relations. The first, as I have suggested, is to seek out activity with other people (i.e., the football team), and the second is to maintain a low level of emotional involvement in these relationships. The low emotional involvement appears in the writer's use of conventional metaphors, even clichés, and in the depiction of the ready transformation of potential conflict into harmonious decisions. In this case, Junior, Mommy, and Daddy agree to give up the violin for manly sports.

These two themes may seem paradoxical, but their coexistence supports what a manager does, including reconciling differences, seeking compromises, and establishing a balance of power. A further idea demonstrated by how the manager wrote the story is that managers may lack empathy, or the capacity to sense intuitively the thoughts and feelings of others. To illustrate attempts to be empathic, here is another story written to the same stimulus picture by someone considered by his peers to be a leader:

> This little boy has the appearance of being a sincere artist, one who is deeply affected by the violin, and has an intense desire to master the instrument.
>
> He seems to have just completed his normal practice session and appears to be somewhat crestfallen at his inability to produce the sounds which he is sure lie within the violin.
>
> He appears to be in the process of making a vow to himself to expend the necessary time and effort to play this instrument until he satisfies himself that he is able to bring forth the qualities of music which he feels within himself.
>
> With this type of determination and carry through, this boy became one of the great violinists of his day.[11]

Empathy is not simply a matter of paying attention to other people. It is also the capacity to take in emotional signals and to make them mean something in a relationship with an individual. People who describe another person as "deeply affected" with "intense desire," as capable of feeling "crestfallen" and as one who can "vow to himself," would seem to have an inner perceptiveness that they can use in their relationships with others.

Managers relate to people according to the role they play in a sequence of events or in a decision-making *process,* while leaders, who are concerned with ideas, relate in more intuitive and empathetic ways. The manager's orientation to people, as actors in a sequence of events, deflects his or her attention away from the substance of people's concerns and toward their role in a process. The distinction is simply between a manager's attention to *how* things get done and a leader's to *what* the events and decisions mean to participants.

In recent years, managers have taken over from game theory the notion that decision-making events can be one of two types: the win-lose situation (or zero-sum game) or the win-win situation in which everybody in the action comes out ahead. As part of the process of reconciling differences among people and maintaining balances of power, managers strive to convert win-lose into win-win situations.

As an illustration, take the decision of how to allocate capital resources among operating divisions in a large, decentralized organization. On the face of it, the dollars available for distribution are limited at any given time. Presumably, therefore the more one division gets, the less is available for other divisions.

Managers tend to view this situation (as it affects human relations) as a conversion issue: how to make what seems like a win-lose problem into a win-win problem. Several solutions to this situation come to mind. First, the manager focuses others' attention on procedure and not on substance. Here the actors become engrossed in the bigger problem of *how* to make decisions, not *what* decisions to make. Once committed to the bigger problem, the actors have to support the outcome since they were involved in formulating decision rules. Because the actors believe in the rules they formulated, they will accept present losses in the expectation that next time they will win.

Second, the manager communicates to his subordinates indirectly, using "signals" instead of "messages." A signal has a number of possible implicit positions in it while a message clearly states a position. Signals are inconclusive and subject to reinterpretation should people become upset and angry, while messages involve the direct consequences that some people will indeed not like what they hear. The nature of messages heightens emotional response, and, as I have indicated, emotionally makes managers anxious. With signals, the question of who wins and who loses often becomes obscured.

Third, the manager plays for time. Managers seem to recognize that with the passage of time and the delay of major decisions, compromises emerge that take the sting out of win-lose situations; and the original "game" will be superseded by additional ones. Therefore, compromises may mean that one wins and loses simultaneously, depending on which of the games one evaluates.

There are undoubtedly many other tactical moves managers use to change human situations from win-lose to win-win. But the point to be made is that such tactics focus on the decision-making process itself and interest managers rather than leaders. The interest in tactics involves costs as well as benefits, including making organizations fatter in bureaucratic and political intrigue and leaner in direct, hard activity and warm human relationships. Consequently, one often hears subordinates characterize managers as inscrutable, detached, and manipulative. These adjectives arise from the subordinates' perception that they are linked together in a process whose purpose, beyond simply making decisions, is to maintain a controlled as well as rational and equitable structure. These adjectives suggest that managers need order in the face of the potential chaos that many fear in human relationships.

In contrast, one often hears leaders referred to in adjectives rich in emotional content. Leaders attract strong feelings of identity and difference, or of love and hate. Human relations in leader-dominated structures often appear turbulent, intense, and at times even disorganized. Such an atmosphere intensifies individual motivation and often produces unanticipated outcomes. Does this intense motivation lead to innovation and high performance, or does it represent wasted energy?

Senses of Self

In *The Varieties of Religious Experience,* William James describes two basic personality types, "once-born" and "twice-born."[12] People of the former personality type are those for whom adjustments to life have been straightforward and whose lives have been more or less a peaceful flow from the moment of their births. The twice-borns, on the other hand, have not had an easy time of it. Their lives are marked by a continual struggle to attain some sense of order. Unlike the once-borns they cannot take things for granted. According to James, these personalities have equally different world views. For a once-born personality, the sense of self, as a guide to conduct and attitude, derives from a feeling of being at home and in harmony with one's environment. For a twice-born, the sense of self derives from a feeling of profound separateness.

A sense of belonging or of being separate has a practical significance for the kinds of investments managers and leaders make in their careers. Managers see themselves as conservators and regulators of an existing order of affairs with which they personally identify and from which they gain rewards. Perpetuating and strengthening existing institutions enhances a manager's sense of self-worth: he or she is performing in a role that harmonizes with the ideals of duty and responsibility. William James had this harmony in mind—this sense of self as flowing easily to and from the outer world—in defining a once-born personality. If one feels oneself as a member of institutions, contributing to their well-being, then one fulfills a mission in life and feels rewarded for having measured up to ideals. This reward transcends material gains and answers the more fundamental desire for personal integrity which is achieved by identifying with existing institutions.

Leaders tend to be twice-born personalities, people who feel separate from their environment, including other people. They may work in organizations, but they never belong to them. Their sense of who they are does not depend upon memberships, work roles, or other social indicators of identity. What seems to follow from this idea about separateness is some theoretical basis for explaining why certain individuals search out opportunities for change. The methods to bring about change may be technological, political, or ideological, but the object is the same: to profoundly alter human, economic, and political relationships.

Sociologists refer to the preparation individuals undergo to perform in roles as the socialization process. Where individuals experience themselves as an integral part of the social structure (their self-esteem gains strength through participation and conformity), social standards exert powerful effects in maintaining the individual's personal sense of continuity, even beyond the early years in the family. The line of development from the family to schools, then to career is cumulative and reinforcing. When the line of development is not reinforcing because of significant disruptions in relationships or other problems experienced in the family or other social institutions, the individual turns inward and struggles to establish self-esteem, identity, and order. Here the psychological dynamics center on the experience with loss and the efforts at recovery.

In considering the development of leadership, we have to examine two different courses of life history: (1) development through socialization, which prepares the individual to guide institutions and to maintain the existing balance of social relations; and (2) development through personal mastery, which impels an individual to struggle for psychological and social change. Society produces its managerial talent through the first line of development, while through the second leaders emerge.

Development of Leadership

The development of every person begins in the family. Each person experiences the traumas associated with separating from his or her parents, as well as the pain that follows such frustration. In the same vein, all individuals face the difficulties of achieving self-regulation and self-control. But for some, perhaps a majority, the fortunes of childhood provide adequate gratifications and sufficient opportunities to find substitutes for rewards no longer available. Such individuals, the "once-borns," make moderate identifications with parents and find a harmony between what they expect and what they are able to realize from life.

But suppose the pains of separation are amplified by a combination of parental demands and the individual's need to the degree that a sense of isolation, of being special, and of wariness disrupts the bonds that attach children to parents and other authority figures? Under such conditions, and given a special aptitude, the origins of which remain mysterious, the person becomes deeply involved in his or her inner world at the expense of interest in the outer world. For such a person, self-esteem no longer depends solely upon positive attachments and real rewards. A form of self-reliance takes hold along with expectations of performance and achievement, and perhaps even the desire to do great works.

Such self-perceptions can come to nothing if the individual's talents are negligible. Even with strong talents, there are no guarantees that achievement will follow, let alone that the end result will be for good rather than evil. Other factors enter into development. For one thing, leaders are like artists and other gifted people who often struggle with neuroses; their ability to function varies considerably even over the short run, and some potential leaders may lose the struggle altogether. Also, beyond early childhood, the patterns of development that affect managers and leaders involve the selective influence of particular people. Just as they appear flexible and evenly distributed in the types of talents available for development, managers form moderate and widely distributed attachments. Leaders, on the other hand, establish, and also break off, intensive one-to-one relationships.

It is a common observation that people with great talents are often only indifferent students. No one, for example, could have predicted Einstein's great achievements on the basis of his mediocre record in school. The reason for mediocrity is obviously not the absence of ability. It may result, instead, from self-absorption and the inability to pay attention to the ordinary tasks at hand. The only sure way an individual can interrupt reverie-like preoccupation and self-absorption is to form a deep attachment to a great teacher or other benevolent person who understands and has the ability to communicate with the gifted individual.

Whether gifted individuals find what they need in one-to-one relationships depends on the availability of sensitive and intuitive mentors who have a vocation in cultivating talent. Fortunately, when the generations do meet and the self-selections occur, we learn more about how to develop leaders and how talented people of different generations influence each other.

While apparently destined for a mediocre career, people who form important one-to-one relationships are able to accelerate and intensify their development through an apprenticeship. The background for such apprenticeships, or the psychological readiness of an individual to benefit from an intensive relationship, depends upon some experience in life that forces the individual to turn inward. A case example will make this point clearer. This example comes from the life of Dwight David Eisenhower, and illustrates the transformation of a career from competent to outstanding.[13]

Dwight Eisenhower's early career in the Army foreshadowed very little about his future development. During World War I, while some of his West Point classmates were already experiencing the war firsthand in

France, Eisenhower felt "embedded in the monotony and unsought safety of the Zone of the Interior ... that was intolerable punishment."[14]

Shortly after World War I, Eisenhower, then a young officer somewhat pessimistic about his career chances, asked for a transfer to Panama to work under General Fox Connor, a senior officer whom Eisenhower admired. The Army turned down Eisenhower's request. This setback was very much on Eisenhower's mind when Ikey, his first-born son, succumbed to influenza. By some sense of responsibility for its own, the Army transferred Eisenhower to Panama, where he took up his duties under General Connor with the shadow of his lost son very much upon him.

In a relationship with the kind of father he would have wanted to be, Eisenhower reverted to being the son he lost. In this highly charged situation, Eisenhower began to learn from his mentor. General Connor offered, and Eisenhower gladly took, a magnificent tutorial on the military. The effects of this relationship on Eisenhower cannot be measured quantitatively, but, in Eisenhower's own reflections and the unfolding of his career, one cannot overestimate its significance in the reintegration of a person shattered by grief. As Eisenhower wrote later about Connor,

> Life with General Connor was a sort of graduate school in military affairs and the humanities, leavened by a man who was experienced in his knowledge of men and their conduct. I can never adequately express my gratitude to this one gentleman. ... In a lifetime of association with great and good men, he is the one more or less invisible figure to whom I owe an incalculable debt.[15]

Some time after his tour of duty with General Connor, Eisenhower's breakthrough occurred. He received orders to attend the Command and General Staff School at Fort Leavenworth, one of the most competitive schools in the army. It was a coveted appointment, and Eisenhower took advantage of the opportunity. Unlike his performance in high school and West Point, his work at the Command School was excellent; he was graduated first in his class.

Psychological biographies of gifted people repeatedly demonstrate the important part a mentor plays in developing an individual. Andrew Carnegie owed much to his senior, Thomas A. Scott. As head of the Western Division of the Pennsylvania Railroad, Scott recognized talent and the desire to learn in the young telegrapher assigned to him. By giving Carnegie increasing responsibility and by providing him with the opportunity to learn through close personal observation, Scott added to Carnegie's self-confidence and sense of achievement. Because of his own personal strength and achievement, Scott did not fear Carnegie's aggressiveness. Rather, he gave it full play in encouraging Carnegie's initiative.

Mentors take risks with people. They bet initially on talent they perceive in younger people. Mentors also risk emotional involvement in working closely with their juniors. The risks do not always pay off, but the willingness to take them appears crucial in developing leaders.

Can Organizations Develop Leaders?

The examples I have given of how leaders develop suggest the importance of personal influence and the one-to-one relationship. For organizations to encourage consciously the development of leaders as compared with managers would mean developing one-to-one relationships between junior and senior executives and, more important, fostering a culture of individualism and possibly elitism. The elitism arises out of the desire to identify talent and other qualities suggestive of the ability to lead and not simply to manage.

The Jewel Companies, Inc., enjoy a reputation for developing talented people. The chairman and chief executive officer, Donald S. Perkins, is perhaps a good example of a person brought along through the mentor approach. Franklin J. Lunding, who was Perkins's mentor, expressed the philosophy of taking risks with young people this way: "Young people today want in on the action. They don't want to sit around for six months trimming lettuce."[16]

The statement runs counter to the culture that attaches primary importance to slow progression based on experience and proved competence. It is a high-risk philosophy, one that requires time for the attachment between senior and junior people to grow and be meaningful, and one that is bound to produce more failures than successes.

The elitism is an especially sensitive issue. At Jewel the MBA degree symbolized the elite. Lunding attracted Perkins to Jewel at a time when business school graduates had little interest in retailing in general, and food distribution in particular. Yet the elitism seemed to pay off: not only did Perkins become the president at age 37, but also, under the leadership of young executives recruited into Jewel with the promise of opportunity for growth and advancement, Jewel managed to diversify into discount and drug chains and still remain strong in food retailing. By assigning each recruit to a vice president who acted as sponsor, Jewel evidently tried to build a structure around the mentor approach to developing leaders. To counteract the elitism implied in such an approach, the company also introduced an "equalizer" in what Perkins described as "the first assistant philosophy." Perkins stated:

> Being a good first assistant means that each management person thinks of himself not as the order-giving, domineering boss, but as the first assistant to

those who 'report' to him in a more typical organizational sense. Thus we mentally turn our organization charts upside-down and challenge ourselves to seek ways in which we can lead ... by helping ... by teaching ... by listening ... and by managing in the true democratic sense ... that is, with the consent of the managed. Thus the satisfactions of leadership come from helping others to get things done and changed—and not from getting credit for doing and changing things ourselves.[17]

While this statement would seem to be more egalitarian than elitist, it does reinforce a youth-oriented culture since it defines the senior officer's job as primarily helping the junior person.

A myth about how people learn and develop that seems to have taken hold in the American culture also dominates thinking in business. The myth is that people learn best from their peers. Supposedly, the threat of evaluation and even humiliation recedes in peer relations because of the tendency for mutual identification and the social restraints on authoritarian behavior among equals. Peer training in organizations occurs in various forms. The use, for example, of task forces made up of peers from several interested occupational groups (sales, production, research, and finance) supposedly removes the restraints of authority on the individual's willingness to assert and exchange ideas. As a result, so the theory goes, people interact more freely, listen more objectively to criticism and other points of view and, finally, learn from this healthy interchange.

Another application of peer training exists in some large corporations, such as Philips, N.V. in Holland, where organization structure is built on the principle of joint responsibility of two peers, one representing the commercial end of the business and the other the technical. Formally, both hold equal responsibility for geographic operations or product groups, as the case may be. As a practical matter, it may turn out that one or the other of the peers dominates the management. Nevertheless, the main interaction is between two or more equals.

The principal question I would raise about such arrangements is whether they perpetuate the managerial orientation, and preclude the formation of one-to-one relationships between senior people and potential leaders.

Aware of the possible stifling effects of peer relationships on aggressiveness and individual initiative, another company, much smaller than Philips, utilizes joint responsibility of peers for operating units, with one important difference. The chief executive of this company encourages competition and rivalry among peers, ultimately appointing the one who comes out on top for increased responsibility. These hybrid arrangements produce some unintended consequences that can be disastrous. There is no easy way to limit rivalry. Instead, it permeates all levels of the operation and opens the way for the formation of cliques in an atmosphere of intrigue.

A large, integrated oil company has accepted the importance of developing leaders through the direct influence of senior on junior executives. One chairman and chief executive officer regularly selected one talented university graduate whom he appointed his special assistant, and with whom he would work closely for a year. At the end of the year, the junior executive would become available for assignment to one of the operating divisions, where he would be assigned to a responsible post rather than a training position. The mentor relationship had acquainted the junior executive firsthand with the use of power, and with the important antidotes to the power disease called *hubris*—performance and integrity.

Working in one-to-one relationships, where there is a formal and recognized difference in the power of the actors, takes a great deal of tolerance for emotional interchange. This interchange, inevitable in close working arrangements, probably accounts for the reluctance of many executives to become involved in such relationships. *Fortune* carried an interesting story on the departure of a key executive, John W. Hanley, from the top management of Proctor & Gamble, for the chief executive officer position at Monsanto.[18] According to this account, the chief executive and chairman of P&G passed over Hanley for appointment to the presidency and named another executive vice president to this post instead.

The chairman evidently felt he could not work well with Hanley, who, by his own acknowledgement, was aggressive, eager to experiment and change practices, and constantly challenged his superior. A chief executive officer naturally has the right to select people with whom he feels congenial. But I wonder whether a greater capacity on the part of senior officers to tolerate the competitive impulses and behavior of their subordinates might not be healthy for corporations. At least a greater tolerance for interchange would not favor the managerial team player at the expense of the individual who might become a leader.

I am constantly surprised at the frequency with which chief executives feel threatened by open challenges to their ideas, as though the source of their authority, rather than their specific ideas, were at issue. In one case a chief executive officer, who was troubled by the aggressiveness and sometimes outright rudeness of one of his talented vice presidents, used various indirect methods such as group meetings and hints from outside directors to avoid dealing with his subordinate. I advised the executive to deal head-on with what irritated him. I suggested that by direct, face-to-face confrontation, both he and his subordinate would learn to validate the distinction between the authority to be preserved and the issues to be debated.

To confront is also to tolerate aggressive interchange, and has the net effect of stripping away the veils of ambiguity and signaling so characteristic of managerial cultures, as well as encouraging the emotional relationship leaders need if they are to survive.

Retrospective Commentary*

It was not so long ago that Bert Lance, President Jimmy Carter's budget director and confidant, declared, "If it ain't broke, don't fix it." This piece of advice fits with how managers think. Leaders understand a different truth: "When it ain't broke may be the only time you can fix it."

In the splendid discipline of the marketplace, past formulas for success today contain the seeds of decay. The U.S. automobile industry has been cited so often as the prime example of the suicidal effect of continuing to do what one has been doing in the wake of success that its story borders on the banal. But it's true. Top executives in the automobile industry, along with managers in many other industries in the United States, have failed to understand the misleading lessons of success, revealing the chronic fault of the managerial mystique.

As a consequence of placing such reliance on the practical measure of continuing to do today and tomorrow what had proven successful yesterday, we face the chilling fact that the United States's largest export during the last decade or more has been jobs. We live with the grim reality that the storehouse of expertise called know-how has diminished. Perhaps most dismal of all, our children and our children's children may not be able to enjoy the same standard of living we worked so hard to achieve, let alone enjoy a higher standard of living as a legacy of the generations.

When "Managers and Leaders: Are They Different?" first appeared in *HBR*, practicing managers and academics, including many of my colleagues at the Harvard Business School, thought I had taken leave of my senses. Don't ordinary people in an organization with superior structure and process outperform superior people operating in an ordinary organization? To those indoctrinated in the "managerial mystique," talent is ephemeral while organization structure and process are real. The possibility that it takes talent to make a company hum counts for less than acting on those variables managers feel they understand and can control.

Talent is critical to continued success in the marketplace. Yet most organizations today persist in perpetuating the development of managers over leaders. Fortunately, however, there may be an awakening. The chairman of IBM, John Akers, startled the business community with his announcement that IBM intended to abandon its long-held course of running its business as one large corporation. Akers intends to break IBM up into a number of corporations. And while "Big Blue" will continue to be big by most standards, the businesses will run under a leadership and not a managerial mentality. The corporation will no longer rest on the false comforts of economy of scale. Nor will executives be preoccupied with coordination and control, with decentralized operations and centralized financial controls. Process will take a backseat to substance, and the power will flow to executives who are creative and, above all, aggressive.

If other large companies follow this lead, corporate America may recharge, and its ability to compete may rebound. But if left to professional management, U.S. corporations will continue to stagnate.

Since "Managers and Leaders: Are They Different?" was first published, strategy has catapulted itself into the number one position on the managerial hit parade. No aspect of corporate life is indifferent to strategy. Every problem leads to strategic solutions, ranging from how to position products to how to compensate executives. We have a plethora of marketing strategies, employee benefit strategies, and executive development strategies. Strategy, it seems, has replaced business policy as the conceptual handle for establishing a corporation's directives.

In relying on strategy, organizations have largely overlooked results. Strategy is an offspring of the branch of economics called industrial organization; it builds models of competition and attempts to position products in competitive markets through analytic techniques. The aggregation of these product positions establishes mission statements and direction for businesses. With the ascendancy of industrial organization in the 1980s, management consultants prospered and faith in the managerial mystique was strengthened, despite the poor performance in the U.S. economy.

To me, the most influential development in management in the last 10 or 15 years has been Lotus 1-2-3. This popular software program makes it possible to create spreadsheets rapidly and repetitively, and that has given form and language to strategic planning. With this methodology, technicians can play with the question, "What if?" Best of all, everyone with access to a computer and the appropriate software can join in the "what if" game.

Alas, while everyone can become a strategist, few can become, and sustain, the position of creator. Vision, the hallmark of leadership, is less a derivative of spreadsheets and more a product of the mind called imagination.

And vision is needed at least as much as strategy to succeed. Business leaders bring to bear a variety of imaginations on the growth of corporations. These imaginations—the marketing imagination, the manufacturing imagination, and others—originate in perceptual capacities we recognize as talent. Talented leaders grasp the significance of anomalies, such as unfulfilled customer needs, manufacturing operations that can be improved significantly, and the potential of technological applications in product development.

Business imaginations are substantive. A leader's imagination impels others to act in ways that are truly, to use James MacGregor Burns's felicitous term, "transformational." But leaders often experience their talent as restlessness, as a desire to upset other people's applecarts, an impelling need to "do things better." As a consequence, a leader may not create a stable working environment; rather, he or she may create a chaotic workplace, with highly charged emotional peaks and valleys.

In "Managers and Leaders: Are They Different?", I argued that a crucial difference between managers and leaders lies in the conceptions they hold, deep in their psyches, of chaos and order. Leaders tolerate chaos and lack of structure and are thus prepared to keep answers in suspense, avoiding premature closure on important issues. Managers seek order and control and are almost compulsively addicted to disposing of problems even before they understand their potential significance. In my experience, seldom do the uncertainties of potential chaos cause problems. Instead, it is the instinctive move to impose order on potential chaos that makes trouble for organizations.

It seems to me that business leaders have much more in common with artists, scientists, and other creative thinkers than they do with managers. For business schools to exploit this commonality of dispositions and interests, the curriculum should worry less about the logics of strategy and imposing the constraints of computer exercises and more about thought experiments in the play of creativity and imagination. If they are successful, they would then do a better job of preparing exceptional men and women for positions of leadership.

Notes

1. John D. Rockefeller, 3rd., *The Second American Revolution* (New York: Harper & Row, 1973), p. 72.

2. Theodore Levitt, "Management and the Post Industrial Society," *The Public Interest*, Summer 1976, p. 73.

3. Alfred P. Sloan, Jr., *My Years with General Motors* (New York: Doubleday & Co., 1964), p. 429.

4. Ibid. p. 429.

5. Ibid. p. 440.

6. Ibid. p. 91.

7. Ibid. p. 91.

8. Ibid. p. 93.

9. Stanley and Inge Hoffmann, "The Will for Grandeur: de Gaulle as Political Artist," *Daedalus*, Summer 1968, p. 849.

10. Abraham Zaleznik, Gene W. Dalton, and Louis B. Barnes, *Orientation and Conflict in Career* (Boston: Division of Research, Harvard Business School, 1970), p. 326.

11. Ibid. p. 294.

12. William James, *Varieties of Religious Experience* (New York: Mentor Books, 1958).

13. This example is included in Abraham Zaleznik and Manfred F. R. Kets de Vries, *Power and the Corporate Mind* (Boston: Houghton Mifflin, 1975).

14. Dwight D. Eisenhower, *At Ease: Stories I Tell to Friends* (New York: Doubleday, 1967), p. 136.

15. Ibid. p. 187.

16. "Jewel Lets Young Men Make Mistakes," *Business Week*, January 17, 1970, p. 90.

17. "What Makes Jewel Shine so Bright," *Progressive Grocer*, September, 1973, p. 76.

18. "Jack Hanley Got There by Selling Harder," *Fortune*, November, 1976.

4

The Credibility Factor: What People Expect of Leaders

JAMES M. KOUZES
BARRY Z. POSNER

What you have heard about leadership is only half the story. Leadership is not only about leaders, but about followers, or better yet constituents. Successful leadership depends far more upon the constituent's perception of the leader than upon the leader's own perceptions. Constituents determine when someone possesses the qualities of leadership.

Unfortunately, most writings about leadership ignore the constituent. We know what Lee Iacocca, Harold Geneen, Donald Trump, Roger Smith, Harvey Mackay and other executives say about leadership. But what do their constituents have to say about the subject?

What Do People Admire in Leaders?

Over the past six years we have investigated the expectations people have of leaders. We have asked over 10,000 managers, nationwide, to tell us what they look for or admire in their leaders, in people they would be willing to follow. According to our research, the majority of us admire and look for leaders who are honest, competent, forward-looking, and inspiring.

Honesty in Leaders

In every survey we conducted, honesty was selected more often than any other leadership characteristic. Honesty is the most essential requirement

Adapted for the W. K. *Kellogg Foundation Journal* (Fall–Winter 1990), pp. 26–29, from J. M. Kouzes and B. Z. Posner, *The Leadership Challenge: How to Get Extraordinary Things Done in Organizations* (San Francisco: Jossey-Bass, 1987). Reprinted with permission of the publisher.

for leadership. After all, if we are willingly to follow someone, whether it be into battle or into the boardroom, we first must assure ourselves that the person is worthy of our trust. But how is something as subjective as honesty measured? Whatever leaders may say about their integrity, honesty, or ethical practices, constituents will judge leaders by their deeds.

People consider leaders honest when the leaders do what they say they are going to do. Agreements not followed through, false promises, cover-ups, and inconsistency between word and deed are all indicators that an ostensible leader is not honest.

Competency Ranks High

The leadership attribute chosen next most frequently is competence. To enlist in another's cause, we must believe that person is capable and effective. If we doubt the leader's abilities, we are unlikely to enlist in the crusade.

Leadership competence does not necessarily refer to the leader's technical abilities in the core technology of the business. The abilities to challenge, inspire, enable, and encourage must also be demonstrated if leaders are to be viewed as capable.

The competence we look for also varies with the leader's position and the condition of the organization. For example, the higher the rank of the leader, the more people demand to see abilities in strategic planning and policymaking. At the line function level, where subordinates expect guidance in technical areas, these same abilities will not be enough.

We have come to refer to the kind of competence needed by leaders as *value-added competence*. Functional competence may be necessary, but it is insufficient. The leader must bring some added value to the position.

A Forward-Looking Vision

Over half of our respondents selected "forward-looking" as one of their most sought-after leadership traits. People expect leaders to have a sense of direction and a concern for the future of the organization.

Senior executives affirm their managerial colleagues' requirement of vision for leadership. A study we conducted of 284 senior executives found "developing a strategic planning and forecasting capability" as the most critical concern. These same senior managers, when asked to select the most important characteristic in a CEO, cited "a leadership style of honesty and integrity" first, followed by "long-term vision and direction."

Forward-looking does not mean possessing the magical power of a visionary. The reality is far more down to earth; it is the ability to set or select a desirable destination for the organization.

It is the vision of a leader—the magnetic north—that sets the course. A leader's "vision" is, in this way, similar to an architect's model of a new building or an engineer's prototype of a new product. It is an ideal image of a unique future for the common good.

The Inspirational Quotient

It is not enough for our leaders to dream about the future. They must be able to communicate the vision in ways that encourage us to sign on for the duration.

Some people react with discomfort to the idea that "inspiring" is an essential leadership quality. They say, "I don't trust people who are inspiring"—no doubt in response to past crusaders who led their followers to death or destruction. Other executives are skeptical of their ability to inspire others and, therefore, dismiss the quality as unnecessary.

In the final analysis it is essential that leaders inspire our confidence in the validity of the goal. Enthusiasm and excitement signal the leader's personal commitment to pursuing that dream. If a leader displays no passion for a cause, why should others care?

The Credibility Factor

Put together, these four characteristics offer clear insight into the foundation of leadership from the constituent's perspective. These characteristics are generally the basis of what social scientists and communications experts refer to as "credibility." What we found in our investigation of admired leadership qualities was that, more than anything, we want leaders who are credible.

When we believe a leader is credible—when we believe he or she is honest, competent, has a sense of the future and personal conviction about the path—then we somehow feel more trusting and secure around that leader. And more willing to commit and work hard to achieve a shared vision.

Credibility, however, is extremely fragile. It takes years to be earned, growing through persistent, consistent, patient exhibition of the four most admired leadership qualities. Yet credibility can be lost with one thoughtless remark, inconsistent act, or one broken agreement.

Actions Speak Louder Than Words

Leadership is a unique and special bond between leaders and their constituents. The development of this relationship requires our constant attention. Credibility is earned, not conferred by title or position. The following are five fundamental actions we have found that help build credibility:

1. *Know your constituents.* Building any relationship begins with getting to know those we desire to lead. Find out what is important to your constituents. Only in this way can you show them how their interests can be served by aligning them with yours.

A recent study points out that the ability—or inability—to understand other people's perspectives is the most glaring difference between successful and unsuccessful managers. How do you get to know the aspirations of others? There's no substitute for spending time with and listening to your constituents.

2. *Stand up for your beliefs.* In our culture we tend to appreciate people who clearly take a position. We resolutely refuse to follow people who lack confidence in their own decisions. People feel stress when confused about what you stand for; not knowing what you believe leads to conflict, indecision, and political rivalry.

There is, however, a danger in always standing on principle. It can make you rigid and insensitive, precisely the attributes that lead to derailment and termination. The key to escaping rigidity is to remain open to others and to new information.

3. *Speak with passion.* To gain the commitment of others you must communicate your excitement about the dream. If the leader is a wet match, there will be no spark to ignite passion in others. Effective leadership means delivering the message in a way that lives and breathes. Napoleon is reported to have said, "If you want to lead the people, you must first speak to their eyes." Paint word pictures. Tell stories. Relate anecdotes. Weave metaphors. Enable others to see, hear, taste, smell, and feel what you experience. Martin Luther King, Jr. taught the world that when the dream lives inside others, it lives forever.

4. *Lead by example.* Leaders are role models. We look to them for clues on how we should behave. We believe their actions over their words, every time.

If you ask others to observe certain standards, then you need to live by the same rules. That is exactly what we were told many times by exemplary leaders: You can only lead by example.

Leadership is not a spectator sport. Leaders don't sit in the stands and watch. But hero myths aside, neither are leaders in the game substituting for the players. Leaders coach. They show others how to behave, on and off the field. You demonstrate to others what is important by how you spend your time, by the priorities on your agenda, by the questions you ask and the people you see.

5. *Conquer yourself.* Jim Whitaker was the first American to reach the summit of Mt. Everest. He learned from his experience that "You never conquer a mountain. Mountains can't be conquered," he told us. "You conquer yourself—your hopes, your fears."

The real struggle of leadership is internal. Do you understand what is going on in your organization and the world in which it operates? Are you prepared to handle the problems the organization is facing? Can you make the right decision? Where should the organization be headed? These and more make up the internal struggle of leadership.

This everyday struggle places enormous stress upon the leader. We will not place our confidence in someone who appears weak, uncertain, or lacking in resolve. People need to sense that the leader's internal struggle—if they know it to exist—has been fought and won.

What Is a Leader to Do?

The self-confidence required to lead has at its core two sources: knowledge and integrity.

Conquering yourself means learning about yourself—your skills and inadequacies, beliefs and prejudices, talents and shortcomings. Self-confidence develops as you build on strengths and overcome weaknesses.

Self-confidence also comes with worldliness. The leader is usually the first to encounter the world outside the boundaries of the organization. The more the leader knows about that world, the easier it is to approach it with assurance. Thus, you should seek to learn as much as possible about the forces that affect your organization, be they political, economic, social, moral, or artistic.

With knowledge of the inner and outer worlds comes an awareness of the competing value systems, of the many different ways to run an organization. The internal resolution of these competing beliefs is what leads to personal integrity. A leader with integrity has one self, at home and at work. The late industrialist, John Studebaker, stated it clearly: "To have integrity, the individual cannot merely be a weathervane turning briskly with every doctrinal wind that blows. The individual must possess key loyalties and key convictions which can serve as a basis of judgment and a standard of action."

There is no well-cut path to the future, only wilderness. Strongly held beliefs compel leaders to take a stand and go out in front. Credibility begins with a credo. If, as a leader, you are to have the self-confidence needed to step out into the unknown, you might begin each day by looking in the mirror and asking yourself, "Just what do I stand for?"

5

Power and Leadership in Organizations

EDWIN P. HOLLANDER
LYNN R. OFFERMANN

Over the past decade or more, significant developments have occurred in thinking about the participation of followers in leadership and the exercise of power in organizations. Concepts of empowerment and power sharing reflect a shift in focus from a leader-dominated view to a broader one of follower involvement in expanding power (see e.g., Burke, 1986; Kanter, 1981). This development has been affected by the greater attention to groups and team effort in the workplace attributable in part to Japanese management practices (e.g., Ouchi, 1981), which had precursors in the "human relations" approach (e.g., Likert, 1961; McGregor, 1960). Accordingly, there now is a context of thinking encouraging the value of participative leadership, at least in organizational psychology. In this article, we present the background of the expanding power of followers, review some of its current features and applications, and point to new directions of effort.

Leadership clearly depends on responsive followers in a process involving the direction and maintenance of collective activity. Central to this process are one or more leaders who are the primary actors serving vital functions, especially defining the situation and communicating it to followers. Other leadership functions are such roles as problem solver and planner, adjudicator of conflict, advocate, and external liaison. Because the leader cannot do everything alone, these functions need to be dispersed and involve sharing power and engaging others' talents through empowerment. Leadership is therefore a system of relationships with constraints as well as opportunities (see Stewart, 1982). System constraints include not only task demands but also the expectations and commitments of followers.

Power is not the same as leadership, but often is seen as a feature of it (see Maccoby, 1976, 1981; McClelland, 1975; Zaleznik & Kets deVries, 1975). Power in organizations has three identifiable forms, which often exist together as a result of an individual's position in a time and place, as well as his or her personal qualities. The most familiar form is *power over*, which is explicit or implicit dominance. Clearly, leadership in organizations involves such power in varying degrees. But Freud (1921/1960), for one, compared dominance unfavorably with leadership, and Cowley (1928) called such authority-based power "headship." A leader's dependence on this kind of power has costs in undermining both relationships with followers and goal achievement (Kipnis, 1976). A second form is *power to*, which gives individuals the opportunity to act more freely within some realms of organizational operations, through power sharing, or what is commonly called *empowerment*. A third form is *power from*, which is the ability to resist the power of others by effectively fending off their unwanted demands. High status carries the potential for all of these power forms, while lower status participants may at best have one or two of the latter forms available to them.

Both leadership and followership can be active roles, given the reality that hierarchical organizations require both at every level. The traditional view of the follower role as mainly passive is misconstrued. Although leaders command greater attention and influence, there is more awareness now of follower influence on leaders, especially insofar as follower expectations and perceptions affect the process of leadership (see Hollander, 1985, 1986; Lord & Maher, 1990), as will be discussed in more detail later.

Historical Developments

From Traits to Attributions

The original trait conception of leadership was founded on the major assumption that leaders possessed universal characteristics that *made* them leaders. These characteristics were seen to be fixed, largely inborn, and applicable across situations. Broadly speaking, this was the essence of the "Great Man Theory" promulgated by Galton (1869) and his disciples. Among its failings were an absence of consideration of the situation faced by the leader, including the followers to be led and any concern with the quality of the leader's *performance*. On the latter point, interest developed in the particular behaviors or skills needed to perform well as a leader, rather than those needed to become one.

Almost four decades ago, the situational approach to leadership came on the scene and largely displaced the dominant trait approach (e.g., Hemphill, 1949). Its primary thrust was that situations varied in the qualities demanded of leaders, so those qualities were appropriate to a particular task and interpersonal context. This development marked a change from the traditional trait conception and was furthered by research describing leader behavior begun in 1947 at Ohio State University (see Fleishman's, 1973, review of consideration and initiation of structure). A counterpart to this work was the development of assessment centers to evaluate leader skills (see Thornton & Byham, 1982).

Many situational elements are now recognized as affecting the process of leadership, in addition to the characteristics of the leader and followers. Among them are the nature of the task or activity, its history, the availability of human and material resources, and the quality of leader-follower relations. These relations are affected by the leader's attributes, including his or her perceived competence, motivation, and personality characteristics, as they relate to followers. All can play a part in shaping followers' perceptions of and responses to the leader. Indeed, this link between perceptions and behavior is the essence of the current interest in leader attributes perceived by followers, and the followers' implicit leadership theories (ILTs; e.g., Calder, 1977; Rush, Thomas, & Lord, 1977). Basically, ILTs are followers' preconceptions of what a leader ought to be like, such as *competent* and *considerate*. However, bias can be introduced into leadership ratings by followers if they make their ILTs the basis for rating leaders, rather than the leaders' actual behavior.

Today, the emphasis has shifted from traits to follower attributions of leaders that make followers respond affirmatively or otherwise to their leader's qualities (Lord, DeVader, & Alliger, 1986). These perceptions are checked against prototypes held by followers of leader attributes and how leaders should perform (see Lord & Maher, 1990). This line of work is part of the greater attention being given to cognitive elements in leader-follower relations, exemplified by follower expectations and attributions. Such an integration of cognition and leadership is but one example of how the increasing prominence of cognitive approaches in psychology in general can be seen in organizational research (e.g., Gioia & Sims, 1986).

A related approach to leader cognition considers it to be based on relatively stable cognitive qualities, a style. This is illustrated by the work on "integrative complexity" in cognition by Suedfeld and Tetlock (1977), which refers to the richness of a leader's cognitive elements, revealed by content analyzing his or her verbal materials. Another approach is the work of Fiedler and Garcia (1987) on "cognitive capacity," essentially intelligence, whose applicability Fiedler and Leister (1977) found was limited by what a leader's superior would allow.

Leader and Follower Roles

Ideas about leadership have viewed the leader and followers in highly differentiated roles, although being a follower can be an active role that holds the potential of leadership. Indeed, behaviors seen to represent effective leadership include attributes of good followership, such as dependability and responsiveness (see Hollander & Webb, 1955; Kouzes & Posner, 1987). Granting that there is an imbalance of power, influence can be exerted in both roles, as part of a social exchange (Homans, 1961). To some degree, effective leadership depends on reciprocity and the potential for two-way influence and power sharing. This is so despite the extremes of leaders' shrinking from using power and seeing it as necessarily bad or, alternatively, seeking it at the expense of abusing less powerful others and damaging their relationships with those others. The latter difficulty is seen in Kipnis's (1976) work on the "metamorphoses of power," dealing with the changes that may be brought about in the "powerholder" by having high power over others, including exalted self-worth and isolation from and devaluation of less powerful others.

About 25 years ago, two especially important conceptual and research approaches were developed: contingency models and transactional approaches to leadership. Both added to understanding the complexities of leadership and were a departure from the traditional dichotomy of individual traits or situational conditions as determiners of (a) who becomes a leader and (b) who performs well as a leader.

Contingency Models

The contingency model approach to leadership was initiated by the Fiedler (1967) least preferred coworker (LPC) contingency model, followed by the Evans (1970) and House (1971) path-goal model, and the Vroom and Yetton (1973) normative model of leadership and decision making. These and other contingency models considered leadership effectiveness to be a joint function of leader qualities and situational demands as contingencies interacting to make leader qualities variously appropriate to the task at hand.

Fiedler's LPC model distinguishes between two leader styles, task oriented and relationship oriented, using the LPC measure. Respondents are asked to rate the person in their lives with whom they could work least well. High LPC scores are associated with favorable ratings and relationship orientation, and low LPC scores with unfavorable ratings and task orientation. Fiedler and his colleagues found that such orientations are associated with greater or lesser effectiveness depending on three situational contingencies: (a) leader-member relations, (b) task structure, and (c) leader position power. According to Fiedler (1967), when these factors are either all favorable or unfavorable, task-oriented leaders should perform best. When they are mixed or intermediate, relationship-oriented leaders should perform best. As the first and most prominent contingency model, the LPC has continued to generate interest and controversy (e.g., Fiedler, 1977; Rice & Kastenbaum, 1983; Schriesheim & Kerr, 1977).

Path-goal theory (House, 1971; House & Mitchell, 1974) is a contingency model based on the leader's effectiveness in increasing subordinates' motivation along a path leading to a goal. The three contingencies seen to face the leader are the task, the characteristics of the subordinates, and the nature of the subordinates' group. The emphasis is on the leader's behavior as a source of satisfaction to subordinates. Among the model's predictions are (a) that leader consideration behavior will be more effective when there is low role ambiguity for subordinates, whereas initiating structure will be superior under conditions of high role ambiguity and high job complexity and (b) that subordinates will respond better to leader directive behavior when the task is unstructured, and less when it is structured (see House & Dessler, 1974).

The Vroom and Yetton (1973) normative contingency model emphasizes increased follower involvement in decision making ranging from autocratic, consultative, to group leadership styles. Choice of style is based on situational factors, including importance of decision quality, availability of information to the leader and followers, clarity of the problem, and the degree to which followers' acceptance is necessary to implementing the decision. Studying the model may give leaders an awareness of how they make decisions, what goes into them, and how to improve that process (Baker, 1980).

Transactional Approaches

A process-oriented *transactional* approach to leadership developed out of a social exchange perspective. It emphasizes the implicit social exchange or transaction over time that exists between the leader and followers, including reciprocal influence and interpersonal perception (see Hollander, 1964, 1978; Hollander & Julian, 1969; Homans, 1961). The leader gives benefits to followers, such as a definition of the situation and direction, which is reciprocated by followers in heightened esteem for and responsiveness to the leader. This transactional approach fits other contemporary social science views emphasizing the significance of persuasive influence, rather than coercive power and compliance in organizational leadership.

Furthermore, a transactional approach gives special emphasis to the significance of followers' perceptions of the leader. Relatedly, Graen (1975) developed a Leader Member Exchange (LMX) model of leader-follower relationships emphasizing role-making between a leader and particular followers (see Dienesch & Liden, 1986). Briefly, the LMX model distinguishes between followers who are close to the leader and those who are more distant. The first have a better quality relationship with the leader, but the leader also has higher expectations for their performance and loyalty. For the others, the leader makes fewer personal demands and gives fewer benefits. For example, subordinates who reported a high-quality relationship with their supervisors assumed more job responsibility, contributed more, and were rated as higher performers than those with low-quality relationships (Liden & Graen, 1980).

Transactional approaches center on the followers' perceptions of and expectations about the leader's actions and motives, in accordance with attributional analysis. Heider's (1958) earlier work on the attribution of intentions through interpersonal perception is exemplified in the distinction between *can* and *will*. If a leader is perceived to be able to achieve a favorable outcome, but does not because of an apparent failure of will, this causes a greater loss of following than if he or she is unable to achieve something desirable but has made an evident effort, nonetheless.

This is related to the "idiosyncrasy credit" model of innovative leadership (Hollander, 1958), dealing with a leader's latitude to initiate change as a function of followers' perceptions of that leader's competence and signs of loyalty that engender trust. Specifically, the idiosyncrasy credit model focuses on a dynamic process of interpersonal evaluation in leadership. It emphasizes the leader's sources of credits earned in the eyes of followers that allow latitude for deviations that would be unacceptable for those without such credit. Credits come from perceived competence and conformity to group norms, as a sign of loyalty, and then can be used for innovative actions expected within the leader's role. Unused credits can be drained by failing to fulfill followers' role expectations, including inaction in the face of need, self-serving and other negatively viewed behaviors, and perceptions of weak motivation, incompetence, and responsibility for failure (cf. Alvarez, 1968).

A closely associated question concerns how followers perceive the leader's source of authority, or "legitimacy," in responding to that leader. A leader's legitimacy affects group performance, the followers' perceptions of the leader (e.g., Ben-Yoav, Hollander, & Carnevale, 1983), and the leader's perception of followers (cf. Green & Mitchell, 1979). Generally, election creates a heightened psychological identification between followers and the leader, insofar as they have a greater sense of involvement with someone for whom their responsibility is greater. But they also have higher expectations about the leader and may make more demands on the leader. Elected leaders who fail to perform well are more vulnerable to criticism than appointed leaders, particularly if they are seen to be competent in the first place (Hollander & Julian, 1970, 1978). Although election and appointment can create different psychological climates between leaders and followers, this does not deny the very real possibility for organization leaders to attain a "following" by doing more than exercising authority, as Katz and Kahn (1978) have observed in saying that organizational *leadership* is an increment of influence above compliance based in authority. This would be seen in showing attributes such as trustworthiness and credibility that engage followers and evoke commitment from them.

One effect of the current attributional view is to make even more explicit the significance of followers' and others' perceptions of the leader. These perceptions set up expectancies that may affect the leader's own sense of latitude to take or not take actions affecting followers. In this way, follower perceptions can serve as a constraint or check on leader behavior. There also are associated expectations about leader characteristics such as appropriate competence and motivation, as well as the perceived motives behind leader behavior, especially in dealing with followers, peers, superiors, and adversaries. However, the reverse perspective of the leader's perception of followers also is significant in determining leader behavior (see Mitchell, Green, & Wood, 1981). For example, when an employee's performance is unsatisfactory, coercive corrective actions are seen as most appropriate if failure is perceived to be due to the subordinate's lack of effort; by contrast, taking no immediate corrective action is seen as more appropriate when failure is perceived to be due to factors outside the subordinate's control, such as luck or task difficulty (Pence, Pendleton, Dobbins, & Sgro, 1982).

From Charismatic to Transformational Leadership

An older trait-based concept, which has now been revitalized, is *charismatic* leadership, founded on an emotional appeal. Sociologist Max Weber (1921/1946) based the concept on the Greek word *charisma*, which means divine gift, and considered such a leader to have considerable power over followers, especially in a time of crisis when there are strong needs for direction. In a newer guise, House (1977) has proposed that the leader-follower bond is due less to an emotional appeal than to the leader gripping followers with a program of action, that is, a goal and the path to achieve it. From his political science perspective, Burns (1978) developed a related concept in his idea of the "transformational leader" who changes the outlook and behavior of followers.

Burns's idea of the leader as a transforming agent has been applied to organizational leadership by Bass (1985), Bennis and Nanus (1985), and Conger and Kanungo (1988), especially to account for exceptional performance. The essential point is that the leader strives to go beyond the bounds of the usual to bring about a change in follower thinking that will redirect follower actions (see Fiedler & House, 1988). Ideas of excellence, exemplified in the popular book by Peters and Waterman (1983), are another example of this thrust, as is Vaill's (1982) work on "high-performing systems."

Transformational leadership can be seen as an extension of transactional leadership, but with greater rewards in leader intensity and follower arousal. Indeed, according to Bass (1985) transformational leadership has two transactional factors (i.e., contingent reward and management by exception), in addition to charisma, intellectual stimulation, and individual attention to followers. However, it is important to note whether charisma is primarily directed to the service of the leader's self-oriented ends or to mission-oriented ends, which is a distinction Burns (1978) had made. Coupled with personalized power needs, the outcome of a charismatic appeal can be destructive, as Hogan, Raskin, and Fazzini (1988) have observed in their paper, "The Dark Side of Charisma."

Organizational Culture and Leader Style

Also significant today is the attention being given to *organizational culture*, as seen in the recent works of Deal and Kennedy (1982), Schein (1985), and Kilmann, Saxton, Serpa, and Associates (1985). This emphasis has broadened an earlier interest in organizational climate, exemplified by Likert's (1961) observation that the top leader sets a climate or tone in an organization that permeates the leader style there. For instance, a highly placed autocratic leader, who is low on input and participation from subordinates, can set a climate that limits the ability of leaders below to be participative. Therefore, style in some degree is a function of the climate and culture of the organization.

Individual differences among leaders are perceived as real and do play a role in follower satisfaction and performance outcomes. Leader style now is understood to be more complex than just being typical behavior, as was thought earlier. Obviously, it is affected by such situational constraints as role demands, which are related to the leader's level in the organization (see Boyatzis, 1982) and the expectations of followers. Style also is a function of the particular followers with whom the leader interacts, as pointed out in the leader-member exchange model already noted.

Newer Developments and Orientations

The conceptual and research developments described show increasing attention to the follower in the leadership process. Although the study of leadership has always presumed the existence of followers, their roles were viewed as essentially passive. Recent models have increasingly sought to integrate followers more fully into an understanding of leadership, building on the foundation provided by contingency and transactional models.

Attribution approaches provide a richer perspective on the leader-follower dynamic, focusing both on follower behavior as the stimulus for leader behavior and the obverse, thus expanding leadership as a process worthy of study as either a dependent or an independent variable. As noted earlier, ILTs examine the way in which follower perceptions and expectations about leaders may structure the leader-follower relationship and may adversely affect the validity of subordinate evaluations of leader behavior. Dynamic leader-member exchange relationships are key features in models by Hollander (1958, 1978) and Graen (1975; Graen & Scandura, 1987), with an increasing interest in follower influence and follower perceptions of leaders. Furthermore, charismatic leaders and, therefore, the charismatic component of transformational leaders, are identified by the effects they have on their followers.

Do these changes in views of leadership benefit organizations that seek to use current leadership concepts? Clearly, they do. Greater attention to followers, and their role in understanding and promoting leadership, is compatible with changes in the organizational environments faced by today's leaders. A climate of participative management with greater follower involvement in decision making appears to be more common in organizations and appears to increase commitment and profitability (Burke, 1986).

Quality circles, groups of employees meeting regularly to discover and solve work problems in their areas, are on the rise (Ledford, Lawler, & Mohrman, 1988). Employee stock ownership programs (ESOPs), such as the one at Weirton Steel in West Virginia, are breaking down traditional distinctions between management and labor. The development of self-managed work teams (Goodman, Devadas, & Hughson, 1988) shows that there may be new roles for corporate leaders, with some functions associated with traditional leadership being performed by committed peer groups. All of these workplace trends underline the importance of developing and expanding the roles of followers in the leadership of organizations. These trends also presume the willingness of leaders themselves to embrace the notion of sharing power with subordinates.

The Role of Power

Underlying the concern for developing the role of followers in the leadership process is the reality of power, in the several forms discussed earlier. As already noted, power plays a major part in the interactions occurring in organizational life (see Pfeffer, 1981). It cannot be ignored if we hope to understand and improve the functioning of organizations from within (Kanter, 1981; Mintzberg, 1983). Power over others is also especially intertwined with an understanding of leadership processes, with regard both to its appropriateness and limitations (Hollander, 1985).

Yet, despite the relevance of power to organizations in general, and to an understanding of leadership in particular, research studies of power and leadership are not well integrated. Also, assumptions about power often remain unstated and untested. Like love, its importance and existence are acknowledged, but its study is often resisted. And those with the most power and influence in organizations have typically been most able to shield themselves from study (Kipnis, 1976).

Sharing Power

One of the clearest bridges between the study of power and leadership in organizations has been in the area of subordinate participation in decision making (PDM). Advocates of PDM have theoretical roots in a human relations approach to management that stresses social interaction and power equalization. Unfortunately, little agreement exists on a definition of participation, and wide variations exist in its content, degree, scope, formality, and on whether it should be mandatory or voluntary (Locke & Schweiger, 1979). To some extent, however, all forms of participation embody the idea that employees should be permitted or even encouraged to influence their working environment. Accordingly, a continuum of employee influence can be offered ranging from no influence (autocratic decisions) through various levels of opinion-giving (consultative decisions) to truly joint decision making (power sharing) (e.g., Tannenbaum & Schmidt, 1958).

Evidence of positive relationships between participative decision making and outcomes such as subordinate productivity, motivation, and satisfaction is mixed. In a recent meta-analysis, Miller and Monge (1986) reported a notable positive relationship between participation and satisfaction (mean correlation .34) and a small, but significant, correlation between participation and performance (mean correlation .15). Yet the results of another recent meta-analysis by Wagner and Gooding (1987) suggest that positive participation-outcome relationships may be largely due to methodological artifacts including use of percept-percept correlations, those obtained from the same individual with the same questionnaire at the same time, rather than correlations based on multiple sources and differences between the types of subjects used, for example, students versus workers.

In examining both laboratory and field studies of PDM, Schweiger and Leana (1986) concluded that contextual variables are important in moderating the relationship between PDM and performance and that no one degree of participation, from autocratic to fully participative, can be employed effectively for all subordinates in all situations. This is, of course, what contingency theorists such as Vroom and Yetton (1973) have long maintained. To some, the mixed effects of PDM, particularly in extending beyond subordinate satisfaction, is reason to question the use of participation, or at least to consider it as just one of a number of possible organizational interventions geared to organizational productivity. To others, participation is valued for fulfilling human psychological needs and promoting employee health and should be encouraged whether or not it increases productivity. According to Sashkin (1984), nonparticipation may be psychologically and physiologically damaging, and because participation may increase productivity, or at minimum not decrease it, participation is therefore an ethical imperative.

In cases in which employees express opinions or give suggestions that may or may not be accepted or acted on by their supervisors, participation can be more accurately thought of as an influence-sharing option with the leader retaining power. Decisions made may or may not reflect follower input because subordinates may participate but have little influence on decision making (Hoffman, Burke, & Maier, 1965; Mulder, 1971). Indeed, one potential drawback of such a consultative form of participation is that it may unduly raise the expectations of followers that their suggestions and ideas will be regularly accepted. Routine failure to accept follower influence may make followers believe that participation is a sham designed to give them a sense of involvement that will motivate them without giving them any real influence. For example, members of quality circles receiving largely negative responses to their suggestions tend to become discouraged and stop meeting (Ledford et al., 1988).

Implementing participation by followers also may require skills a given leader does not possess. Recent work by Crouch and Yetton (1987) has suggested that high performance costs may be incurred by managers with poor conflict management skills who attempt to bring subordinates together to resolve conflict. Alternatively, performance increments may be associated with such meetings convened by leaders with good conflict management skills. If participation by subordinates is to be encouraged, then organizations need to consider ways in which managers can be trained in the skills required to implement meaningful participation.

Distributing Power

True follower development needs to go beyond encouraging follower influence (sharing power) to allowing followers to have decision responsibility (distributing power). For this purpose, delegation may be a better model than participation for truly empowering others. Delegation involves decisions that managers allow subordinates to make on their own (Heller & Yukl, 1969). It typically involves decision making by individual subordinates rather than by subordinate groups or manager-subordinate dyads and stresses subordinate autonomy in decision making (Locke & Schweiger, 1979). Yet delegation has received far less research attention than participation. Although it is often depicted as the extreme end of the participation continuum, delegation has been shown to be a very different process than participation (Leana, 1986, 1987).

Unlike the human relations background of participation, delegation derives from a cognitive growth approach to job enrichment advocating individual development through expanded use of skills, autonomy, and responsibility. In a recent study comparing delegation and participation, Leana (1987) found that managers reported the use of delegation under highly circumscribed conditions, specifically when less important decisions were involved, the subordinate was seen as capable, and the manager was too overloaded to participate. Furthermore, she found that delegation was correlated with higher subordinate performance, whereas participation was correlated with lower performance. These potentially superior organizational outcomes for delegation may be due to the fact that unlike participation, delegation is not indiscriminate but considers the ability and responsibility of followers for the task at hand. High performers should have more functions delegated to them than low performers. Therefore, although delegation distributes power, it does so selectively rather than equally.

Self-managed work teams are current examples of follower groups to whom authority has been delegated with successful results (Goodman et al., 1988). Self-managed teams differ from traditional work crews in the greater degree of control they exert over both the management and execution of group tasks, which may include allocating jobs to members, having responsibility for production levels, solving local production problems, selecting and training new members, and delivering finished goods (see Goodman et al., 1988, for specific case examples). The existence of such self-managed groups does not, however, *necessarily* preclude a role for an external leader, sometimes referred to as a *coordinator* or *consultant.* The role of the external leader differs from the traditional leader role in that the key leadership functions are in monitoring and facilitating the team in performing its own regulation. The most important leadership behaviors in these cases have been suggested to be encouraging self-reinforcement, self-observation, and self-evaluation (Manz & Sims, 1987).

Barriers to Empowerment

There are clear barriers to promoting the distribution of power in organizations. Although Tannenbaum (1968) found that power in organizations is not finite but can expand, there remains a pervasive belief that to empower others is to lose power oneself. In short, although power is not a zero-sum quality, it is often perceived as such. This likely perceived loss of power may be a deterrent for many leaders, particularly those who have a high need for power. At the Ford Motor Company, effective implementation of a large-scale employee involvement program necessitated dispelling the misperceptions of supervisors that employee involvement would undermine their authority or eliminate their jobs (Banas, 1988).

Some managers may perceive the strong use of power as necessary to do their jobs. In dealing with poor performance, bank managers in one study were found to report greater satisfaction with their handling of events and their outcomes when they were more punishing (Green, Fairhurst, & Snavely, 1986). Subordinates may well have felt differently about the experience. Greater managerial awareness of the negative effects of punishment on subordinates may be needed.

Organizations should be aware, however, that it is unrealistic to expect leaders to distribute power to others when negative consequences of actions taken will fall on the leader. The unwillingness of many leaders to delegate is understandable considering that, in many organizations, no matter who actually makes decisions, leaders retain responsibility for decisions made in their units. When the team loses, it is often the coach or manager who gets fired (Pfeffer, 1977).

In Vroom and Yetton's (1973) normative model of decision making in leadership, leaders are urged to expand participation and delegation for individuals when (a) they lack the information necessary to make decisions themselves and subordinates have enough information to make high-quality decisions, (b) subordinates share the organization's goals, and (c) subordinate acceptance and commitment are needed. Yet each of these components requires an assessment by the leader that may be biased toward the leader's preferred outcome, whether autocratic, participative, or something in between. Thus, autocratically oriented leaders may be more inclined than participatively oriented leaders to feel that their own information is sufficient, that subordinates lack information and commitment, and that subordinate commitment is not needed or important for most decisions.

In fact, research has shown that leaders contemplating participation pay close attention to how much information they have themselves and whether subordinates share the organization's goals, involving others when they lack information and when others share the goals, as the model suggests they should. Leaders are also more likely to underestimate the need for subordinate commitment to the effective implementation of decisions, making guidelines dealing with the importance of obtaining subordinate commitment the most commonly violated provision of Vroom and Yetton's (1973; Vroom & Jago, 1988) model. Furthermore, it would be difficult for subordinates ever to obtain enough information to make quality decisions if leaders use their own information power in a way that deprives subordinates of what they need to participate (see Mulder, 1971).

Empowerment as Career Development
Through Modeling and Mentoring

By sharing power and allowing themselves to be influenced by followers and by distributing power through delegation, leaders may foster the development of leadership in others. In recent years, increasing attention has been paid to leaders as models and mentors. Modeling has been proposed as a mechanism to help persons learn to lead themselves (Manz & Sims, 1988), although it has been shown to be a complex phenomenon involving multiple linkages going beyond mere imitation. Thus, leaders who had previously viewed videotaped supervisors reprimanding a subordinate later showed less positive reinforcement and goal-setting behavior in their own interaction with a subordinate, as might be expected (Manz & Sims, 1986). However, goal-setting behavior observed on videotape unexpectedly increased leader reprimand behavior. Interestingly, these effects were found as a result of exposure to a videotaped supervisor without explicit instructions to model the behaviors displayed. Given some of the effects of leader-modeled behavior found, further study is necessary. Such study should examine modeling both for its usefulness as a mechanism of leader development and for its effects on subordinates' satisfaction and performance.

Modeling can be considered part of the concept of mentoring (see Kram, 1985), in which a key component of the leader role is seen to be the advancement and development of talented subordinates. In some organizations, managers are evaluated in part on their abilities to develop subordinates. For example, Southwestern Bell accomplishes this by including subordinate development items in the performance appraisal instrument for middle and lower level managers (Vandaveer & Varca, 1988). Managers are rated on such items as delegating responsibility with commensurate authority and follow-up; effectively involving subordinates in decisions affecting them; and providing information, guidance, and development opportunities for their subordinates. In these environments, leaders need to identify subordinates' potential, model appropriate behavior by serving as a referent, increasingly share power by giving subordinates access and participation, and ultimately distribute power to subordinates through delegation with appropriate follow-up.

One of the most difficult, but important, elements of delegation may be allowing subordinates to make mistakes (Manz & Sims, 1988). Southwestern Bell also incorporates a performance appraisal item dealing with the encouragement and positive reward of intelligent risk-taking, without punishing occasional failure. Some executives know this lesson well.

When faced with a manager who had made a $100,000 mistake and who suggested that maybe he should be fired, one executive said, "Why should I fire you when I've just invested $100,000 in your development?" (McCall, Lombardo, & Morrison, 1988, p. 154).

Expanding the role of subordinates may expand the role of leader as well. Although employees gain in expertise and knowledge through participation and delegation, leaders may be freer to engage in other profitable activities such as long-term planning, market forecasting, and entrepreneurship. General Electric chairman John F. Welch, Jr. has advocated stretching managers thin to force them to delegate less critical decisions to subordinates so they can concentrate on the important ones. This involves increasing responsibility at lower levels in the organization. In spreading this message widely across his organization, Welch hopes to encourage lower level managers to push their superiors for more freedom (Potts, 1988). Time-management advocates have long expressed the same hope of better use of management talent for major decisions by delegating responsibility downward (e.g., Patten, 1981). More research on the effects of delegation and follow-up is needed to assess the impact of such power distribution.

Informal Influence

The discussion so far has centered on power sharing and distribution through relatively formal mechanisms in organizations, usually at the leader's initiative. Yet a thriving area of current research deals with informal influence, which occurs without formal authority and usually at the follower's initiative. In keeping with a general trend toward focusing on the duality of good leadership and responsive/proactive followership, more studies are being done on the informal processes of upward influence in organizations. For example, one study of public sector supervisors and their managers (Waldera, 1988) showed that better quality supervisor-manager relationships and a greater range of supervisory influence strategies were associated with greater self-rated upward influence.

We are learning a great deal about associations between numerous variables and measures of organizational influence (see Porter, Allen, & Angle, 1981, for a review). For example, women typically have been shown to have less upward influence than men (e.g., Brass, 1985; Trempe, Rigny, & Haccoun, 1985). This difference has been attributed to the less central positions in organizational networks and lower access that women have to the main powerholders in an organization (Brass, 1985). Because information and access are essential to organizational functioning, they are keys to power.

Strategies of upward influence also are gaining attention. Strategies used have been shown to be influenced by numerous individual characteristics, including the person's level in the organization (e.g., Kipnis, Schmidt, & Wilkinson, 1980; Offermann & Schrier, 1985), their years of experience (Mowday, 1979), their own perceived power (Kipnis, Schmidt, Swaffin-Smith, & Wilkinson, 1984), their own need for power (Mowday, 1979) or apprehension about power (Offermann & Schrier, 1985), and their investment in the influence objective (Sussman & Vecchio, 1982).

Subordinate influence strategies also have been found to be affected by the goal desired by the subordinate and the supervisor's leadership style. Waldera (1988) found that more direct strategies were used in influence attempts dealing with attaining organizational objectives than were used for achieving personal objectives. Ansari and Kapoor (1987) reported that when desiring personal benefits, subordinates tended to use ingratiation, whereas organizational goals were sought through the use of combinations of rational and nonrational strategies such as persuasion, blocking, and upward appeals. Nonrational strategies were more commonly used with authoritarian leaders, whereas rational persuasion was more common with participative leaders. Thus, participation may be viewed not only as a leader method of sharing influence, but also as a style that affects the ways in which subordinates attempt to influence the leader.

Subordinate strategies may also be affected by characteristics of the target of influence. For example, when attempting to influence a supervisor, employees are more likely to use self-presentation, supporting data, coalitions, and rational tactics than when trying to influence peers or subordinates (Kipnis et al., 1980). The gender of the target supervisor may also affect the strategies used by subordinates, with subordinates less likely to withdraw and more likely to try to reason with a male rather than a female supervisor (Offermann & Kearney, 1988). These studies indicate that followers need not be passive compliers, and their results provide added support for a two-way influence conception of leadership (e.g., Ben-Yoav et al., 1983; Elgie, Hollander, & Rice, 1988). There is much to be learned about leadership from an understanding of leaders as both initiators and targets of influence.

Challenges to Leadership Research

Although there has been an encouraging increase in interest in power in organizations, and steady activity in leadership research and application, further work is needed to improve integration of research on power and leadership. Expanding the follower role requires an understanding of power sharing, power distribution, and informal influence and their effects. We have suggested the importance of empowering followers in the leadership process. As described, leadership research and applications have moved consistently in this direction over time, yet cautions need to be acknowledged. Employee involvement may make for more effective use of human resources, but should not be expected to be a panacea for all organizational problems. Furthermore, in an era of "down-sizing," developing employees who then have nowhere to go within the organization can be destructive.

Methodological problems in the measurement of power are common and in need of resolution (Podsakoff & Schriesheim, 1985). Further work is needed to understand the dynamics of formal and informal subordinate influence as these affect subordinates, leaders, and organizations. In addition, the resurgence of interest in charismatic and transformational leadership ought to be viewed with appropriate caution. A major question to consider is how such leader-centric approaches mesh with the growing trend toward empowerment and subordinate influence.

Another critical shortcoming is the failure of most leadership models to consider levels of leadership. Most models use the term *leader* to designate individuals occupying a wide range of supervisory positions, from first-line supervisors to executives. In the past, most leaders studied were at the lowest levels of organizations (cf. Boyatzis, 1982). Recently, more attention has been given to more senior-level leaders and executives (e.g., Kotter, 1982; Levinson & Rosenthal, 1984). Unfortunately, it is often difficult to make comparisons across studies in regard to "supervisors," "leaders," and "executives." Not atypically, the term *executives* is operationalized as individuals to whom the responding firms attached the term, even with an awareness that these individuals encompass many levels and that the term is variably applied in different organizations. Despite this problem, understanding leadership at the top of the organizational hierarchy is important, as well as studying the empowerment of lower level participants.

Jacobs and Jaques (1987) have developed a model expressly to consider the level of leadership within an organization and to understand the requisite skills needed for success at a given level. Looking at leadership as *value added* to the resources of the system at any level, what leaders must do to add value to an organizational system will differ depending on their organizational level and the nature of the organization (e.g., public vs. private). Tasks, goals, and time frames will differ considerably by level, with higher level leadership requiring greater conceptual effort in dealing with uncertainty, abstraction, and longer time frames.

The concept of leadership as value-added, or incremental to basic management components, should help address the issue of whether managers and leaders are different (see Zaleznik, 1977). Rather than worrying about distinctions between leaders and managers, leadership researchers need to consider seriously whether the "leaders" being studied are perceived as such by their subordinates and peers. Focusing on follower perceptions indicates that supervisors and leaders may be perceived differently. Recent work on ILTs suggests that although people use the same dimensions to describe supervisors and leaders, ratings in response to the cue *supervisor* are significantly less favorable than those given in response to the cue of *leader* (Offermann & Kennedy, 1987). This points to the need to study those individuals identified as leaders by subordinates, perhaps comparing them not only with followers but also with persons of comparable organizational authority and position who are not so identified. These "leaders" may or may not be managers, because the exercise of authority alone is not the hallmark of leadership. But they should be those at any level who are perceived as leaders and whose actions move their organizations toward achieving their goals.

There also is a need to examine the dynamic features of leadership over time. Time frames considered could range from an episode to an entire career. Recent examples of work with a greater span of time include the development of an episodic model of power (Cobb, 1984), looking at supervisory control as a chain or sequence of events (Green et al., 1986), work on managerial careers (e.g., Howard & Bray, 1988), and leadership succession (Gordon & Rosen, 1981).

Future research must also address the issue of *leadership toward what ends* (Hollander, 1985). Just as the issue of power in organizations raises questions of moral right to participation, leadership processes cannot escape questions about ultimate goals and outcomes. Although power over others is inevitable in organizational life, it always carries with it the specter of abuse. In the wake of scandals about insider trading and corporate violations, courses in business ethics are on the rise (Eyde & Quaintance, 1988). The role of leaders as transmitters and upholders of organizational values is increasingly being stressed (e.g., Kouzes & Posner, 1987). Whether all this activity results in more ethical, responsive, and humane leadership remains to be seen.

In reviewing the considerable activity that has gone on in leadership research and practice in recent years, we believe there is good reason for optimism. Progress has been made toward applying what we know about leadership processes to ongoing organizational problems, such as simulation training.

Research on power and leadership is alive and well. Substantial gains have been made in understanding leaders and their followers, as seen in Fiedler and House's (1988) review of gains. Granting a bias toward believing in leadership as a causal force in organizational performance, even when the cause is indeterminant (Meindl, Ehrlich, & Dukerich, 1985), effective leadership *can* make a difference in important organizational outcomes (e.g., Smith, Carson, & Alexander, 1984). Our ready willingness to attribute outcomes to leadership underscores the importance of the concept both to individuals and to their organizations. Psychologists can and have played important roles in both the understanding and development of leadership in organizations. Although much remains to be done, studying leadership and followership from a power perspective shows promise of considerable return.

References

Alvarez, R. (1968). Informal reactions to deviance in simulated work organizations: A laboratory experiment. *American Sociological Review, 33,* 895–912.

Ansari, M. A., & Kapoor, A. (1987). Organizational context and upward influence tactics. *Organizational Behavior and Human Decision Processes, 40,* 39–49.

Baker, C. (1980). The Vroom-Yetton model of leadership—Model, theory or technique. *Omega, 8,* 9–10.

Banas, P. A. (1988). Employee involvement: A sustained labor/management initiative at the Ford Motor Company. In J. P. Campbell & R. J. Campbell (Eds.), *Productivity in organizations* (pp. 388–416). San Francisco: Jossey-Bass.

Bass, B. M. (1985). *Leadership and performance beyond expectations.* New York: Free Press.

Bennis, W. G., & Nanus, B. (1985). *Leaders.* New York: Harper & Row.

Ben-Yoav, O., Hollander, E. P., & Carnevale, P. J. D. (1983). Leader legitimacy, leader-follower interaction, and followers' ratings of the leader. *Journal of Social Psychology, 121,* 111–115.

Boyatzis, R. E. (1982). *The competent manager.* New York: Wiley-Interscience.

Brass, D. J. (1985). Men's and women's networks: A study of interaction patterns and influence in an organization. *Academy of Management Journal, 28,* 327–343.

Burke, W. W. (1986). Leadership as empowering others. In S. Srivasta & Associates (Eds.), *Executive power: How executives influence people and organizations* (pp. 51–77). San Francisco: Jossey-Bass.

Burns, J. M. (1978). *Leadership.* New York: Harper & Row.

Calder, B. J. (1977). An attribution theory of leadership. In B. M. Staw & G. R. Salancik (Eds.), *New directions in organizational behavior* (pp. 179–204). Chicago: St. Clair Press.

Cobb, A. T. (1984). An episodic model of power: Toward an integration of theory and research. *Academy of Management Review, 1,* 482–493.

Conger, T. A., & Kanungo, R. N. (1988). *Charismatic leadership: The elusive factor in organizational effectiveness.* San Francisco: Jossey-Bass.

Cowley, W. H. (1928). Three distinctions in the study of leaders. *Journal of Abnormal Social Psychology, 23,* 144–157.

Crouch, A., & Yetton, P. (1987). Manager behavior, leadership style, and subordinate performance: An empirical extension of the Vroom-Yetton conflict rule. *Organizational Behavior and Human Decision Processes, 39,* 384–396.

Deal, T. E., & Kennedy, A. A. (1982). *Corporate cultures: The rites and rituals of corporate life.* Reading, MA: Addison-Wesley.

Dienesch, R. M., & Liden, R. C. (1986). Leader-member exchange model of leadership: A critique and further development. *Academy of Management Review, 11,* 618–634.

Elgie, D. M., Hollander, E. P., & Rice, R. W. (1988). Appointed and elected leader responses to favorableness of feedback and level of task activity from followers. *Journal of Applied Social Psychology, 18,* 1361–1370.

Evans, M. G. (1970). The effects of supervisory behavior on the path-goal relationships. *Organizational Behavioral Human Performance, 5,* 277–298.

Eyde, L. D., & Quaintance, M. K. (1988). Ethical issues and cases in the practice of personnel psychology. *Professional Psychology, 19,* 148–154.

Fiedler, F. E. (1967). *A theory of leadership effectiveness.* New York: McGraw-Hill.

Fiedler, F. E. (1977). A rejoinder to Schriesheim and Kerr's premature obituary of the contingency model. In J. G. Hunt & L. L. Larson (Eds.), *Leadership: The cutting edge* (pp. 45–51). Carbondale: Southern Illinois University Press.

Fiedler, F. E., & Garcia, J. E. (1987). *New approaches to effective leadership.* New York: Wiley.

Fiedler, F. E., & House, R. J. (1988). Leadership theory and research: A report of progress. In C. L. Cooper & I. Robertson (Eds.), *International review of industrial and organizational psychology* (pp. 73–92). London: Wiley.

Fiedler, F. E., & Leister, A. F. (1977). Leader intelligence and task performance: A test of a multiple screen model. *Organizational Behavior and Human Performance, 20,* 1–14.

Fleishman, E. A. (1973). Twenty years of consideration and structure. In E. A. Fleishman & J. G. Hunt (Eds.), *Current developments in the study of leadership* (pp. 1–37). Carbondale: Southern Illinois University Press.

Freud, S. (1960). *Group psychology and the analysis of the ego.* New York: Bantam. (Originally published in German in 1921.)

Galton, F. (1869). *Hereditary genius: An inquiry into its laws and consequences.* London: Macmillan. (Paperback edition by Meridian Books, New York, 1962)

Gioia, D., & Sims, H. P. (1986). *The thinking organization.* San Francisco: Jossey-Bass.

Goodman, P. S., Devadas, R., & Hughson, T. L. (1988). Groups and productivity: Analyzing the effectiveness of self-managing teams. In J. P. Campbell & R. J. Campbell (Eds.), *Productivity in organizations* (pp. 295–327). San Francisco: Jossey-Bass.

Gordon, G. E., & Rosen, N. (1981). Critical factors in leadership succession. *Organizational Behavior and Human Performance, 27,* 227–254.

Graen, G. (1975). Role-making processes within complex organizations. In M. D. Dunnette (Ed.), *Handbook of industrial and organizational psychology* (pp. 1201–1245). Chicago: Rand McNally.

Graen, G. B., & Scandura, T. A. (1987). Toward a psychology of dyadic organizing. In B. Staw & L. L. Cummings (Eds.). *Research in organizational behavior* (Vol. 9, pp. 175–208). Greenwich, CT: JAI Press.

Green, S. G., & Mitchell, T. R. (1979). Attributional processes of leaders in leader-member interactions. *Organizational Behavior and Human Performance, 23,* 429–458.

Green, S. G., Fairhurst, G. T., & Snavely, B. K. (1986). Chains of poor performance and supervisory control. *Organizational Behavior and Human Decision Processes, 38,* 7–27.

Heider, F. (1958). *The psychology of interpersonal relations.* New York: Wiley.

Heller, F. A., & Yukl, G. (1969). Participation, managerial decisionmaking, and situational variables. *Organizational Behavior and Human Performance, 4,* 227–241.

Hemphill, J. K. (1949). *Situational factors in leadership.* Columbus: Ohio State University, Personnel Research Board.

Hoffman, L. R., Burke, R. J., & Maier, N. R. F. (1965). Participation, influence, and satisfaction among members of problem-solving groups. *Psychological Reports, 16,* 661–667.

Hogan, R., Raskin, R., & Fazzini, D. (1988, October). *The dark side of charisma.* Paper presented at the Conference on Psychological Measures and Leadership, San Antonio, TX.

Hollander, E. P. (1958). Conformity, status, and idiosyncrasy credit. *Psychological Review, 65,* 117–127.

Hollander, E. P. (1964). *Leaders, groups, and influence.* New York: Oxford University Press.

Hollander, E. P. (1978). *Leadership dynamics: A practical guide to effective relationships.* New York: Free Press/Macmillan.

Hollander, E. P. (1985). Leadership and power. In G. Lindzey & E. Aronson (Eds.), *The handbook of social psychology* (3rd ed., pp. 485–537). New York: Random House.

Hollander, E. P. (1986). On the central role of leadership processes. *International Review of Applied Psychology, 35,* 39–52.

Hollander, E. P., & Julian, J. W. (1969). Contemporary trends in the analysis of leadership processes. *Psychological Bulletin, 71,* 387–397.

Hollander, E. P., & Julian, J. W. (1970). Studies in leader legitimacy, influence, and innovation. In L. L. Berkowitz (Ed.), *Advances in experimental social psychology* (Vol. 5, pp. 33–69). New York: Academic Press.

Hollander, E. P., & Julian, J. W. (1978). A further look at leader legitimacy, influence, and innovation. In L. Berkowitz (Ed.), *Group processes* (pp. 153–165). New York: Academic Press.

Hollander, E. P., & Webb, W. B. (1955). Leadership, followership, and friendship: An analysis of peer nominations. *Journal of Abnormal and Social Psychology, 50,* 163–167.

Homans, G. C. (1961). *Social behavior: Its elementary forms.* New York: Harcourt, Brace & World.

House, R. J. (1971). A path-goal theory of leader effectiveness. *Administrative Science Quarterly, 16,* 321–338.

House, R. J. (1977). A 1976 theory of charismatic leadership. In J. G. Hunt & L. L. Larson (Eds.), *Leadership: The cutting edge* (pp. 189–207). Carbondale: Southern Illinois University Press.

House, R. J., & Dessler, G. (1974). The path goal theory of leadership: Some post hoc and a priori tests. In J. G. Hunt & L. L. Larson (Eds.), *Contingency approaches to leadership* (pp. 29–55). Carbondale: Southern Illinois University Press.

House, R. J., & Mitchell, T. R. (1974). Path-goal theory of leadership. *Journal of Contemporary Business, 3*(4), 81–97.

Howard, A., & Bray, D. (1988). *Managerial lives in transition: Advancing age and changing times.* New York: Dorsey.

Jacobs, T. O., & Jaques, E. (1987). Leadership in complex systems. In J. Zeidner (Ed.), *Human productivity enhancement* (pp. 7–65). New York: Praeger.

Kanter, R. M. (1981). Power, leadership, and participatory management. *Theory Into Practice, 20,* 219–224.

Katz, D., & Kahn, R. L. (1978). *The social psychology of organizations* (2nd ed.). New York: Wiley.

Kilmann, R. H., Saxton, M. J., Serpa, R., & Associates. (1985). *Gaining control of the corporate culture.* San Francisco: Jossey-Bass.

Kipnis, D. (1976). *The powerholders.* Chicago: University of Chicago Press.

Kipnis, D., Schmidt, S., Swaffin-Smith, C., & Wilkinson, J. (1984, Winter). Patterns of managerial influence: Shotgun managers, tacticians, and bystanders. *Organizational Dynamics,* pp. 58–67.

Kipnis, D., Schmidt. S., & Wilkinson, I. (1980). Intraorganizational influence tactics: Explorations in getting one's way. *Journal of Applied Psychology, 65,* 440–452.

Kotter, J. P. (1982). *The general managers.* New York: Free Press.

Kouzes, J. M., & Posner, B. Z. (1987). *The leadership challenge: How to get extraordinary things done in organizations.* San Francisco: Jossey-Bass.

Kram, K. E. (1985). *Mentoring at work: Developmental relationships in organizational life.* Glenview, IL: Scott, Foresman.

Leana, C. R. (1986). Predictors and consequences of delegation. *Academy of Management Journal, 29,* 754–774.

Leana, C. R. (1987). Power relinquishments versus powersharing: Theoretical clarification and empirical comparison of delegation and participation. *Journal of Applied Psychology, 72,* 228–233.

Ledford, G. E., Jr., Lawler, E. E., III, & Mohrman, S. A. (1988). The quality circle and its variations. In J. P. Campbell & R. J. Campbell (Eds.), *Productivity in organizations* (pp. 255–294). San Francisco: Jossey-Bass.

Levinson, H., & Rosenthal, S. (1984). *CEO: Corporate leadership in action.* New York: Basic Books.

Liden, R. C., & Graen, G. (1980). Generalizability of the vertical dyad linkage mode of leadership. *Academy of Management Journal 23,* 451–465.

Likert, R. (1961). *New patterns of management.* New York: McGraw-Hill.

Locke, E. A., & Schweiger, D. M. (1979). Participation in decision-making: One more look. In B. M. Staw (Ed.), *Research in organizational behavior* (Vol. 1, pp. 265–339). Greenwich, CT: JAI Press.

Lord, R. G., DeVader, C. L., & Alliger, G. M. (1986). A meta-analysis of the relation between personality traits and leadership perceptions: An application of validity generalization procedures. *Journal of Applied Psychology, 71,* 402–409.

Lord, R. G., & Maher, K. J. (1990). Leadership perceptions and leadership performance: Two distinct but interdependent processes. In J. Carroll (Ed.), *Advances in applied social psychology: Business settings* (Vol. 4, pp. 129–154). Hillsdale, NJ: Erlbaum.

Maccoby, M. (1976). *The gamesman, the new corporate leaders.* New York: Simon & Schuster.

Maccoby, M. (1981). *The leader.* New York: Simon & Schuster.

Manz, C. C., & Sims, H. P., Jr. (1986). Beyond imitation: Complex behavioral and affective linkages resulting from exposure to leadership training models. *Journal of Applied Psychology, 71,* 571–578.

Manz, C. C., & Sims, H. P., Jr. (1987). Leading workers to lead themselves: The eternal leadership of self-managed work teams. *Administrative Science Quarterly, 32,* 106–128.

Manz, C. C., & Sims, H. P., Jr. (1988). *Superleadership: Leading people to lead themselves.* Englewood Cliffs, NJ: Prentice-Hall.

McCall, M. W., Jr., Lombardo, M. M., & Morrison, A. M. (1988). *The lessons of experience.* Lexington, MA: Lexington Books.

McClelland, D. (1975). *Power: The inner experience.* New York: Irvington.

McGregor, D. (1960). *The human side of enterprise.* New York: McGraw Hill.

Meindl, J. R., Ehrlich, S. B., & Dukerich, J. M. (1985). The romance of leadership. *Administrative Science Quarterly, 30,* 78–102.

Miller, K. I., & Monge, P. R. (1986). Participation, satisfaction, and productivity: A meta-analytic review. *Academy of Management Journal, 29,* 727–753.

Mintzberg, H. (1983). *Power in and around organizations.* Englewood Cliffs, NJ: Prentice-Hall.

Mitchell, T. R., Green, S. G., & Wood, R. E. (1981). An attributional model of leadership and the poor performing subordinate: Development and validation. In L. L. Cummings & B. M. Staw (Eds.), *Research in organizational behavior* (Vol. 3, pp. 197–234). Greenwich, CT: JAI Press.

Morrison, A., & Von Glinow, M. A. (1990). Women and minorities in management. *American Psychologist, 45,* 200–208.

Mowday, R. T. (1979). Leader characteristics, self-confidence, and methods of upward influence in organizational decision situations. *Academy of Management Journal, 22,* 709–725.

Mulder, M. (1971). Power equalization through participation? *Administrative Science Quarterly, 16,* 31–38.

Offermann, L. R., & Kearney, C. T. (1988). Supervisor sex and subordinate influence strategies. *Personality and Social Psychology Bulletin, 14,* 360–367.

Offermann, L. R., & Kennedy, J. K., Jr. (1987, April). *Implicit theories of leadership: A look inside.* Paper presented at the meeting of the Society for Industrial and Organizational Psychology, Atlanta.

Offermann, L. R., & Schrier, P. E. (1985). Social influence strategies: The impact of sex, role, and attitudes toward power. *Personality and Social Psychology Bulletin, 11,* 286–300.

Ouchi, W. G. (1981). *Theory Z: How American business can meet the Japanese challenge.* Reading, MA: Addison-Wesley.

Patten, T. H., Jr. (1981). *Organizational development through team-building.* New York: Wiley.

Pence, E. C., Pendleton, W. C., Dobbins, G. H., & Sgro, J. A. (1982). Effects of causal explanations and sex variables on recommendations for corrective action following employee failure. *Organizational Behavior and Human Performance, 29,* 227–240.

Peters, T. J., & Waterman, R. H. (1983). *In search of excellence.* New York: Harper & Row.

Pfeffer, J. (1977). The ambiguity of leadership. In M. W. McCall, Jr., & M. M. Lombardo (Eds.), *Leadership: Where else can we go?* Durham, NC: Duke University Press.

Pfeffer, J. (1981). *Power in organizations.* Marshfield, MA: Pitman.

Podsakoff, P. M., & Schriesheim, C. A. (1985). Field studies of French and Raven's bases of power: Critique, reanalysis, and suggestions for future research. *Psychological Bulletin, 97,* 387–411.

Porter, L. W., Allen, R. W., & Angle, H. L. (1981). The politics of upward influence in organizations. In L. L. Cummings & B. M. Staw (Eds.), *Research in organizational behavior* (Vol. 3, pp. 109–149). Greenwich, CT: JAI Press.

Potts, N. (1988, May 22). GE's management mission. *The Washington Post,* pp. H1–H4.

Rice, R. W., & Kastenbaum, D. R. (1983). The contingency model of leadership: Some current issues. *Basic and Applied Social Psychology, 4,* 373–392.

Rush, M. C., Thomas, J. C., & Lord, R. G. (1977). Implicit leadership theory: A potential threat to the internal validity of leader behavior questionnaires. *Organizational Behavior and Human Performance, 20,* 93–110.

Sashkin, M. (1984). Participative management is an ethical imperative. *Organizational Dynamics, 12,* 4–22.

Schein, E. (1985). *Organizational culture and leadership: A dynamic view.* San Francisco: Jossey-Bass.

Schein, E. (1990). Organizational culture. *American Psychologist, 45,* 109–119.

Schriesheim, C. A., & Kerr, S. (1977). R.I.P. LPC: A response to Fiedler. In J. G. Hunt & L. L. Larson (Eds.), *Leadership: The cutting edge* (pp. 51–56). Carbondale: Southern Illinois University Press.

Schweiger, D. M., & Leana, C. R. (1986). Participation in decision making. In E. A. Locke (Ed.), *Generalizing from laboratory to field settings* (pp. 147–166). Lexington, MA: Heath.

Smith, J. E., Carson, K. P., & Alexander, R. A. (1984). Leadership: It can make a difference. *Academy of Management Journal, 27,* 765–776.

Stewart, R. (1982). *Choices for the manager.* Englewood Cliffs, NJ: Prentice-Hall.

Suedfeld, P., & Tetlock, P. E. (1977). Interactive complexity of communication in international crises. *Journal of Conflict Resolution, 21,* 169–184.

Sussman, M., & Vecchio, R. (1982). A social influence interpretation of worker motivation. *Academy of Management Review, 7,* 177–186.

Tannenbaum, R. (1968). *Control in organizations.* New York: McGraw-Hill.

Tannenbaum, R., & Schmidt, W. H. (1958). How to choose a leadership pattern. *Harvard Business Review, 36,* 95–101.

Thornton, G. C., & Byham, C. C. III (1982). *Assessment centers and managerial performance.* New York: Academic Press.

Thornton, G. C., & Cleveland, J. N. (1990). Developing managerial talent through simulation. *American Psychologist, 45,* 190–199.

Trempe, J., Rigny, A., & Haccoun, R. (1985). Subordinate satisfaction with male and female managers: Role of perceived supervisory influence. *Journal of Applied Psychology, 70,* 44–47.

Vaill, P. B. (1982). The purposing of high-performing systems. *Organizational Dynamics, 11*(2), 23–39.

Vandaveer, V. V., & Varca, P. E. (December, 1988). *Managing performance: Development of a new performance appraisal system for managers* (Tech. Rep.). St. Louis, MO: Southwestern Bell Telephone Company.

Vroom, V. H., & Jago, A. G. (1988). *The new leadership: Managing participation in organizations.* Englewood Cliffs, NJ: Prentice-Hall.

Vroom, V. H., & Yetton, P. W. (1973). *Leadership and decision-making.* Pittsburgh, PA: University of Pittsburgh Press.

Wagner, J. A., III, & Gooding, R. Z. (1987). Shared influence and organizational behavior: A meta-analysis of situational variables expected to moderate participation-outcome relationships. *Academy of Management Journal, 30,* 524–541.

Waldera, L. (1988). *The effects of influence strategy, influence objective, and leader-member exchange on upward influence.* Unpublished doctoral dissertation, George Washington University.

Weber, M. (1946). The sociology of charismatic authority. In H. H. Gerth & C. W. Mills (Eds. and Trans.), *From Max Weber: Essays in sociology* (pp. 245–252). New York: Oxford University Press. (Original work published 1921)

Zaleznik, A. (1977). Managers and leaders: Are they different? *Harvard Business Review, 55,* 67–78.

Zaleznik, A., & Kets de Vries, M. F. R. (1975). *Power and the corporate mind.* Boston: Houghton Mifflin.

6

A New Leadership Paradigm

MARSHALL SASHKIN
WILLIAM E. ROSENBACH

Looking through the history of the study of leadership, we find that the earliest coherent thrust centered on an approach now referred to as the "Great Man" or "Great Person" theory. For a full generation, leadership scholars concentrated on identifying the traits associated with great leadership. At first it seemed obvious; are not great leaders exceptionally intelligent, unusually energetic, far above the norm in their ability to speak to followers, and so on? However, when these "obvious" propositions were subjected to test, they all proved false. Yes, leaders were found to be a bit more intelligent than the average, but not much more. And yes, they were more energetic and dynamic—but not significantly so. True, they were better-than-average public speakers, but again their overall advantage was not very great. And so it went: Each of these and other leadership myths evaporated under the glare of scientific scrutiny.

What followed was a focus on the behavior of leaders. If the key was not *who* they were, perhaps the crux of leadership could be found in *what* they did. In fact, researchers were able to identify two crucial types of leader behavior: behavior centered on task accomplishments and behavior directed toward interpersonal relations. Individuals who consistently exhibited high levels of both of these types of behavior were typically reported as leaders by their peers. Those who engaged in a high level of task-related activity but only an average level of relationship-centered behavior were sometimes still designated leaders. Those who engaged only in a high level of relationship behavior were rarely designated leaders by their peers. Finally, those who did little in the way of either task- or relationship-centered activity were never seen as leaders.

Perhaps, then, the essence of effective leadership is engaging in high levels of both task-oriented and relationship-centered activity. To test this possibility, researchers trained factory foremen in the two types of behavior and put them back on the job. For a while things did seem to improve, but the effects were short-lived. After only a few weeks the foremen went back to their old behaviors; performance and productivity also returned to their prior levels. Although further research showed that even sustained high levels of the new behaviors had limited long-term effects on employees' performance, productivity, or satisfaction, the leadership-training programs developed in the early 1960s are still popular. Serious students of leadership, however, soon recognized the need to look further for answers to the riddle of effective leadership.

Some took a new path, suggesting that leadership effectiveness might require different combinations of task and relationship behavior in different situations. Theoretically, the most effective combination would depend upon certain situational factors, such as the nature of the task or the ability level of employees reporting to a certain supervisor. Another somewhat different path was to combine the situational hypothesis with some variations of the personal characteristics approach. Like earlier attempts, however, these efforts to explain effective leadership met with limited results. The puzzle remained unsolved.

Earlier in this century, Chester Barnard commented that leadership "has been the subject of an extraordinary amount of dogmatically stated nonsense." More recently, Joseph Rost observed that leadership as good management is what the "twentieth-century school of leadership" is all about. Rost argues for the development of a whole new paradigm of leadership that includes the dynamic interplay between leaders and followers. Later on, we will have more to say about Rost's interesting and important ideas. But first we will examine the ground-breaking work of political scientist and historian James MacGregor Burns, who has had the most influence on leadership research and theory over the past fifteen years.

Burns's work served to reacquaint scholars with a critical distinction first raised by the famous German sociologist Max Weber—the difference between economic and noneconomic sources of authority. This important distinction was one basis for Weber's discussion of charisma and charismatic leadership. Burns amplified and focused this issue, using examples such as Gandhi and Roosevelt, illustrations that made the distinction between *leaders* and *managers* so striking that it could not be ignored. The work of Burns led to the development of several new approaches to the study of what many now refer to as "transformational" leadership. That term is now widely used to contrast this "new leadership" with the old "transactional" leadership (or *management*) approach.

The transactional approach is based on economic and quasi-economic transactions between leaders and followers and appeals to followers' self-interest. In contrast, the new transformational approaches appeal to followers beyond their self-interest and incorporate the idea that leadership involves what Weber called noneconomic sources of authority or influence. In his widely acclaimed 1978 book *Leadership*, Burns defined transformational leadership as occurring when one or more persons engage with others in such a way that leaders and followers raise one another to higher levels of motivation and morality. In other words, both leader and followers—as well as the social system in which they function—are transformed.

Explorations in the New Paradigm

Burns's early work was crucial for the establishment of the new transformational paradigm, but he did not carry forward his concept by developing a clear theory or any direct measures. It was left to others, inspired by his original work, to build on it by defining theory and creating measures. The first and one of the most important of these follow-up efforts was initiated by Bernard M. Bass. Bass had long been recognized as a serious leadership researcher and scholar and had taken responsibility for updating and preparing new editions of Ralph Stogdill's classic *Handbook of Leadership*. Perhaps Bass's immense breadth of background knowledge led him to try to turn Burns's new concept into a more rigorous and measurable theory.

Leadership and Performance Beyond Expectations

Bass's first contribution was to identify a serious mistake in Burns's work. Burns thought transactional (managerial) and transformational leadership were the end points of a continuum. This belief resembled an error made many years earlier by traditional leadership researchers, who thought that "relationship orientation" and "task orientation" were end points of one leadership dimension. They soon found, however, that they were really two independent dimensions, that a person could exhibit one, the other, both, or neither. Bass realized that transactional leadership is simply different from, not inconsistent with, transformational leadership. A person might exhibit just one, the other, both, or neither.

Bass demonstrated this point by creating a measuring tool, the Multifactor Leadership Questionnaire (MLQ). The MLQ is filled out by a leader as well as by others who report on that person. This variety of perspectives gives what is called a "360 degree" picture of the leader. The MLQ was developed by getting several hundred people to give descriptions of leaders and leadership, by identifying specific actions and characteristics contained in those descriptions, and by then translating those behaviors and characteristics into specific questions. These questions were put into a single, long questionnaire that was administered to hundreds more people. Their answers were then analyzed using factor analysis, a statistical technique that groups together all the questions that seem to fit with one another, producing a relatively small set of categories. This process helps clarify the underlying meaning of the specific questions.

Bass refined the MLQ repeatedly by revising the questions and administering them to new groups of people. Ultimately, he concluded that the questionnaire was able to measure the two forms of leadership and, within each, to identify several more specific categories.

With respect to the old transactional, or managerial, side of leadership, Bass found three subcategories very much like some of those identified by earlier researchers.

- *Laissez-faire*—This component refers to a tendency for the leader to abdicate responsibility toward his or her followers, who are left to their own devices. Laissez-faire leadership really indicates an absence of leadership.
- *Contingent reward*—Often called reward-and-punishment or simply carrot-and-stick leadership, this approach means that the leader rewards followers for attaining performance levels the leader had specified. Performance-contingent strategies are by no means completely ineffective; in general, they are associated with both the performance and satisfaction of followers.
- *Management by exception*—This type of transactional leadership involves managers taking action only when there is evidence of something not going according to plan. There are two types of MBE: *active* and *passive.* The former describes a leader who looks for deviations from established procedure and takes action when irregularities are identified. The passive form describes a tendency to intervene only when specific problems arise because established procedures are not being followed.

The MLQ also taps four specific aspects of transformational leadership. Each of these is different from the forms of transactional leadership just described, because there is no tit-for-tat, no reward (or punishment) from the leader in exchange for followers' efforts.

- *Charisma*—For Bass and, in a statistical sense, for the MLQ, this is the most important dimension assessed by the instrument. Followers see leaders as charismatic when the leader provides emotional arousal—that is, a sense of mission, vision, excitement, and pride. This feeling is typically associated with respect and trust of the leader.
- *Inspiration*—Transformational leaders who inspire their followers set high expectations, use symbols to focus efforts, express important

purposes in simple ways, and are specifically concerned with communicating a vision to followers.

- *Individualized consideration*—This aspect of transformational leadership is similar to the old notion of relationship behavior. Individualized consideration means that the leader gives personal attention to followers. The leader builds a personal, considerate relationship with each individual, focusing on that person's needs. Leaders who show individualized consideration toward followers also help followers learn and develop by encouraging personal responsibility. In the process, the leader exhibits trust and respect, which followers then come to feel toward the leader.
- *Intellectual stimulation*—Transformational leaders often provide followers with a flow of new ideas, challenging followers to rethink old ways of doing things. In one sense, this aspect of transformational leadership is related to the older form of task-focused managerial (transactional) leadership, because the focus is on the actual content of the work. The difference is that instead of giving structure and directions, transformational leaders stimulate followers to develop their own task structure and figure out problems on their own.

Bass developed these dimensions of leadership to identify specific categories and types of transactional and transformational leadership behavior. The MLQ could then be used as a coaching and development tool, not just to aid in research or to assess individuals' potential in order to hire or promote the person most likely to succeed. Bass and his associates have made substantial contributions in this regard, developing training programs for navy officers and school superintendents, among other groups, based on this approach to transformational leadership and the MLQ.

However, we believe that the MLQ and Bass's theory have some important deficiencies. Although Bass argues that the MLQ is a measure of *behavior,* when one looks at the actual questions it becomes evident that the most important transformational leadership dimension, charisma, is measured by attitudinal questions, not by leader actions. This approach is actually quite sensible, because charisma is the *result* of transformational leadership rather than its *cause.* Max Weber was the first to use the term *charisma* to describe leaders. There was something special about them that he didn't understand, so he used the ancient Greek word meaning "gift of the gods." That seemed the only available explanation.

We now know that charisma is neither magical nor mysterious. It is simply the feeling that most people have about another person when that person behaves toward them in certain ways. (Later, we will look at some of the specific behaviors associated with charisma.) The chief flaw in Bass's approach is his continued acceptance of charisma as some mysterious quality of the leader. It is true that people often attribute certain special characteristics to leaders because of the way those leaders behave and the feelings they arouse. However, this doesn't really tell us anything about either the personal qualities or behaviors leaders display that produce charismatic effects. To understand transformational leadership we must explore, identify, and measure both the specific actions and the personal characteristics of leaders.

Although Bass's work has been very important in helping to clarify and make concrete Burns's ideas, it ignores some important aspects of transformational leadership that are rooted in the *personal characteristics* of individual leaders. Nor does Bass address the *culture* of the organization. However, before looking at characteristics of leaders or organizational culture, we need to examine transformational behavior more closely. We will draw on the empirical and behavior-focused work of two other leadership researchers, James M. Kouzes and Barry Z. Posner.

Five Behavioral Dimensions of Leadership

Not long after Bass began theorizing about transformational leadership, researchers on the other side of the country took up the same general problem. Kouzes and Posner were also affected by Burns's work; however, rather than having people describe great leaders and then using those descriptions to construct a questionnaire, they asked managers to write detailed memoirs of their own greatest, most positive leadership experience. These "personal best" cases, some of which ran on for ten pages or more, were analyzed to identify common threads. Only then did the researchers begin to construct questions about leadership behavior.

Kouzes and Posner, like Bass, developed a very long list of questions. They asked hundreds of managers to answer these questions, describing exceptional leaders they had known personally (instead of concentrating on great leaders in history as did Bass). Like Bass, Kouzes and Posner examined the results using factor analysis. They identified five clear factors, all describable in terms of reasonably concrete behaviors. Ultimately (and again like Bass) Kouzes and Posner constructed a questionnaire to measure transformational leadership: the Leadership Practices Inventory (LPI).

The LPI has five scales, one for each of the five types of leadership behavior. We will briefly define each.

- *Challenging the process*—This means searching for opportunities and experimenting, even taking sensible risks, to improve the organization.
- *Inspiring a shared vision*—This sounds a lot like Bass's category, but it is focused less on inspiration per se and more on what leaders actu-

ally do to construct future visions and to build follower support for the vision.

- *Enabling others to act*—Leaders make it possible for followers to take action by fostering collaboration (as opposed to competition) and supporting followers in their personal development.
- *Modeling the way*—Leaders set examples by their own behaviors. They also help followers focus on step-by-step accomplishments of large-scale goals, making those goals seem more realistic and attainable.
- *Encouraging the heart*—Leaders recognize followers' contributions and find ways to celebrate their achievements.

The five practices of exemplary leadership identified by Kouzes and Posner are, in our view, much more specific and behaviorally focused than the transformational leadership dimensions developed by Bass. We don't mean that Bass's dimensions or his MLQ are not useful: His ideas were crucial for moving beyond Burns's ground-breaking concepts, and the MLQ can be a valuable tool for executive development. Still, Kouzes and Posner have taken a big step beyond Bass toward a much clearer behavioral explanation of transformational leadership. Yet even this work is not the final word. There's more to transformational leadership than behavioral practices.

The Visionary Leader

At about the same time Bass and Kouzes and Posner were working on their models of transformational leadership, Marshall Sashkin was constructing the first draft of his Leader Behavior Questionnaire (LBQ). Sashkin originally based the LBQ on the work of Warren Bennis, who studied ninety exceptional leaders. Bennis looked for some common factors, some things that would explain just what these leaders did that made them so successful. He identified several commonalities that he called, at various times, "competencies," "behaviors," and "strategies." Sashkin took five of those behavior categories and developed a questionnaire based on them. The categories were:

- *Clarity*—Sashkin's first category of transformational leadership behavior involves focusing the attention of others on key ideas, the most important aspects of the leader's vision. In practice, this means (for example) coming up with metaphors and analogies that make clear and vivid what might otherwise be abstract ideas.
- *Communication*—The second behavior is more general, dealing with skills such as active listening and giving and receiving feedback effectively. These actions ensure clarity of communication.

- *Consistency*—Leaders establish trust by taking actions that are consistent both over time and with what the leader says. Trust, of course, exists in the minds and hearts of followers and is not an obvious aspect of leader behavior. But consistency over time and between words and actions produces trust in followers.
- *Caring*—The fourth behavior is demonstrating respect and concern for people. Psychologist Carl Rogers called this behavior "unconditional positive regard." By this he meant caring about and respecting another person regardless of one's feelings or judgments about that person's actions. Caring is shown not just by "big" actions such as ensuring job security but also by many everyday actions, such as remembering people's birthdays or even something as basic as learning and using their names.
- *Creating opportunities*—Bennis originally associated this behavior with risk taking and risk avoidance, but the underlying issue is more complicated. Transformational leaders do empower followers by allowing them to accept challenges—taking on and "owning" a new project, for example. But transformational leaders also are careful to plan ahead and not to ask more of followers than they know the followers are capable of. Followers might honestly feel a sense of risk in accepting a challenge, but a transformational leader does all that is possible to ensure that any risk is relatively low, that with the right resources and (if necessary) help the follower can and will be successful.

The similarity between these categories and the five leadership practices identified by Kouzes and Posner are striking; in some cases even the words are the same. Sashkin used the categories identified by Bennis to create a questionnaire with a scale for each category and five questions on each scale. Then, like Kouzes and Posner, he collected data and used factor analysis to show that the five dimensions are replicated in people's real experience.

However, there is an interesting difference between the approach taken by Kouzes and Posner and that taken by Sashkin. Kouzes and Posner started by capturing significant experiences and, from those experiences, generated questions that identified their five practices. Sashkin, however, came from the opposite direction, developing measures of the five behaviors on the basis of Bennis's concepts and then validating his measure by analyzing reports of significant experiences. The fact that these two independent research efforts, coming from different directions, wound up in essentially the same place gives us confidence that these researchers are on to something, that the behaviors they've identified are real and important.

In the course of his study of leadership, Sashkin concluded that there had to be more to transformational leadership than just the five behaviors.

He identified three specific personal characteristics that mark the differences among exceptional transformational leaders, average leaders, transactional leaders (managers), and nonleaders. None of these characteristics is a *trait* in the strictest sense, because all of them are learnable and changeable. Sashkin developed questionnaire scales to assess the extent to which leaders act on the basis of each of these three characteristics. The three scales were then added to the LBQ.

The first and perhaps most basic characteristic is self-confidence. Psychologists call this "self-efficacy" or "internal control." It is, in essence, the belief that one controls one's own fate. The second characteristic concerns the need for power and the way that need is manifested. Getting things done in organizations depends on one's power and influence and how that power is used. Finally, exceptional leaders have vision, but that vision is not an aspect of charisma or inspiration or some trait like creativity. Vision is based on the ability to think through what's happening, to determine causes, and to identify how complicated chains of cause and effect actually work. Only then can a person begin to figure out how to bring about the outcomes he or she wants. We will briefly describe the nature of each of these three personal characteristics.

Self-confidence. The great American writer Mark Twain probably said it best: "If you think you can ... or think you *can't* ... you're probably right." Often we defeat ourselves before we start. Sometimes it's almost intentional. In the comic strip *Calvin and Hobbes,* Calvin, a precocious seven-year-old, asks his best friend, a stuffed tiger named Hobbes, whether he believes the stars control our fate. "Naw," says Hobbes. "Oh, I do," replies Calvin. "Life's a lot more fun when you're not responsible for your actions." However, by denying control, Calvin denies all of the vast possibilities of leadership. How can someone who has no faith in himself or herself become a leader of others?

Self-confidence or self-efficacy is a prerequisite to leadership. And it is not a trait. Self-efficacy is learned. Did you ever hear someone scold a child by saying, "Johnny, that's not how you do it! Can't you do anything right?!" Well, every time that happens, Johnny learns that he cannot control his fate. That's not a good lesson for success, let alone leadership. Parents and teachers must help children learn that they *can* control their own fate. But it's never too late; even adults can learn, and that's one of the most important jobs of leaders—teaching followers that they can do things for themselves. This is the first paradox of leadership: To become a leader, one must believe in one's own ability to achieve results for one's self, but the *real* job of a leader is not doing it but teaching others that *they* can do it.

Power. Harvard psychologist David McClelland has studied human motivation for about half a century. Early on he came to believe that three motives, or needs, play particularly important roles: the need to achieve, the need for power and control, and the need for friendship and human interaction. McClelland thought of needs not as fixed or inborn traits but rather as habits that people develop in the course of their lives. His particular focus for many years was on the need to achieve, which he believed might relate to business success. He thought it might be possible to actually "teach" people to need achievement, which should make it more likely for them to actually attain their goals.

In an important real-world experiment, McClelland found that small-business entrepreneurs could learn to "need" achievement and that this enhanced their business success. But when he looked at managers in organizations, he found that the need for *power*, not achievement, was most strongly associated with success. Organizations are set up because there is work to do that can't be done by just one person, that requires people to work together to achieve goals. The process is controlled by the exercise of power and influence. Managers who have an extremely high need to achieve tend to burn out; they get frustrated about things not getting done and try to do everything themselves. But that's not really possible; one gets things done, in large organizations, by using influence and relying on others.

McClelland went on to observe that some managers with a high need for power appeared to be quite effective, while others were very ineffective. Looking more closely at this second group, McClelland characterized them as using power primarily to benefit themselves—to get status, to get "perks," and even just to get others to obey them and be subservient. In contrast, the effective managers used power to empower others, to delegate and to legitimate employees' taking charge and taking real responsibility for accomplishments.

People who use power to manipulate others to serve their own self-centered ends are often seen as charismatic. In fact, that's often how such leaders dupe others into doing as they, the leaders, wish. This helps explain why one must be careful about measures of charisma, such as that contained in Bass's MLQ, and about reasonable-sounding theories that glorify charismatic leadership. In the United States people tend to associate charisma with admirable leaders such as Franklin Roosevelt and John Kennedy. But in Europe charisma is often identified with tyrants such as Napoleon and Hitler. Roosevelt and Kennedy certainly used charisma, but they did not use it to control followers by promising that the followers could become more like *them* (i.e., the leaders) by obeying the leader's every command. Instead, these and other great leaders who might be cited as positive models, people such as Gandhi or Churchill, appealed to what Abraham Lincoln called "the better angels of our nature." These are simply the basic values about what is right, what is good, what should be done, and what should be avoided that guide us toward positive long-run goals.

Nontransformational leaders who use charisma to get what they want appeal primarily to the self-serving side of human nature. They say (in effect), "If you do as I wish you'll be like me and have all the wonderful things I have." Psychologists call this an appeal to narcissism, or self-love. Of course, such leaders are really lying—their narcissistic appeals are designed only to get followers to do as the leader wants. Their charisma is artifice, a result of behaviors that they have carefully learned and rehearsed for the specific purpose of manipulating followers.

In contrast, transformational leaders seek power not for self-aggrandizement but in order to share it. They empower others to take an active role in carrying out the value-based mission or vision defined by the leader. That vision is based on what the organization and followers need, not what the leader wants personally. Thus, transformational leaders appeal to followers' *values*, emphasizing that certain important values serve as the common basis for our ideals and goals.

This brings us to the second paradox of leadership: While it may seem that charismatic and transformational leaders are complete opposites, the power need is common to both. Thus the paradox: The same power need that gives us a Gandhi can also produce a Hitler. Those who have worked closely with even an exceptional transformational leader have probably seen in that person at least a touch of the self-serving tyrant. Again, the paradox: The source is the same—the power need—but how that need is channelled makes all the difference.

Vision. The term *vision* is commonly applied to leadership. Many speak of leaders' vision and the importance of constructing a vision. Few observers, however, are able to explain exactly what vision means. Some seem to think it means that leaders come up with an image of an ideal future condition and then explain it to others and convince them to do what's necessary to attain the vision. But visionary leaders don't simply think up a vision and sell it to followers. If it is more than just a slick sales pitch, the long-term ideal that leaders come up with will always derive (at least in part) from followers' ideas.

Developing a vision doesn't mean dreaming. It means thinking, and thinking hard. That's what the ground-breaking work of social psychologist Elliott Jaques tells us. After years of study, Jaques concluded that when organizations are working well, they have leaders who possess the perspective necessary to deal with problems of the degree of complexity common to their particular hierarchical level.

Most organizations, Jaques found, need no more than six levels of hierarchy. But they also need people at each level who can think about chains of cause and effect and see how things work. At the higher levels these leaders must figure out how several causal chains affect one another over relatively long periods of time and must decide what to do to achieve desired outcomes. Jaques calls this ability "cognitive power," the ability to think in complex ways. Cognitive power isn't the same thing as intelligence, nor is it a fixed, unchangeable trait. Successful leaders *learn* to use cognitive power effectively. What's the time span over which you are comfortable in planning? A few months? A year? Two years? What's the longest-term project you are working on right now? That should tell you something about the time-span limits you're comfortable with.

Transformational leaders transform organizations by first using their cognitive power to understand complex causal chains and then acting to design outcomes that will benefit the organization and advance the leader's vision. But transformational leadership is much more than that. While a substantial degree of cognitive power is required in order for top-level leaders to be effective, such effectiveness results as much from the leader's success in developing followers' cognitive abilities as from the exercise of his or her own. A transformational leader with the degree of cognitive power required for a top-level position makes important long-term strategic decisions. But how much do these decisions affect what actually goes on in the organization on a daily, weekly, monthly, and yearly basis? It is the thought and action of managers and employees at lower levels that most affect current and short-term future operations. The finest long-term plan and the wisest long-range actions will surely fail if those who must act today and tomorrow are not capable of doing so. Thus, it is more important for top-level leaders with great cognitive power or vision to help followers expand and improve on their *own* vision than it is for leaders to simply exercise their cognitive power. This is the third paradox of leadership.

Personal Characteristics. The personal characteristics of effective leaders are somewhat different from what traditional "trait" theories of leadership addressed. These characteristics are not obvious as the foundations of leadership, yet that's exactly what they are. More important, these foundations are not something people are born with; they are developed. At least to some extent, that development can be planned and carried out over one's life and career. Indeed, transformational leaders teach followers to develop these characteristics for themselves, rather than simply using their own capabilities to do things *for* followers.

Incorporating the three personal characteristics into his Visionary Leadership Theory (VLT), Sashkin modified his LBQ to include a total of eight scales—the five original scales developed to assess certain types of leader behavior, along with three new scales designed to examine how the three specific characteristics important for transformational leadership show up in leaders' actions. But there was still more to the transformational leadership equation. Behavior is a function of the person and the situation or context. What about that context? Sashkin addressed this question by looking at organizational culture in terms of the situational context of transformational leadership.

The Leader's Role in Shaping the Organization's Culture

Edgar H. Schein has said that the *only* important thing leaders do may well be constructing culture. They somehow help define and inculcate certain shared values and beliefs among organizational members. Values define what is right or wrong, good or bad; beliefs define what people expect to happen as a consequence of their actions. The values and beliefs shared by people in an organization are the essence of that organization's culture.

The elements of organizational culture are not just selected by chance or at random. They deal with the most important and fundamental issues faced by people in organizations. These issues include *adaptation*—how people deal with external forces and the need to change; *goal achievement*—the nature of organizational goals, how they are defined, and their importance; *coordination*—how people work together to get the job done; and *the strength of shared values and beliefs*—that is, the degree to which people in the organization generally agree that these values and beliefs are important and should guide their actions. We will briefly consider each issue and the values and beliefs relevant to that issue.

Adaptation. Consider two specific beliefs about change and adaptation. The first goes like this: "We really just have to go along with outside forces; what we do can't really make much difference." Such a belief has some pretty clear implications for action—or inaction. After all, why bother? Contrast this outlook with the belief, "We can control our own destiny." The former belief may be more accurate in an objective sense. However, it also pretty much ensures that nothing will be done and that what is done will not, in fact, make a difference, because no one expects it to. Even if the second belief is not as accurate, it certainly helps make it more likely that action will be taken. And perhaps that action will have a positive effect, especially because people expect it to.

These beliefs dealing with change and adaptation are actually the organizational analog of self-efficacy, the belief that one's destiny is a matter of self-control. Therefore, it is crucial that leaders teach followers self-efficacy. Only then is it likely that the organization will develop the sort of culture that makes successful adaptation to change more likely.

Goal Achievement. "Every person, every department, has its own goals; the organization is best served by competition among them." Does that sound like a typical organizational value? Unfortunately it is; it's unfortunate because organizations are not well served by such a value. Contrast it with this one: "We are all here to serve our customer by identifying and meeting the customer's needs, whatever they may be." That value says a lot about how goals are defined and what goal achievement is all about. And, unlike the first value, this one really does benefit the organization.

The issue of goals relates to the leader's need for power and how that need can be played out—to benefit the organization by empowering others, or to benefit only the individual through narcissistic self-aggrandizement. Leaders' empowerment of others is so important because it models the value of achievement in a larger, organizational sense, not just for their own benefit or the benefit of their department.

Coordination. Many organizations seem to operate on the maxim, "Every person for him- or herself; we all compete to be best." But this is not a very functional value when the very essence of organization is to perform tasks that require the coordinated work of several individuals and groups. In contrast, the value "We all must work together" is a much better expression of the reality of organization. Only when people work together effectively can an organization prosper.

We spoke of vision or cognitive power as the means by which leaders think through complicated cause-and-effect chains and decide how to create desirable outcomes. This process entails looking at the organization as a system and thinking about how it fits together, which happens, of course, through the coordinated efforts of organization members. Leaders, then, must help followers develop their cognitive power, their own vision so that followers are able to coordinate their efforts effectively.

Shared Values and Beliefs. In some organizations one hears people say, "Everyone has the right to his or her own philosophy." Although that might seem to be a sound democratic ideal, it makes poor organizational sense. Such a principle destroys the potentially positive effect of the three issue-focused beliefs and values just identified. If everyone can buy into or reject them at will, how can these values and beliefs be expected to have any consistent impact? "Everyone here is expected to adhere to a common core of values and beliefs" is itself a value that strengthens a positive, functional approach toward adapting, achieving goals, and coordinating efforts. Of course, such a value would make alternative beliefs and values even more dysfunctional. That's why "cultural strength," the degree to which values are shared among the members of an organization, is a poor predictor of organizational effectiveness.

But How?

All this may seem reasonable, especially because it is relatively easy to see how the personal characteristics required for effective leadership relate to the fundamental aspects of organizational culture. Still, we must ask how leaders construct cultures—that is, how they go about defining and inculcating values and beliefs. There are many ways that leaders do this, but three general approaches are of special importance and impact. First, leaders develop a clear, simple, value-based *philosophy*, a statement of organizational purpose or mission that everyone understands. This task is anything but simple. A philosophy does not spring fully formed from the brow of the leader. Leaders must use their cognitive power to assess the organization's context, its environment, and the key factors in that environment; they must solicit input from others; and they must convince top-level executives that all this is possible.

Second, leaders empower others to define organizational *policies* and develop *programs* that are explicitly based on the values and beliefs contained in the philosophy that in fact put those values and beliefs into organizational action. For example, hiring and promotion policies should take into account values consistent with those in the organization's philosophy as well as applicants' knowledge and skill. Reward systems and bonus programs must be based on the values of cooperation and innovative action instead of on competition over a limited pool of resources.

Finally, leaders inculcate values and beliefs through their own individual behaviors, their personal *practices*. Leaders model organizational values and beliefs by living by them constantly and consistently. That is why the leadership behaviors we described earlier are extremely important. Many people think of these behaviors as tools with which leaders explain their vision to followers and convince them to carry out that vision. Although this is not totally untrue, the far more significant reason these behaviors are important is that leaders use them to demonstrate and illustrate the values and beliefs on which their visions are founded. That's why transformational leadership takes so much time and effort—and why transformational leaders must be good managers with strong management skills. These leaders use everyday managerial activities—a committee meeting, for example—as opportunities to inculcate values. In a meeting the leader may guide a decisionmaking process while making it clear that final authority and responsibility rests with the group. By so doing, the leader takes what might otherwise be a bureaucratic process and instills the value of empowerment into it. Whenever possible, leaders "overlay" value-inculcating actions on ordinary bureaucratic management activities. Without a sound base of management skills, this would not be possible.

The Visionary Leader Again

Thus, Sashkin's Visionary Leadership Theory brings us full circle, from the easiest-to-observe behaviors to a deeper understanding of the personal source of visionary leadership to the more subtle and fundamental expression of leadership through culture building. Ultimately, VLT leads to the recognition that transformational leaders' own personal behaviors play a large part in shaping organizational culture. This comprehensive theory goes beyond behavior to incorporate personal characteristics. Even more, it includes the organizational context of transformational leadership—that is, culture building. It is the only analysis of leadership that attends to all three factors—behavior, personal characteristics, and the organizational context—thus paying heed to the basic equation of behavior as a function of person and environment.

Is There Really Such a Thing as Transformational Leadership?

We began by trying to define what most of those now involved in studying transformational leadership refer to as a "paradigm shift." A paradigm is a way of thinking, a frame of reference. Sometimes—generally not very often—we are forced to change the way we look at and think about things. When this happens it's most often because of some major change in scientific knowledge. When Copernicus, for example, concluded that the sun, not the earth, was the center of the solar system, he caused a radical scientific paradigm shift. Similarly, the proposal that what we had thought of as leadership is really something rather different—management/supervision—forced many researchers to take a step back and rethink their basic assumptions about leadership in organizations. Others concluded that this "discovery" was nothing more than a wrong-headed assertion, that a full understanding of leadership could still be had in the context of the existing paradigm.

The existing paradigm, of course, is based on the notion of transactions or exchanges: Leaders provide followers with rewards for doing as the leader wishes or administer punishments if the wishes are not heeded. In the 1950s various social scientists, George Homans (a sociologist) and Edwin Hollander (a social psychologist) in particular, developed detailed models of "social exchange." These models show how people exchange not just money for doing a job but also "sentiments." A person might, for example, exchange friendship for certain favors. This sounds a bit crass, and the fact is that whenever such exchanges become obvious they automatically lose their value. No one would consciously say, "I'll be your buddy if you'll drive me to work." But that's exactly what people do all the time without explicitly saying so.

The examples above are purposely simplistic and extreme for the sake of clarity. The social exchange model is really more subtle and complex than we have made it appear. Still, it may seem at first glance that transformational leadership is obviously more than an exchange of work for money and certainly goes beyond an exchange of sentiments, such as commitment and caring from the leader in exchange for followers' acceptance of the leader's agenda. Edwin Hollander has recently suggested that there *is* an exchange, an exchange that goes beyond money *or* sentiments.

In exchange for their willingness to carry out the leader's vision, followers receive intangible but very real and useful rewards, such as a new, clear, and practical understanding of how to design and carry out projects that require interdepartment coordination. Thus, exchange can take at least three forms. At its simplest, leader-follower exchange involves concrete rewards for actions. In its simple social version, leader-follower exchange consists of sentiments for actions, friendship for favors. But in what may be its most sophisticated form, leader-follower exchange balances followers' committed actions against the intangible but practically useful insights and understandings they receive from leaders.

Is it possible, then, that what we have called transformational leadership could be reinterpreted within the traditional paradigm of transaction and exchange? We are not convinced. Our objection is based on the essence and nature of transformation. Leaders transform organizations, but they also transform followers, a process that involves much more than simply exchanging useful insights for followers' actions. Followers are transformed because they accept and internalize the key values and beliefs that leaders have identified as the basis of the organization's culture. Leaders teach followers self-confidence (self-efficacy), and followers become more capable of independent, autonomous action (though that action will still be based on the shared values identified by the leader). Moreover, leaders empower followers to act by sharing power and expanding influence throughout the organization. In this process followers, like leaders, come to value and use power and influence not for self-aggrandizement or narcissistic goals but to accomplish organizationally and socially desirable ends. They learn a more mature use of power and influence. Finally, it is easy to see how leaders might use their cognitive abilities, their vision, to come up with clear plans and strategies that followers can implement. But, as we discussed in the context of the paradoxes of leadership, leaders don't simply use their cognitive abilities to figure out what's coming next and how to control it in ways that benefit the organization. Leaders construct organizational contexts that permit followers to exercise and expand their own cognitive abilities, and to become more capable of defining and enacting their own visions.

Note that each of the three specific transformational effects we just defined is an outcome of one of the paradoxes of leadership. These effects, individually and in sum, involve far more than any exchange relationship could explain. Thus, although some may have tried to expand our understanding of leadership while retaining the basic transactional paradigm, we contend that this paradigm still does not and cannot encompass what we think of as transformational leadership. Understanding this form of leadership *requires* a paradigm shift.

Transformational leadership, then, is more than a form of transactional leadership in which the transactions are subtle and intangible. But that doesn't mean that Hollander's extended social exchange model can be dismissed. It's easy to say that simple observation of a transformational leader in action yields no sign of social exchange, but it would be foolish to reject the social exchange model on that basis, because if social exchange is actually operating, that is exactly how it would have to appear. Remember, when a social exchange process is obvious, it tends to lose its utility; most people reject the thought of an exchange that involves "buying" feelings. Anyone actually involved in the transformational "exchange" would be expected to deny that such an exchange existed.

Our disagreement with the social exchange approach is not based on the notion that there is an "obvious" difference between transactional and transformational leadership. Rather, our view is based on evidence—the evidence provided by Bass's research. Remember, Bass was able to define and measure several aspects of transactional leadership and to show that these were clearly independent of the dimensions of transformational leadership. If there were really no difference—if these were all simply transactions, with some just more open than others—it's hard to imagine that Bass would have been able to show such a clear separation. Some of our own recent research adds support to Bass's work by showing that two very different approaches to measuring transformational dimensions yield consistent results.

We believe that the conceptual distinctions we have made provide clear theoretical support for our view. Transformational leadership is used to construct a value-based culture. But it requires the context of transactional leadership, the everyday bureaucratic and managerial activities that form the "text," with values and culture the "subtext." It is clear to us that these are very different activities and processes. Transactional leadership—management—is the "paper" on which transformational leaders define values and describe organizational cultures. Without management there could be no leadership. Thus, both are important—but they are different.

Current "Transformational" Leadership Approaches as Wolves in Sheep's Clothing

Some may argue that there is no such thing as transformational leadership or that it is simply a form of charisma; others insist that current transformational theory is still ill-defined. One scholar, Joseph Rost, feels that a paradigm shift has not yet occurred; he views the present transformational leadership theories as merely providing an *opportunity* for a transition. What is especially lacking in current transformational theories, according to Rost, is a full and complex consideration of the role of followership. Leadership, he argues, involves more than leaders getting followers to carry out leaders' wishes. A distinction between leaders and followers is crucial, but the concept of follower must, according to Rost, take on a new meaning. Followers must be seen as active, not passive, and as themselves engaging in leadership, not just in followership. In addition, Rost has pointed out that there is typically more than one leader just as there must be more than one follower.

Rost has emphasized that both leaders and followers make important contributions. Although we agree with Rost that there must be mutual contributions, we disagree on the *nature* of those contributions. Rost appears to us to say or suggest that leaders' and followers' contributions are similar in nature. We, however, believe that leaders' essential contributions are quite different from the contributions of followers. Leaders' contributions include synthesizing and extending the purposes of followers as well as constructing conditions under which followers can be transformed into leaders. Thus, in terms of a vision or common purpose, the relationship between leaders and followers need not and cannot be equal— but it *must* be *equitable*, that is, fair. To us this means that the contributions of leaders and of followers, which are inherently unequal in kind, must be equal in effort and in commitment to one another and to a shared vision.

We do not disagree with Rost's definition of leadership as "an influence relationship among leaders and followers who intend real changes that reflect their mutual purposes." We do, however, find this definition to be incomplete; what gets lost in Rost's argument, we think, is the leader as a source of vision or motive. Rost and some others seem to think that transformational leaders exist primarily to focus and help carry out the visions of followers. There is some truth to this and in this sense leaders are, as Robert Greenleaf has so beautifully said, servants. However, transformational leaders do not simply identify and build a clear vision from the visions of followers. They also identify what followers themselves might wish to envision but have not and perhaps cannot. And they provide followers with conditions that permit followers to achieve the goals and aims they share with leaders; leaders enable followers themselves to change, to realize more fully their potential. In sum, transformational leadership involves real, unique contributions from both followers and leaders, a point that Rost says he agrees with but which seems to us to be missing in meaningful detail from his approach.

Conclusion

We believe that a paradigm shift has indeed occurred over the past decades with respect to leadership research, theory, and practice. This shift has as its source Burns's pioneering ideas. That work led to a variety of new transformational approaches; we have reviewed the most important in this chapter. While different in many ways, these new approaches are nonetheless consistent. The new transformational leadership paradigm

TABLE 6.1   Transformational Leadership Measures

Multi-Factor Leadership Questionnaire (Bass & Avolio)	*Leadership Practices Inventory* (Kouzes & Posner)
Laissez-faire	Challenging the Process
Transactional Leadership	—Search for opportunities
—Contingent-reward	—Experiment and take risks
—Management by exception	Inspiring a Shared Vision
—active	—Envision the future
—passive	—Enlist others
Transformational Leadership	Enabling Others to Act
—Charisma	—Foster collaboration
—Individual consideration	—Strengthen others
—Intellectual stimulation	Modeling the way
—Inspiration	—Set the example
	—Plan small wins
	Encouraging the Heart
	—Recognize contribution
	—Celebrate accomplishments

Leadership Behavior Questionnaire
    (Sashkin)
Leadership Behaviors
—Focused leadership (Clarity)
—Communicative leadership (Communication)
—Trust leadership (Consistency)
—Respectful leadership (Caring)
—Risk leadership (Creating opportunities)
Leadership Characteristics
—Bottom-line leadership (Self-confidence
—Empowered leadership (Power)
—Long-term leadership (Vision)
Culture Building Leadership
—Organizational leadership
—Cultural leadership

confirms the unity of the concepts of leadership and followership. It accomplishes this in ways that, on the surface, appear to be paradoxical. However, the paradoxes we have described are paradoxes only if one tries to look at them from the perspective of the old transactional, or management, paradigm. When we apply the new transformational paradigm we see that what at first appeared to be paradoxical actually makes logical sense.

The most general paradox involves the apparent inconsistency between being a manager and being a leader. This apparent paradox is resolved by recognizing that effective transformational leaders use transactional, managerial roles not simply to define, assign, and accomplish tasks and achieve goals but also to educate, empower, and ultimately transform followers. By doing so, leaders wind up transforming their organizations. The transactional approach views the sort of skills and behaviors defined and described by Bass, Kouzes and Posner, and Sashkin as essential managerial activities, important for communicating clearly the terms of exchange between managers and their subordinates. But leaders don't just communicate directions, they communicate values. What the transactional paradigm cannot explain is that leaders use these interaction skills not to convince followers to do as the leaders want but to become more self-confident, to use power and influence in a positive way, and to develop more complex thinking skills. These outcomes are more than rewards accepted in exchange for compliance; they are true transformations in followers, transformations that lead to transformation in the organization.

Our outlook does not, however, deny the need for management. From the vantage point of the new paradigm, management is more important than ever; only by using the context of management activities can leaders transform followers and organizations. Through this new transformational leadership paradigm, the study and practice of leadership itself has been transformed.

Notes

1. The authors gratefully acknowledge the helpful comments on earlier drafts of this chapter from Edwin P. Hollander, Barry Z. Posner, Joseph C. Rost, and Walter F. Ulmer, Jr. We accept full responsibility for our interpretation and presentation of their views.

2. The views expressed here are those of the authors and do not necessarily represent the positions or policies of the Office of Educational Research and Improvement or the U.S. Department of Education.

Suggested Readings

Organizations and Management by Chester I. Barnard (Cambridge, MA: Harvard University Press, 1948). Chester Barnard was an executive at AT&T for many years. He was also a serious management thinker and his work is still considered important by both scholars and thoughtful managers.

Bass & Stogdill's Handbook of Leadership (3rd edition) by Bernard M. Bass (New York: Free Press, 1990). This is a comprehensive reference resource that organizes just about everything ever written on the topic of leadership.

Leadership and Performance Beyond Expectations by Bernard M. Bass (New York: Free Press, 1985). This was the first formal attempt to apply Burns's idea of transformational leadership to leadership in organizations instead of nations.

Leaders: The Strategies for Taking Charge by Warren Bennis and Burt Nanus (New York: Harper & Row, 1985). This very readable book reports the authors' study of ninety exceptional chief executives and a model of organizational leadership based on what they learned.

Leadership by James McGregor Burns (New York: Harper & Row, 1978). Burns's work is the most important original source for the concept of transformational leadership. His book is also very readable and won a Pulitzer Prize.

"Legitimacy, Power, and Influence: A Perspective on Relational Features of Leadership" by Edwin P. Hollander, in *Leadership Theory and Research: Perspectives and Directions,* edited by Martin M. Chemers and R. Ayma (New York: Academic Press, 1993). This is the most clear and current statement of the "pure" transactional approach. The author tries to interpret and explain transformational leadership in terms of the older transactional paradigm (though misunderstanding the nature of transformational leadership by confusing it with charisma).

Executive Leadership by Elliott Jaques and Stephen D. Clement (Arlington, VA: Cason Hall, 1991). This very readable explication of Jaques's important theory of organization and leadership is based on his concept of "cognitive power" and the notion that individuals' levels of cognitive power must be matched to their positional levels in the organizational hierarchy.

The Leadership Challenge by James M. Kouzes and Barry Z. Posner (San Francisco: Jossey-Bass, 1987). These authors used much the same approach as Bass did to create a tool for measuring leadership, but they did not start from a theoretical base, and their focus was more behavioral. The five aspects of leadership they identified and measured, however, are very similar to and consistent with the five "strategies" originally defined by Bennis and the five behavior categories defined and measured by Sashkin.

"Power Is the Great Motivator," by David C. McClelland and David H. Burnham (*Harvard Business Review,* March–April 1976, pp. 100–110). This is a very readable report of McClelland's ground-breaking work on how the need for power comes into play in organizations and how it can be used for good or for ill.

Structure and Process in Modern Societies by Talcott Parsons (New York: Free Press, 1960). This is a very *un*readable (but important) reference source. Parsons was one of the most important modern social scientists. He developed a very simple, perhaps even elegant, way of understanding what goes on in organizations and why.

Leadership for the Twenty-first Century by Joseph Rost (New York: Praeger, 1991). Rost provides an exceptional overview of the history of leadership study, as well as a leading-edge analysis of the new paradigm of transformational leadership.

"Understanding and Assessing Organizational Leadership" by Marshall Sashkin and W. Warner Burke, in *Measures of Leadership,* edited by Kenneth E. Clark and Miriam B. Clark (West Orange, NJ: Leadership Library of America/Center for Creative Leadership, 1990). This is the most accessible synopsis of Sashkin's Visionary Leadership Theory, including extensive data and research results up to 1990.

"Assessing Transformational Leadership and Its Impact" by Marshall Sashkin, William E. Rosenbach, Terrence E. Deal, and Kent D. Peterson, in *Impact of Leadership,* edited by Kenneth E. Clark, Miriam B. Clark, and David P. Campbell (Greensboro, NC: Center for Creative Leadership, 1992). This update of Sashkin's earlier report focuses on additional research evidence for his approach and explains *how* transformational leaders achieve their effects.

Organizational Culture and Leadership (2nd edition) by Edgar H. Schein (San Francisco: Jossey-Bass, 1992). Schein applies Parson's concepts in an understandable manner, clarifying the underlying nature of organizational culture and identifying many of the values and categories of values that are the most important ingredients of organizational culture.

PART TWO

FOLLOWERSHIP: MAKING LEADERSHIP POSSIBLE

Leaders come from the ranks of followers. In fact, few leaders can be successful without first having learned the skills of following. Aristotle's *Politics*, Plato's *Republic*, Homer's *Odyssey*, and Hegel's *Phenomenology of Mind* affirm the mastery of followership as the sine qua non of leadership. Hence, the contemporary study of leadership must examine followership and leader development as they affect organizational success.

Most of us are followers more often than we are leaders: Followership dominates our lives and our organizations. All too often, however, followers are taken for granted; preoccupation with leadership often keeps us from considering the nature and importance of the follower. Qualities that make effective followers are the same qualities found in effective leaders— in fact, effective followers and leaders move easily from one role to the other. In many organizations, the leadership role is the only path to success, and therefore it is developed, encouraged, and rewarded whereas followership is not. Fortunately, some organizations also nurture and reward effective followers.

In an attempt to sidestep the stereotypes associated with followership, many organizations refer to followers with loftier-sounding terms such as "constituents," "associates," "partners," "team members," or "colleagues." The word "subordinate" has almost been eliminated from our vocabulary. However, what we call people matters far less than how we treat them. We have observed "constituents," "associates," "partners," "team members," or "colleagues" treated shabbily by those in charge. These people clearly were regarded as subordinates in the mind of the leader. Regardless of the nomenclature, followers don't want to be treated as inferior; they do want leaders, as partners, to help define direction and create a path to the future. There is no reason to suggest that theirs is somehow a lesser role—the truth is that every leader is also a follower. Thus, a major tenet of developing effective leadership is understanding and experiencing effective followership.

Followers' expectations are changing. New social, economic, and technological conditions have created a better educated and more sophisticated constituency; superior education, technical skills, and access to information are no longer solely within the purview of the leader. As a result of the narrowing gap between their followers' abilities and their own, leaders must more actively involve followers in organizational processes.

If leadership consists of getting things accomplished through others, then these "others" are critical to the leader's effectiveness. One cannot be an effective leader if one has not been (and is not) an effective follower. The experience of following gives leaders perspective and enables them to share vision, communicate with empathy, treat people as individuals, and empower others to achieve shared goals and objectives. Empowerment implies that the followers are central to the organization rather than tangential to it. Empowered followers believe that they make a difference, that their actions have significance and meaning. They have discretion in what they do but are also accountable for their actions. Empowered organizations are characterized by a culture of mutual trust, integrity, and multidirectional communication.

If leaders are to develop good followers, they must encourage participation in the creation of goals and objectives, allowing their ideas to be modified and "owned" by everyone. Separating the individual from leadership creates "we," building a true sense of involvement and empowerment among followers.

Failure to recognize interdependencies between leader and follower can have serious consequences for both. These interdependencies are critical to a leader's success and ensure an ongoing pattern of leadership development. In many ways, leaders serve followers—certainly a reversal of traditional perceptions. But effective leaders create opportunities, help provide necessary resources, delegate authority, and vigorously support the decisions made and actions taken. Often, leaders must watch while others do things differently than they would have. Helping people learn by allowing them to make mistakes takes true courage and results in organizational learning. This is how leaders develop effective followers who, in turn, are learning the elements of effective leadership.

Some people evaluate leaders on the basis of who they have around them. We see many leaders who like to be the smartest, the most decisive, and all-powerful. They thrive on having followers revere them. Unfortunately, the organization becomes completely dependent on such a leader—everything happens because of her or him. Truly effective leaders have people around them who are bright, critical, and independent. Decisions are made at the organizational level having the most information. Followers are given the means and the responsibility to do the job; creativity and innovation are prized. Thus, leaders are best evaluated on the basis of organizational success and how well they develop their followers.

Leadership Perspectives

In "Followership: The Essence of Leadership" (Chapter 7), Chris Lee notes that leaders have tended to be viewed in isolation, as if they were the only truly active participants. The followers, if considered at all, are usually seen as empty vessels waiting to be filled with the leaders' inspiration. Lee suggests that the focus on leadership has been myopic and describes a variety of ongoing research that finds effective followers exhibiting the same sorts of characteristics that describe good leaders.

Robert Kelley describes how exemplary followers get along with their coworkers and leaders to benefit the organization in "How Followers Weave a Web of Relationships" (Chapter 8). These followers are attuned to other people's interests, enabling them to nurture a network of social relationships that contributes to the organization's success. According to Kelley, the follower's three most important relationships are with teams, organizational networks, and leaders. He describes the best followers as strong, independent partners with leaders.

James M. Kouzes, in "When Leadership Collides with Loyalty" (Chapter 9), describes the results of a study he did with Barry Z. Posner, which indicates that leaders are expected to be forward-looking and inspiring. Leaders and followers each want the other to be capable and effective; they need to be able to depend on and trust one another and set aside their own agendas for that of the organization. Yet being forward-looking and inspiring is often incompatible with being cooperative and dependable, which presents another dilemma. The leader who usually is both must make an either-or choice between leading and following.

In Chapter 10, "Followership" (a chapter from his book *Leadership Jazz*), Max De Pree reflects upon his leadership experiences, jazz, and playing second fiddle. He admits that he will never completely understand the relationship between leaders and followers but attests that he learned something about leadership from trying to be a good follower.

In Chapter 11, "Mentoring: Empowering Followers to Be Leaders," William E. Rosenbach reviews the literature on mentorship and its consequences for the mentor, protégé, and organization. Informal mentoring relationships have been very successful in the past, but with the recognition that one of the leader's most important responsibilities is the development of followers, organizations may favor formal mentorship programs in the future.

Finally, the delightful parable "The Wheel and the Light" by W. Chan Kim and Renée A. Mauborgne (Chapter 12) provides a fresh understanding of the essence of leadership from an Oriental master. This parable demonstrates the leader's ability to create an organization that draws out the unique strengths of each member.

7

Followership:
The Essence of Leadership

CHRIS LEE

"Follower" is almost a pejorative term in our culture. We much prefer to focus on the role of leader. John Wayne, inspiring his troops to dash to the rescue, a gun blazing in either hand, his horse's reins in his teeth, is a leader. His faithful charges, hanging back in the weeds and waiting for orders, are followers. Dull. Sheeplike. But essential—for without faithful followers, leaders cannot lead. Without followers even John Wayne becomes a solitary hero, or, given the right script, a comic figure, posturing on an empty stage.

Yet take a step back from the easy stereotypes and what do you see? In recent years, we've heard plenty about leaders and what they do. According to most schools of thought, an effective leader provides a vision, inspires others to commit to that vision, and creates strategies that move them toward the vision.

Leaders have been poked and prodded, their styles analyzed, their childhoods examined, their experiences compared and contrasted, and their successes and failures dissected. In most of this analysis, however, the leader tends to be viewed in isolation, as the only truly active agent in the picture. Those "others," those followers, are objects. If we consider them at all, it's usually as empty vessels, waiting to be filled with the leader's inspiration.

Executives and managers of every stripe have heard the news by now: They should be leading, not managing. They know their job is to spout forth inspirational vision statements like there's no tomorrow, to rally employees around those visions, and to lead them to better productivity and increased market share. In all of this, how many look around and conduct the ultimate litmus test of leadership: Is anyone following?

Could it be that our focus on leadership for the past several years has been myopic? Do followers have more to do with the leadership equation than we've suspected? A few researchers think so. They've begun to take a closer look at those empty vessels.

Without followers, points out Robert Kelley, a business professor at Carnegie Mellon University in Pittsburgh, Napoleon would have been just a man with grandiose ambitions. In a 1988 article in the *Harvard Business Review,* "In Praise of Followers," he describes effective followers as those who engage in "enthusiastic, intelligent and self-reliant participation—without star billing—in the pursuit of an organizational goal."

Kelley has been concentrating on followers and how they contribute to organizational success for some time now. "Like many people, I started out in the leadership area," he explains. "But I came to realize that I was dedicating my attention to that 1 percent to 2 percent of the equation that are leaders. There's plenty of research on what you should look for in a leader, but not on what you should look for in a follower. Why not pay attention to that 98 percent of the people who are followers? After seven years [of concentrating on followers], I've come to the conclusion that followers are more important than leaders."

Kelley has his own theories on why we see scads of leadership training, but essentially nothing in the way of followership training. "There's a lot of negative baggage associated with the term 'follower.' We think of sheep. And maybe 5 percent to 10 percent of followers fit that negative stereotype. We should set aside the term—call them team members, partners, associates, something.

"It's curious," he continues. "We make the assumption that leaders are effective and then give them all this training. We assume that followers are ineffective, yet we don't train them. People are not born with either [skill]. We want people to be independent, critical thinkers, and to have the courage to stand up for what they believe is right. But we don't develop these competencies that are at the core of organizational success. All of these things can be developed if we teach them and then reward people for practicing them."

Organizations that have effective leaders tend to be the kind of places that develop effective followers, although they may call them something more culturally palatable. And there's nothing sheeplike about effective followers. They do more than march lockstep toward fulfilling the vision their leader has laid out for them. Effective followers are partners in creating the vision in the first place. They take responsibility for getting their jobs done. They take the initiative to fix problems or improve processes.

They question leaders when they think they're wrong. In other words, they act a lot like leaders themselves.

Let's put that more strongly. To a suspicious degree, good followers exhibit exactly the sorts of characteristics that pundits talk about when describing good leaders.

Everyone's a Follower

But consider the fact that every leader, regardless of position, also plays the role of follower. As Kelley's *HBR* article noted: "At different points in their careers, even at different times of the working day, most managers play both roles, though seldom equally well. After all, the leadership role has the glamour and attention. We take courses to learn it, and when we play it well we get applause and recognition. But the reality is that most of us are more often followers than leaders. Even when we have subordinates, we still have bosses. For every committee we chair, we sit as a member on several others."

Consider many people's idea of the ultimate business leader—Lee Iacocca. He is in the role of follower when he is held accountable by Chrysler's board of directors and stockholders. Even the president of the United States, accountable to the voters every four years, must excel in the role of follower if he is to read the prevailing winds of public opinion accurately.

In the recent election and the federal budget imbroglio that immediately preceded it, we got an interesting demonstration of the leadership-followership dynamic. While President Bush flip-flopped on what he would and would not accept in a budget package, Congress foundered as well. Failure of leadership or failure of followership?

Perhaps both. Republican congressional leaders seemed unsure how to follow the President's lead, so their followers, in turn, failed to follow them. In a report on the debacle several weeks before the budget finally passed, *The Wall Street Journal* noted: "... neither Democrats nor Republican leaders in Congress could deliver their members. ... The day after the vote, Rep. Silvio Conte of Massachusetts, the senior Republican on the appropriations panel, wore a hat with visors facing opposite directions and the legend, 'I'm their leader, which way did they go?'" But, the *Journal* continued, "it wasn't lack of leadership that was the problem. The leaders led. It was lack of followership."

The problem here, according to Kelley, is that members of Congress "all want to vie for the title of leader—although none want the responsibility of leader—and none want the follower's role. Because of our societal bias against followership, they'd all rather vie for one-535th of the leadership role."

As for presidential leadership, the Monday morning quarterbacking after the November election made short work of that idea. Bush's 1990 election stumping for Republican candidates appeared to be singularly ineffective. Fourteen of the 18 candidates for whom he campaigned lost. In fact, quipped political commentator Daniel Schorr on National Public Radio's "All Things Considered," we witnessed "negative coattails."

In fact, we may have witnessed a failure of followership. In his 1985 book, *The Knowledge Executive: Leadership in an Information Society,* Harlan Cleveland quotes columnist Russell Baker's take on presidential leadership: "The country yearns for new leadership for a new era. If led, will the country follow? If given the right kind of leadership, the country will surely follow. But what kind of leadership is the right kind? The leadership that leads the country in the direction it wants to take. And what specific direction does the country want to take? Who knows? That's for the leader to figure out. If he is the right kind of leader, he will guess correctly. … Am I wrong in concluding that it isn't leadership the country wants in a president but followership?"

Cleveland concurs. "… [M]ajor change in society's sense of direction … is first shaped in an inchoate consensus reached by the people at large," he writes.

This "inchoate consensus" works the same way in organizations, say James Kouzes and Barry Posner in their book *The Leadership Challenge.* "Corporate leaders know very well that what seeds the vision are those imperfectly formed images in the marketing department about what the customers really wanted and those inarticulate mumblings from the manufacturing folks about the poor product quality, not crystal-ball gazing in upper levels of the corporate stratosphere. *The best leaders are the best followers.*" (Emphasis added.)

If this view stands the idea of leadership on its head, that's intentional. "This notion of leaders as followers may take some getting used to," acknowledge Kouzes and Posner. "It flies in the face of the leaders-as-heroes myth perpetuated so long in comic books, novels and movies. It also contradicts the newest myth of the entrepreneur as lone savior of the national economy. Yet, if we look closely, we see that even the entrepreneur is an astute listener and follower of others' desires."

James Georges, president and CEO of Par Training Corp., a consulting firm based on Atlanta, emphasizes the symbiotic relationship between leaders and followers. "To be a leader, you'd better know what following is all about because the substance of leadership is followership. But the idea of followership has gotten a bad reputation because people associate it with being a second-class citizen, a servant in the pejorative sense. To serve is the ultimate value a human being has. The leader is a servant," he says, citing Robert Greenleaf's essay "The Servant as Leader."

Peter Block echoes that idea. "If you have power over people you are accountable to them," says the Plainfield, NJ–based consultant and author. If followership can be defined as an act of commitment to an organization, to something outside oneself, then it's something that must be developed among our leaders as well, he adds.

"E" Words

What links effective, independent-thinking followers with effective leaders? Empowerment, an idea that has earned buzzword status in the past few years, seems to describe many of the dynamics inherent in the relationship. Mounting evidence from a wide variety of organizations has demonstrated that when individuals have a say in how their jobs are designed, when they are involved in making decisions about how their work is conducted, they are more effective. In other words, a more empowered work force is a more productive work force.

So is an effective follower essentially an empowered individual?

Kelley, for one, objects to applying the concept of empowerment to followers. "Effective followership is not the same as empowerment," he says. "I prefer enabling rather than empowering. You're not giving people power. People have power; the organization simply gets in their way."

Nevertheless, he acknowledges that some followers are more effective than others. He has developed an instrument designed to measure two dimensions of behavior that contribute to effective or ineffective followership. One dimension measures the test-taker's degree of independent, critical thinking; the other is an active/passive scale.

Once plotted on a grid, these dimensions yield several types of followers: Sheep, who are low on both scales; Yes People, who are more active but uncritical; Alienated Followers, who are critical and independent thinkers but who don't act; Survivors, who balance on the middle ground on both dimensions; and Effective Followers, who think for themselves and carry out tasks with enthusiasm.

To Kelley, the point is that if "we have effective, independent-thinking followers, we have less need for effective leaders. If we have effective leaders, too, that's a plus."

Warren Bennis, distinguished professor of business administration at the University of Southern California School of Business Administration and author of *On Becoming a Leader,* cites willingness to tell the truth as the single most important characteristic of an effective follower. "It is the good follower's obligation to share his or her best counsel with the person in charge. And silence—not dissent—is the one answer that leaders should refuse to accept," he wrote in an opinion piece in the *New York Times* last year.

While he puts the obligation for encouraging and even rewarding dissent on the leader, Bennis acknowledges that followers who question leaders may be putting their jobs on the line. "Perhaps the ultimate irony is that the follower who is willing to speak out shows precisely the kind of initiative that leadership is made of," he concludes.

If we identify independent thinking and a willingness to question leaders as earmarks of effective followers, several other qualities become givens. "If you consider a leader a servant to people," says Georges, "that implies empowerment. A person is empowered when they are totally willing and able, [that is to say] committed and competent. If you take either one away, they have no power." In fact, they will no longer be followers at all, to Georges' way of thinking, because he considers commitment and competence the necessary preconditions to the act of following a leader.

Stephen Lundin, a professor at Metropolitan State University in Minneapolis, and Lynne Lancaster of Lancaster Consulting Group in St. Paul, MN, are working on a book that focuses on the importance of followership. An article in *The Futurist* last year summarized some of their observations about effective followers:

- They have personal integrity that demands both loyalty to the organization and the willingness to act according to their beliefs.
- They "own the territory," meaning they understand the organization and their contributions to it.
- They are versatile—skillful and flexible enough to adapt to a changing environment.
- They "take responsibility for their own careers, their own actions and their own development."

Like Kelley, Lundin contends that the term empowerment implies something leaders do *to* followers. "Effective followership is something you do to yourself," he says.

A few other researchers have drawn a distinction between empowering and enabling that may be helpful here. "The Empowerment Process: Integrating Theory and Practice," an article by Jay A. Conger and Rabindra N. Kanungo published in *Academy of Management Review* in 1988, acknowledged that empowerment is often thought of as delegating or sharing power with subordinates. But empowerment in the sense of enabling (the term Kelley prefers), they wrote, implies motivating through a sense of personal efficacy. Thus, they arrived at a definition of empowerment that calls it a "process of enhancing feelings of self-efficacy among organizational members through the identification of conditions that foster powerlessness and through their removal. ..."

As a matter of fact, the definition of empowerment Peter Block used in his 1987 book *The Empowered Manager* sounds very much like a description of the effective follower whose picture is emerging here: "Empowerment is a state of mind as well as a result of position, policies and practices. ... To feel empowered means several things: We feel our survival is in our own hands. ... It requires that we in every sense take responsibility for our situation. ... We have an underlying purpose. Work is something more than paying the mortgage. Granted, we work because we have to, but if we are going to put in time, we have a goal or vision of something worthwhile. ... We commit ourselves to achieving that purpose. ... As managers, our task is to empower ourselves and to create conditions under which others can do the same."

Pick the label you prefer. The point remains that effective followers tend to act in similar ways.

Consider Federal Express, a company that regularly underlines its culture of empowerment by publicizing heroics its employees perform, apparently as a matter of course. In an article in *Quality Progress* late last year, Fred Smith, chairman and CEO of FedEx, related a typical story: "As the building rumbled and shook at the whim of the October 1989 San Francisco earthquake, Federal Express courier Maurice Jane't continued to scan each package he was picking up at Hitachi Data Systems. He then struggled to get them down nine flights of rubble-filled stairs to his waiting van and on to the airport just in time for the plane. ..."

Smith, who would appear on many short lists of effective business leaders, obviously understands the importance of effective followers to his organization's success. "... [W]e learned long ago that employee satisfaction is a prerequisite to customer satisfaction," he writes. And that belief is reflected in the company's philosophy statement: "People, Service, Profit."

FedEx's dedication to fostering effective followers doesn't end with stirring stories of individual heroics and noble-sounding philosophies. The company has programs and processes designed to answer basic questions for employees. Smith enumerated them: "What do you expect of me? What's in it for me? Where do I go with a problem?"

The company recognizes that people want to do a good job and will do so if they are properly trained and know what is expected of them, he wrote. FedEx goes to the employees themselves to find out how to improve processes. As Smith noted, "It is well-known that tapping employee expertise on an ongoing basis is a sure way to make the job a reward in itself, which is what the second question, 'What's in it for me?' is all about."

Of course, FedEx also rewards performance with bonuses based on individual and company performance. Its management evaluation system, called SFA (Survey/Feedback/Action), polls employees and ensures that managers discuss the results with their work groups. Together, they develop written action plans for the manager to use to become more effective. And this process is not some showy-but-meaningless exercise in employee participation. It has teeth in it: Up to 25 percent of each manager's performance-appraisal rating is based on the evaluations handed in by his subordinates.

Partnerships

All of which brings us to an idea that is integral to the concept of effective followership: ownership.

If, in Georges' words, commitment and competence are requirements for following a leader, how do leaders ensure that followers share their goals and possess the abilities to reach them? The answer is, they can't. But they can create an environment in which followers can develop their own goals (in other words, a culture of empowerment), as well as provide the training to develop competence. It then becomes the leader's task to sense where followers want to go, align their goals with the larger goals of the organization, and invite them to follow.

But alignment is only possible when followers have goals of their own, Georges emphasizes. "How can anyone lead you without taking you somewhere you want to go?" he asks. People with no goals of their own cannot be led because they have nowhere they want to go.

Thus, the idea of "feeling like you own" a process, a product, a service, a goal, whatever, is intrinsic to the concept of taking responsibility for it. Georges calls it "an emotional state of confidence." Just how do you go about creating that?

At San Francisco–based Levi Strauss & Co., president and CEO Bob Haas has long been dedicated to creating a sense of ownership among employees. The company's mission and aspiration statement, published several years ago, formalized his commitment to that goal.

In essence, it says that the company will balance its goal of profitability with fair treatment, teamwork, open communications, personal accountability and opportunities for growth and development for employees. It describes empowerment by emphasizing "leadership that increases the authority and responsibility of those closest to our products and customers. By actively pushing responsibility, trust and recognition into the organization we can harness and release the capabilities of all our people."

This statement of the company's values has been put into effect in several ways, says Sue Thompson, director of human resources development. The values it describes have been translated into behavioral terms and merged into the performance-appraisal process for exempt employees.

"They are rated by peers, subordinates and superiors on the extent to which their actions are consistent with the aspirations statement," Thompson says.

All 31,000 Levi Strauss employees eventually will participate in leadership training as well. "All employees need to take leadership roles in a different way at different times," Thompson says. "It may mean not waiting for 'them' to take action, or giving open and honest feedback if things aren't going right. It means stepping forward."

Does that description sound like effective followership? Thompson doesn't like the term. She prefers to describe her company's approach as "shared responsibility, really a partnership."

She uses her own department as an example. "The direction of the department is just as much my staff's responsibility as mine," she says. "They have to challenge, question and push if they're going to be committed to it."

Levi Strauss also is building ownership in a more concrete way. It recently introduced gain sharing, the type of plan in which employees share in profits realized through productivity improvements. Currently, the program is in effect at just three of its 30 production facilities, but the company plans to launch the program in the rest of its plants as soon as possible, Thompson says. "We talk about employees as partners," she says, "now we're seeking ways to make them real partners."

Turning the World Upside Down

Jan Carlzon, the president of Scandinavian Airline Systems (SAS) who turned around the airline in the early '80s, was talking about followership when he admonished his managers and staff people, "If you're not serving the customer, you'd better be serving someone who is."

His idea was, as Peters terms it, to turn the organization upside down. He wanted those front-line employees, the ones who create those "moments of truth" for customers, to become the heroes at SAS. He also wanted them to be able to go around their managers to solve problems if necessary.

That's a lesson more companies are learning, as they realize that front-line workers dramatically affect such paramount concerns as quality and customer service. "An autocratic system can't be customer-focused or quality-oriented," says Block.

The result of this redistribution of power may be a new way of looking at organizations and the roles of leaders and followers—regardless of what we agree to call them. "The problem with the idea of following is that it puts the role of leadership outside the person," muses Block. "Someone else is the leader. I say, if you want a leader, look in the mirror."

8

How Followers Weave
a Web of Relationships

ROBERT KELLEY

High achievers—people who add value by doing a great job—pass the first hurdle of followership. But if that was all they did they would be no more than great solo performers. Exemplary followership has an equally important organizational component. The best followers know how to get along with their co-workers and leaders in ways that benefit the organization.

Unlike followers who consistently try to maximize only their own self-interest, the best followers view the organization as a "commons." The term "commons" dates back to pre-industrial England. It refers to the pasture that townspeople shared in "common" with each other for grazing their livestock. The challenge facing the community was to enable everyone to feed their livestock without degrading the commons for future grazing. If one family maximized their feeding at the expense of the community, they gained in the short run. But if everyone followed suit, all the grass would get eaten, destroying the commons for everyone. For all to benefit, each family had to contribute to maintaining the commons by keeping their short-term selfishness in check.

The best followers treat the organization as a commons. Instead of taking a free ride at the organization's expense or focusing solely on their rights, they acknowledge the mutual responsibilities they have with others. Organizational life requires give-and-take if it is going to work. If you are going to drink from the organizational well, you must also help replenish it.

This attitude helps exemplary followers in their organizational relationships. Others do not see them as only trying to maximize their own self-interest. Instead, they are viewed as also being attuned to and keeping other people's interests in mind. This enables them to nurture and leverage a web of important social relationships that then further contribute to the organization's success. The three most important of these relationships are with:

- Teams
- Organizational networks
- Leaders

Building a Team of Individuals

The demands of the workplace are changing. As many bosses now have twenty to thirty people reporting to them rather than the traditional five to seven, followers can count on leaders less for direction or input. Followers must rely on each other more.

For example, in 1987, declining profitability and intensified competition for corporate clients forced a large commercial bank on the East Coast to reorganize its operations and cut its work force. Its most seasoned managers had to spend most of their time in the field working with corporate customers. Time and energies were stretched so thin that one department head decided he had no choice but to delegate the responsibility for reorganization to his staff people, who had recently had training in self-management.

Despite grave doubts, the department head set them up as a unit without a leader, responsible to one another and to the bank as a whole for writing their own job descriptions, designing a training program, determining criteria for performance evaluations, planning for operational needs, and helping to achieve overall organizational objectives.

They pulled it off. The bank's officers were delighted and frankly amazed that rank-and-file employees could assume so much responsibility so successfully. In fact, the department's capacity to control and direct itself virtually without leadership saved the organization months of turmoil. As the bank struggled to remain a major player in its region, valuable management time was freed up to put out other fires.

As this example illustrates, followers increasingly have to work with each other, and teams are the most common vehicle for this joint effort. In the last ten to fifteen years, teams became ubiquitous. It is not unusual for the average worker to belong to several teams, many of which extend beyond their organizational unit. Most people alternate between team leader and team follower several times a day. These teams go by various names: leaderless groups, self-managed work groups, semi-autonomous units, task forces, committees, crisis units, SWAT teams, alliances, joint efforts, and councils. They all add up to the same message. The work of most organizations today is done through teams.

Exemplary followers, as we shall see, are good team players. But they also view teams with a critical eye. From their perspective, teams and the time-consuming meetings they spawn are often an inappropriate knee-jerk response to organizational challenges. Whenever an issue arises, some leaders react with "Let's form a task force to study the issue and have them report back to us." Teams, in some of these cases, are like the proverbial hammer that gets used for every job because it is the only tool in the box.

Before joining a team, then, exemplary followers ask whether the team is necessary at all. First, what is the task? Can it be written down in one or two sentences? Next, is the task itself related to the critical path? What is the likelihood that the outcomes will add value? Finally, if the task passes these two hurdles, is it something that is best handled by a team or by one or two people?

Once convinced that the task and a team are appropriate, exemplary followers question their own participation and that of others. What value do you and each member bring to this team? Are your talents suitable to the tasks? If not, are there better people to include on the team? Are all of you necessary or could you do with fewer members? If some people are on the team simply because they need to be kept informed or you need their political "buy-in," is there another way to achieve it without tying up their time and talents on this team?

Exemplary followers, then, are very particular about their team involvements. As one explained, "I view teams the way Charles Lindbergh viewed packing for his transatlantic flight. The plane would hold only a finite number of things. Excess items created more drag and required more fuel than the plane could carry. For each item he asked: Is this necessary to achieve the goal? I look at my team involvements the same way: Does my being on the team help me and the organization achieve our mutual goals?"

If exemplary followers don't buy into the team's purpose or goals, they share their views with the team leader up front, rather than be a noncontributing member. If they do join, they set about trying to make the team successful. Here in a nutshell is how they do it.

Start by checking to make sure that all the team members share a common understanding of the team's purpose and goals. Exemplary followers will often share their view and then solicit comments to either confirm or disconfirm their view. If team members are not on the same wavelength, keep pushing till a common understanding is reached.

Next, identify what your contribution to the team is and how it relates to the work of other team members. At each team meeting, commit to the timing and specifications of your output. If your work products are to be used by someone else, have them spell out for you what they expect. Then let them know what you can really deliver and when. Seek concurrence then, rather than down the line.

Exemplary followers try to maintain an equitable division of labor. This does not mean that everyone does the same amount of work. People's availability and talents will often dictate their contributions. Instead, it means not trying to weasel out of work at the expense of others and not letting someone else get saddled with more than she or he should have to handle. It also means chipping in to do your share of the grunt work, filling in for others when necessary, and helping to overcome bottlenecks in the team's progress.

After agreeing to your tasks, make sure you produce your work on schedule. If you are having trouble or getting behind on your schedule, let the other team members know as soon as possible, especially if they are depending on your work output. As one team leader explained, "If someone tells me of a problem before the due date, I view it as an acceptable reason. If someone tells me after the due date, I see it as an excuse." Try to show others your work before it is due so that you have time to act on any criticisms. If it turns out that your work doesn't meet the team's expectations, redo it as quickly as possible.

But team membership goes beyond doing your share of the work in a satisfactory manner. It also means helping out your teammates. As in basketball or hockey, this includes making "assists," where you don't do it yourself but you help someone else do it for the good of the team. The best followers gladly contribute by making assists because their focus is on the goal, not self-propulsion.

Willie Wise played forward on my college basketball team—a team that made it all the way to the NCAA semifinals. Willie was not the captain, the highest scorer, or the number one rebounder. He didn't make the most steals, nor was he the playmaker. The only thing that he led the team in was number of assists, setting up a teammate and then passing to him to make the basket. Willie was also the player who was always there when you needed him, whether it be for a pick, a pass, or a fast break.

After the season, Willie was overlooked in the pro draft. They chose the shooters, jumpers, and playmakers instead. Not discouraged, Willie tried out for the now defunct Salt Lake City team in the American Basketball Association. He not only made the cut, he became a starter. Again, he did not lead the team in anything except assists. What the team and coach found, however, was that Willie helped the team gel. He wasn't the leader, but he soon became critical and irreplaceable. His style of playing was the glue that held the "stars" on the team together. As a result, Willie made All-Pro year after year—a tribute to his contributions.

Likewise, exemplary followers are on the lookout for anything that might be useful to other team members. If relevant documents come across their desk or timely information buzzes in the grapevine, they share it. This is in sharp contrast to information hoarding, such as what once occurred at National Semiconductor. One participant described a manager there who received new and exciting results from a market research study he had commissioned. Upon reviewing it, he said, "This is great, but we can't let it leak out to those bastards. They'll try to use it against us." It turned out that he was not referring to competing companies but to the production people down the hall. Unlike this manager, effective followers realize that long-term success requires cooperation.

An important aspect of team membership is contributing to the team's dynamics. Besides coming to meetings prepared, the best followers try to help keep the team on track and all team members actively involved. Rather than focusing only on what you have to say, make sure that everyone gets a chance to speak and be listened to at team meetings. If someone's comments get ignored, point this out to the group so that the person doesn't give up and slide into passivity. If someone's body language suggests they are turned off or in mute disagreement, try to bring them back onto the team by soliciting their views. If you are personally frustrated with the group, others might feel the same way. Bring it up in a nonaccusatory manner to check if you are sensing a wider phenomenon. You might say, "I'm starting to feel frustrated because I think we're getting off track. Does anyone else feel this way?" By talking about it, you can help clear the air.

As part of the group dynamics, the best team players maintain a sense of humor and perspective. They help the team see the lighter side of the serious work. They are able to kid and be kidded, while being sensitive to others' feelings. But they also avoid being the class clown. Most importantly, they can laugh at their own mistakes and predicaments.

Finally, the best team players give credit where credit is due. They acknowledge other team members' contributions whenever they represent the team. If giving a presentation about the team's work, they start out by identifying everyone on the team. They use "we" rather than "I" unless they clearly did the work independently.

Building a Network

Teams and work departments exist within a mostly invisible stratum of organizational interrelationships. For lack of a better term, I refer to this as the organizational network. Networks include knowing the maintenance worker who can get you a hard-to-come-by table when you need one and a guru in another division who knows the ins and outs of the computer data base you are using on your project.

Your network is a series of interpersonal bridges that connect you to others in the organization. These connections seldom show up on formal organization charts. Nor are they heavily influenced by the organizational authority structure. People in your network do things for you because you have a relationship with them, not because their job requires it or the organizational chain commands it. You are much more likely to get a faster and better response from another department if someone over there is part of your network. This almost always beats talking to your boss, who talks to their boss, who then talks to that person.

Each person has his or her own unique network that branches in many directions. Networks crisscross over each other. This collective web of interrelationships is the real foundation of any successful organization. The traffic of organizational work travels over this invisible infrastructure.

Exemplary followers are sensitive to the role of organizational networks. More often than leaders, they see the effect of different decisions on the network itself. For example, executives may decide to reorganize a division because on paper it appears to be more efficient. Or they may decide to move from one building into two distant buildings to cut costs.

But exemplary followers are likely to see the ramifications of such decisions on the organizational network. The organization has an investment in the time and effort that followers expend to build their networks, let alone the benefits they produce. By moving people away from each other, the executives may destroy the very work relationships that are necessary for the organization to reach its goals.

Exemplary followers also strive to build a network because it is critical for personal and organizational goal accomplishment. To learn how, return to your critical path activities. Identify the key people in the organization who can help or hinder you in the completion of those activities. Then reverse the process. Whose work activities do you directly or indirectly help or hinder? The people identified in both directions become the center of your network.

Now think further upstream and downstream from your immediate work. Once you hand off your work to someone else, who will help or hinder it in its contribution to the organization's goals? These people also need to become part of your network.

For example, if you work in R&D, you will probably need other R&D people in your network to give you technical input. But you will also want people in marketing who can give you customer input or put you directly in contact with customers. Likewise, you will need contacts in manufacturing who can keep you posted about factory floor changes that might influence your work.

When you are in meetings, observe who seems knowledgeable about topics important to you and who garners respect from others. Ask people in your department for names of people that you should get to know. Keep a list of the people who call you for information. All these people can be added to your network.

Once you identify the people, then you have to build the relationship. For some people, this is no more than introducing yourself and getting acquainted. Perhaps you share some hobby or have a common background.

But for networks to maintain themselves over the long run, they must be a two-way street. You must have something which the other party values. One good way to establish the relationship is to try to help them out *before* you need their help. Pass along articles or ideas that they have an interest in. Or maybe you have an expertise that they need access to. Perhaps you are a good listener or sounding board. Maybe your network is valuable to them, so that when they need to find something, they can call you for a referral. It could be as simple as being nice to them.

While building your network, pay attention to etiquette. Before you ask strangers for help, be sensitive to their needs and constraints. Ask if it is a good time to bother them. If not, choose a time and place that is convenient for them. So that you don't look like a lazy leech, never ask someone to solve a problem for you that you haven't first tried. Show them the process you used and the results. Pay attention to their answer, writing it down if need be, so that you don't have to bother them twice. If their help was considerable, let their and your bosses know about their contribution. Always give credit to those who help you. Finally, when it is your turn, reciprocate without hesitation.

Another aspect of etiquette is turf checking. Turf battles are much maligned in today's organization. But the best followers understand that people have both legitimate claims and vested interest in certain areas. If someone has spent five years building up an area, he or she expects to be consulted before people start reinventing the same wheel or tampering with it. The best followers will check with relevant people first and get their buy-in if possible. When there are overlapping interests, they will suggest collaborations.

Exemplary followers also collectively monitor the network for the "social loafers" who expect others to pick up their slack. People who try to get others to do their work or who try to get ahead at others' expense will often get a cold shoulder.

The power of networks, then, is enormous in accomplishing your job and helping the organization reach its goals. By cultivating their networks, exemplary followers increase their productivity and their effectiveness considerably.

Working with the Leader

The most important but troublesome relationship for many followers is with the leader. It can cause anxiety, confusion, frustration, and even anger. Conformist followers feel as if they always have to please the boss, while alienated followers continually snipe at the leader.

Effective followers see themselves—except in terms of line responsibility—as the equals of the leaders they follow. In the spirit of the "commons," effective followers take a barn-raising approach to working with the leader. In this era of distributed leadership, they realize that everyone takes turns leading and following. If they want the current leader to support them when the roles are reversed, they must be a fully contributing follower now. All too often, less effective followers do the minimum when following, saving their energy for when they lead. This results in team leaders who have to do all the work because their passive followers are focused only on their own leadership projects.

Exemplary followers begin by understanding the leader's needs, goals, and constraints. They make a point of asking the leader directly and watching where the leader puts his or her efforts. They also see that the people they follow are, in turn, following the lead of others. To the extent possible, they work hard to help their bosses achieve their own goals and the organization's goals.

Less effective followers, on the other hand, have a more limited worldview that only takes into account their specific work environment and immediate needs. They recognize their own work responsibilities and deadlines, but rarely consider the pressures and commitments their leader faces.

Exemplary followers work cooperatively with the leader rather than adversarially. They control their own ego to keep it from interfering with the leader's projects or other followers' effectiveness. For example, they distinguish between their own ego's stubborn preferences and an honest assessment of the ideas under discussion. When their ego is getting in the way of progress, they suppress it. Rather than always having to get their opinions heard, they help meetings move along in a crisp, productive fashion.

But when exemplary followers truly disagree on important issues, they are more apt to openly and unapologetically disagree with leadership and less likely to be intimidated by hierarchy and organizational structure. They do not accept the leader's viewpoint blindly. They make a habit of internally questioning the wisdom of the leader's decision rather than just doing what they are told. They assert their views even though this might produce conflict or reprisals from the leader. They especially speak out when they believe the leader is going down the wrong track or when the group secretly doesn't want to do what has been decided.

In many ways, followers are extended eyes and ears of the leader. They are often closer to the action and will pick up information that the leader doesn't have access to. Deprived of this information, the leader will make mistakes. Exemplary followers feel a responsibility to give leaders honest and candid feedback about their decisions and actions. They help the leader see both the upside potential and the downside risks of ideas or plans, playing the devil's advocate if need be. By disagreeing, exemplary followers help the leader do a better job.

When disagreeing with the leader, exemplary followers use these guidelines:

First, talk to the leader privately rather than unloading on him or her in a public forum. Avoid grandstanding, especially at the leader's expense. Instead, try to be sensitive to the leader's feelings and public image. Help the leader and other followers who might lose an argument to save face by pointing out the positives, as well as the negatives, of their viewpoint.

Next, pay attention to timing. If possible, don't approach the leader when she or he is dealing with a crisis or a deadline. Pick a time and a place that is convenient and without distraction. Disagreements that can hold till she or he is back from a trip or vacation will get a better hearing than those presented as the leader is rushing to the airport.

When you sit down with the leader, present the issue as a joint problem that needs to be discussed, not his or her stupid decision. State the issue clearly and succinctly from your viewpoint. Have your facts straight and at hand. One exemplary follower writes the issue down on paper and asks the leader to look at it. This helps to focus the issue and eliminate unnecessary confusion.

When presenting a problem, come prepared with potential solutions. The boss seldom needs one more burden. If you are the kind of person who frequently dumps problems but no solutions, the leader is going to erect defenses against you. Not every situation, of course, lends itself to ready solutions. If not, at least do the legwork to find out the details of what is possible. Then at least you can suggest an approach to deal with it.

When brainstorming alternatives, consider your boss's point of view. Which alternatives might appeal to him or her? One exemplary follower queries herself, "If I were the boss, would I sign off on this and risk my reputation on its working?"—thus eliminating half-baked ideas. Whenever possible, offer alternative solutions in a form which the leader only has to approve or disapprove. This saves the leader needless brainstorming and analysis.

Also, don't go in angry, because this usually induces anger in the boss. If you want the boss to focus on the merits of your argument, then work out your anger before the visit. Try not to let your bruised ego get in the way of your effectiveness.

Exemplary followers increase the odds that their voices will be heard by creating trust and avoiding the corrosive effects of mistrust. Likewise, they gauge how much they can trust their leader and their co-workers. Sizing up the leader's trustworthiness helps determine how they use their "power of the follower." In other words, they view credibility as a two-way street. They build it for others and demand that others build it with them.

Credibility grows with each action and day by day through consistent demonstration of trustworthiness. In my book *The Gold-Collar Worker*, I described how trust is built by making deposits in each other's emotional bank accounts. Deposits are made when you act responsibly, honestly, and caringly. A powerful emotional deposit is to help others get what they want. It communicates that you care about the person specifically. Extending yourself for another increases considerably the value of your emotional bank account and your credibility.

In Herman Wouk's *The Winds of War*, Pug Henry is a fictional naval office who finds himself in the eye of major historical storms leading up to World War II. At one point, Pug and his wife, Rhoda, are invited to an intimate dinner party at the White House with President Roosevelt and a few other guests, including the British author and intelligence officer Somerset Maugham. During the conversation, Roosevelt asks Pug what he thinks of Hitler after having had a chance to talk at length face to face with him. After Pug gives his assessment, Rhoda blurts out:

> "Pug, when on earth did you have a talk with Hitler? That's news to me." The artless injured tone made the President laugh and laughter swept the table. She turned on Roosevelt. "Honestly, he's always been closemouthed, but to keep something like that from me!"
>
> "You didn't need to know," Pug said across the table.
>
> "Captain Henry," said Somerset Maugham, leaning forward, "I bow to a professional."
>
> The conversation broke into little amused colloquies. Roosevelt said to Rhoda Henry, "My dear, you couldn't have paid your husband a handsomer compliment in public."

Regardless of how you perceive Pug as a husband, his credibility as a follower who could keep confidences went sky-high. Honesty is a critical element of credibility building. Effective followers are honest with themselves, their co-workers, and the leader. When informing another, they tell the whole story, not just the part that makes them look good. They give credit where it is due and own up to their part in any mistakes. Less effective followers shade the truth, leaving others unsure as to what to believe.

Edward R. Murrow summed it up in the following way: "To be persuasive, we must be believable; to be believable, we must be credible; to be credible, we must be truthful." Credible followers, whose emotional bank accounts with their leaders and their co-workers are high, can make occasional withdrawals, such as missing a deadline, without doing irreparable damage. Others give them the benefit of the doubt. Less effective followers with low emotional bank accounts find their credibility extremely fragile. One false step and they may lose whatever credibility they had.

Putting It All Together

If you want to be an exemplary follower, you need to do a handful of very doable things quite well. The important points are to add value consistently in two ways:

- Do a great job on critical path activities.
- Nurture and leverage a web of organizational interrelationships.

The best followers are strong, independent partners with leaders. They think for themselves, self-direct their work, and hold up their end of the bargain. They continuously work at making themselves integral to the enterprise, honing their skills and focusing their contributions, and collaborating with their colleagues.

One interesting finding of my research is that exemplary followers don't believe they have to know everything. Instead, they actively learn by asking tons of questions, of the leader and their co-workers. They watch what happens around them. To them, followership is not an individual sport, like running a marathon. Instead, they get all the help they can without being a boor or a pest.

Hopefully this chapter has saved you some of that legwork by presenting some of what they have learned, the tricks of the trade that helped them become exemplary. If you still want to learn more, observe the best followers in your organization. If possible, ask them for advice.

Exemplary followership is not the exclusive domain of superheroes and demigods. Exemplary followers are ordinary people, not some idealized stereotype to be cloned. All of us are capable of doing the activities described in this chapter. The difference between the best followers and others is that the best actually *do* them. They echo Paderewski, the famous pianist. When asked by the Queen how often he practiced, he replied, "Every day." Impressed, the Queen queried, "Where did you get so much patience?" Paderewski pondered for a moment and then said, "I don't have any more patience than the next person. I simply use mine."

9

When Leadership Collides with Loyalty

JAMES M. KOUZES

Despite our cry for more effective leadership, I've become convinced that we are quite satisfied to do without it. We would much rather have loyalty than leadership. Recall the fight between former General Motors board member H. Ross Perot and G.M.'s chairman, Roger B. Smith, that erupted when someone other than the official leader of the corporation began to articulate a strategic vision for the company.

Or take the case of a friend of mine, a former senior vice president of a large packaged goods company. A few years ago he faced a critical leadership challenge. New technology made it possible to introduce a substitute for his company's food product. His market studies clearly indicated that the future of the industry lay in the new substitute product. He was convinced that his company had to revise its long-range plans and develop its own entry into the market or suffer disastrous consequences.

But the board did not share his point of view. It authorized its own independent studies by two prestigious management consulting firms, which to the board's surprise supported the senior vice president's sense of the market. Still unconvinced, the board asked two law firms to determine whether entry into the new market would pose any antitrust issues. Both sets of lawyers agreed there would be no problem.

Despite the overwhelming evidence, the board then sought the opinion of yet a third law firm. This one gave it the answer it was looking for and it abandoned the new product.

The senior vice president would not be false to his beliefs and subsequently left the company. He has since successfully applied his leadership talents to dramatically improve the performance of a business he now owns in another industry. And he was right about the future of his former company. It experienced serious financial losses, went through a dramatic downsizing, and has yet to recover fully from its myopic strategy.

This critical incident illustrates an extraordinarily difficult choice executives must often make: Do I lead or do I follow? While one is frequently a leader and a follower in the same organization, there are times in executive careers when the choice is either-or. That is because there are distinct differences [in] what we expect of followers. These expectations are in dramatic conflict.

During the course of doing research for a book, my co-author, Barry Posner, and I asked top-level managers to complete a checklist of the characteristics they look for and admire most in a leader. According to our study, the majority of senior managers admire leaders who are: honest, competent, forward-looking and inspiring.

In a separate study, we asked a similar group of executives about what qualities they value in a follower. The majority of executives in our study said they admire honesty, competency, dependability and cooperation.

In every survey we conducted in the United States, honesty and competency ranked first and second in our expectations of what we want from our leaders and our followers. If we are to follow someone willingly, we first want to know that the person is worthy of our trust. Similarly, when a leader inquires into the status of a project he wants to know that the information is completely accurate.

We also want leaders and followers alike to be capable and effective. When a leader delegates a task he naturally wants assurance that it will be carried out with skill and precision.

But we also expect our leaders to have a sense of direction and a concern for the future of the organization. Leaders must know where they are going. We expect them to be enthusiastic, energetic and positive about the future. It is not enough for a leader to have a dream—he must be able to communicate his vision in ways that uplift and encourage people to go along with it.

Leaders want to know they can count on people to be team players. They want to know they will work together willingly and will be able to compromise and subordinate individual needs to the common purpose.

These qualities are absolutely essential for even the most mundane tasks in organizations. We must be able to rely on each other, to trust each other, and to set aside our own agendas for that of the organization. Without dependability and cooperation, nothing would get done, and politics would be rampant.

Yet being forward-looking and inspiring—two essential leadership qualities—is often not harmonious with being cooperative and dependable. That is what happened in the case of the senior vice president of the packaged goods company. His integrity demanded that he stand up for his point of view. The result was that he was perceived not to be a team player.

If an individual's vision of the future is opposed to that of his superiors, he may be perceived as uncooperative and disloyal even if his point of view is correct. Persistently selling a point of view only reinforces this perception and may diminish support within the organization. It may even lead to being branded a renegade, and result in being fired, transferred, or to a "voluntary" departure.

As essential as cooperativeness and dependability are, they can be inhibitors of organizational change. If they are too rigidly adhered to, they can result in faithful allegiance to the status quo and unquestioning loyalty to the party line. They also can inhibit the development of the leadership skills we so need in business today.

There is another crucial difference between a pioneering leader and a dependable follower. While success in both is founded on personal credibility, leadership requires the realization of a unique and ideal vision of the future. Following requires cooperative and reliable adherence to that common vision. When an individual's vision is in conflict with the existing strategic vision of an organization, he may have to make a choice: do I lead or do I follow?

There is no easy path. If organizations inhibit the honest articulation of fresh strategic visions of the future, they will never grow and improve. They will never create a climate that fosters leadership. On the other hand, if individuals cannot learn to subordinate themselves to a shared purpose, then anarchy will rule.

In these times of business transformation, it is wise for executives to encourage and tolerate more internal conflict than we have allowed in the past. If we expect people to show initiative in meeting today's serious business challenges, then we have to relax our expectations of abiding devotion. Instead, we must support the efforts of honest and competent people to find solutions to the problems that are confronting our companies. In short, we must develop the leader in everyone.

10

Followership

MAX DE PREE

Like many companies, Herman Miller started out small and family-owned. My father, D.J., founded the company and for years was its president. My older brother Hugh had always been looked upon as D.J.'s successor in the family business and for seventeen years made a wonderful president. D.J. said more than once to me, "It takes more grace than tongue can tell to play the second fiddle well." I can surely attest to the truth in this. But I did learn something about leadership from trying to be a good follower.

While becoming a good follower is not the only way to become a good leader, it can be very important training. If one is already a leader, the lessons of following are especially appropriate. Leaders understand the essential contributions as well as the limitations of good followers. Experience in this case is the best teacher.

One obvious requirement for doing good work as a leader is to learn the perspective of followers. The first thing to remember: As long as a follower is in the group you lead, she is essential. Work teams, sports teams, and bands have this in common. I've often asked myself, "Are the poorest sandlot baseball players chosen last because they commit so many errors? Or do they commit errors because they're chosen last?"

When Herman Miller was building its base in Europe some years ago, key people would frequently move to Bath, England, for periods of time to help get the new company up and running. Roy Keech, an effective financial person whose avocation is playing the French horn, took his turn in that "green and pleasant land." As traveling people know, the weekends away from home are the longest.

While strolling through downtown Bath one Sunday, Roy came upon the park along the Avon River, where the afternoon band concert was about to take place. He decided to join the crowd and listen. The band was late getting started, and when the conductor finally came to the podium, he announced that the French hornist wasn't there. They could not play their scheduled concert without a French horn. Could anyone in the audience fill in?

After waiting for someone else to volunteer and with great hesitation, Roy walked up to the conductor. He read through the music, picked up the band's French horn, practiced a few passages, and the concert went on. The audience appreciated the concert and Roy so much that the band ended the concert with "The Stars and Stripes Forever" to honor its new member from the States. The conductor, I imagine, had learned something about the fragility of leadership.

What can a leader learn by walking in the shoes of a follower?

- One quickly learns who delivers solutions and who loves to hand over problems.
- One learns that a leader needs to have a high threshold of pain and a low tolerance for what is popularly called BS.
- One learns to recognize the difficulty of holding people accountable while giving them space to make mistakes. One also learns the fundamental necessity of doing so.
- One learns that the story of the emperor and his clothes is more a parable than a fairy tale. If leaders are to stay dressed, they need a lot of help. Leaders cannot function without the eyes and ears and minds and hearts of followers.
- One learns the sometimes startling differences between the perceptions of leaders and the everyday realities of followers. Some months ago, one of the students at the seminary where I'm a member of the board of trustees asked the board, "If you want our help, do you know our needs? Do you know our gifts? Do you know our problems?"
- One learns that leaders only really accomplish something by permission of the followers.
- One finds out that in learning to play second fiddle well—and perhaps someday first fiddle—three questions come to mind: What does a follower owe? What should leaders beware of that inhibits good followership? What do followers need to know to keep their leader dressed?

Let's talk first about what followers owe. To be sure, leaders owe a great deal to their institutions and their followers. By the same token, followers owe a great deal to their institutions and their leaders. It is an issue of fairness, though, of what a leader can rightly expect. It seems to me, in the context of interdependent work, a leader has the right to expect followers to:

- Develop a high degree of literacy about the institution; understand its motives; know whom it serves; accept what must be measured and the constraints around the survival of the organization.
- Take responsibility for achieving personal goals; hold the organization responsible for providing a level playing field.
- *See* work and take ownership in areas consistent with their responsibilities and accountabilities. Connect themselves to those the organization ultimately serves.
- Become loyal to the idea behind the institution or business, even when unable to agree to all the goals and processes.
- Resist the inevitable and understandable fear of the unknown; realize that reality is not to be avoided.
- Understand the contributions of others and accept the authenticity of each member of the group.
- Make a personal commitment to be open to change.
- Take responsibility for civil and constructive relationships.
- Be a builder, not a taker.
- Ask a great deal of a leader.

What should leaders beware of that inhibits good followership? You could list hundreds of things that prevent people from being good followers, but I would like to mention a few basic elements. You can elaborate.

- Leaders can indulge in crimes of the spirit—cynicism, destructive criticism, unnecessary conflict, personal animosity, gossip—that create an atmosphere in which followers cannot survive, much less perform.
- Leaders who expect followers to be mind readers don't produce good second fiddlers; leaders cannot deprive followers of good training, good orientation, and access to necessary information without paying a price.
- A talented young woman with a bright future at Herman Miller left one day, much to my surprise, to work for a competitor. Sadly I called to wish her the best, and she promised to write to me explaining her decision. After some weeks, I received a long letter describing her failure to find a different position in Herman Miller that would allow her to use her gifts, that would give her the chance to advance and to reach her potential. For me, the key sentence in her letter was "I found several managers who said they wanted me, but

nobody said they needed me." There is indeed an important difference: In the workplace, to be needed is the crucial condition.

- Change is essential to organizational survival. Followers are good at change when leaders are good at managing change.
- Leaders structure and practice involvement. They listen to, evaluate, and respond to input; they take action, or participation will not survive.
- Leaders are available to help, especially when it's painful.
- Leaders pay special attention to the equitable division of results. Nothing cankers the souls of followers like an unfair division of the spoils.
- Leaders do not indulge in imprudent and casual evaluations.

What is it that followers should know that will keep their leader dressed? A leader cannot—and should not—be aware of all the details in an organization. (Leadership is a lot like raising a seventeen-year-old. You don't need to know everything.) This, it seems to me, is both a great strength and an obvious weakness. It's up to the followers to fill in the gap.

- First, followers should know that they sabotage the entire organization by protecting the leader. Eliminate that fatuous phrase "no problem." For there *are* problems, and leaders exist to do hard work and be accountable for solutions to hard problems. A leader can do her best only in a truth-telling climate.
- The previous item suggests this one. Good followers don't withhold difficult options. Search for others' points of view. Seek out the "why" of each situation. Give the organization, through your leader, a chance at greatness.
- Don't forget that followers can improve their leader's ability to get the job done. Followers have a great deal to teach leaders. When Tom Davis, a respected veteran salesperson, retired from Herman Miller, I asked him what had given him the most satisfaction. He answered, "I surpassed my quota fifteen years running, and I successfully trained five regional managers [his superiors!] in the process."

I will never completely understand the relationship between leaders and followers. It can be magical and health-giving or dispiriting and fatal. Perhaps the most singular responsibility of followers is never to let their leader feel like a lion in a den of Daniels. Performance of the group is the only real proof of leadership.

11

Mentoring:
Empowering Followers
to Be Leaders

WILLIAM E. ROSENBACH

In *The Odyssey*, the Greek poet Homer described the loyal and wise Mentor who was entrusted by Ulysses with the care and education of his son Telemachus. For generations, mentors have provided guidance, counsel, and discipline to young people and helped them become mature and effective leaders. The concept of mentorship has become familiar in academia, the military, the professions, and even in professional sports. Homer's Mentor helped his young protégé understand the world and human nature, learn courage, prudence, honesty, and a commitment to serving others. Mentoring allows followers to become intimately familiar with a well-developed style of leadership that should enable them to better develop their own style.

Scholars and psychologists who study organizations argue that mentoring is essential for personal and organizational growth and development. At the same time, there are problems and risks associated with mentoring that can have adverse effects on both the individual and organization. But the benefits of mentoring may outweigh the risks in terms of the development of the mentor, protégé, and organization as a whole. If mentoring is to play a crucial role in organizations, then formal mentoring systems should be expanded.

Traditional mentoring involves a close personal relationship between two people. It is unplanned and spontaneous. Most mentoring relationships have been of the informal, unsanctioned variety, and the selection of mentor-protégé pairs has been left to chance. Even when mutually beneficial relationships have been established, no training, support, or recognition has been provided by the organization. Collin (1988) calls it a "love match rather than an arranged marriage."

There are varying definitions of mentoring. Some describe it as little more than coaching; others stress individuality, confidentiality, and long-term commitment. A coach focuses on specific job results during a one-month to one-year period by creating opportunities for the learner to use new skills and explore problems. A mentor, however, aims to help another person throughout a career or a lifetime by being a friend, willing adversary, listener, and stimulus to increased consciousness (Megginson, 1991). Bowen (1986, p. 61) provides a meaningful definition of the mentorship process when he attempts to capture the essence of the mentor-protégé relationship:

> Mentoring occurs when a senior person (mentor) in terms of age and experience undertakes to provide information, advice, and emotional support to a junior person (protege) in a relationship lasting over an extended period of time and marked by substantial emotional commitment by both parties. If opportunity presents itself, the mentor uses both formal and informal forms of influence to further the career of the protege.

The mentor, who can be within the protégé's organization or outside of it, can be a supervisor, company executive, associate, spouse, friend, teacher, or counselor. The mentor opens doors for the protégé and helps that person learn to arrive at decisions through support and feedback. The relationship is based on an intellectual and emotional exchange that offers challenge and excitement.

Mentoring is not only for the benefit of the protégé; the mentor and organization profit as well. Generally, however, the protégé reaps most of the rewards.

Benefits to the Protégé

In a mentor-protégé relationship, the protégé receives such benefits as career skills development, accelerated cultural indoctrination, self-confidence, rapid advancement opportunities, stress reduction, and improved networking ability. Mentors can provide protégés with more focused learning, enabling them to study the managerial and leadership techniques of successful people under real world conditions. This experience promotes rapid progress and permits protégés to learn the ropes without the threat of political or psychological damage. Observing effective mentors allows them to mentally rehearse various cause-and-effect scenarios, providing modeling and vicarious reinforcement (Dreher and Ash, 1990).

The close interpersonal relationship between mentor and protégé can create a forum for exchanging ideas. The protégé receives higher reward and recognition feedback through the support and perspective of the mentor. This support can protect the protégé from making early, career-limiting errors. Access to privileged information can build confidence and create a sense of competence. A newly recruited employee can be sheltered from excess stress and prepared to cope with the requirements of a diverse work force.

Mentors can advise their protégés on the political acumen and ethics required for rapid progression. They may also provide assignments or presentations that effectively demonstrate the protégé's talents to top executives or shield him or her from low-visibility or even suicidal assignments. Protégés also can break into executive social networks, which could have taken much longer without the mentor's support. They are able to build alliances and coalitions that can yield career-enhancing benefits not available through more traditional channels.

The mentor may also provide protection and assistance with regard to promotions by intervening in conflicts and situations that may endanger the protégé's advancement. In addition, the mentor aids in acquiring promotions for the protégé by marketing her or his skills to upper-level management. In a sense, the mentor goes out on a limb for the protégé. Of course, the mentor is only truly effective if he or she is powerful and influential within the organization. And that power and influence can be the deciding factor in whether a protégé gets promoted. Zey (1984, p. 43) summarizes this point:

> Obviously the mentor's position in the organization can be an important determinant of the extent of his influence on the protege's career. The protege's career is almost always unmistakenly connected to the career of the mentor, politics playing a very important role in the ultimate progress of the protege.

Benefits to the Mentor

Some feel that mentors take on the sponsor role because they are fulfilling some deep-seated need to teach, assume a parental role, or indulge various altruistic yearnings. Some executives do desire to teach or pass on their knowledge to younger generations. But they may also receive many other career benefits from the mentoring relationship. The protégé helps the mentor with his or her job, serves as a source of organizational information and intelligence, and often becomes a trusted advisor. Jones (1982, p. 50) notes,

> Mentoring is a two-way exchange; your mentor will benefit enormously from your relationship—sometimes far more than you do. In fact the rewards can be so great that a full understanding of the dynamics in their favor may even make you feel a little shortchanged.

During the relationship the protégé performs various tasks that benefit the mentor. First, a successful and hard-working protégé enhances the mentor's career by performing job duties well, which, in turn, contributes to the mentor's reputation. If the mentor has a number of successful protégés, he or she can build an empire within the organization; this empire will improve the mentor's reputation as a "starmaker." Successful mentors may receive direct rewards for contributing to the grooming of future leaders and can use the process to establish their legacy. Not only will promotions be more likely but the mentor will also increase his or her referent power within the organization. Second, by contributing to the stock of knowledge in the group, the protégé can become a trusted advisor to the mentor. Through such relationships, the mentor can build a following of former protégés. Their alliances provide a powerful support base for both technical innovations and psychosocial welfare: Having bright, ambitious young people on his or her team makes the mentor look better. Third, the successful protégé gives the mentor a sense of pride, a sense of contributing to the organization. Mentors derive personal satisfaction by teaching young leaders. According to Reich's study on mentoring, mentors highly value being able to keep exceptional people on their team and thus improve group performance. They also value personal satisfaction, but less so. Intelligent protégés truly enhance their mentors' careers by their contributions.

Although mentors can benefit greatly from the relationship, they also encounter some risks. There is a large amount of ambiguity and uncertainty in the relationship that often is not recognized from the outset. For example, a protégé that does not live up to the mentor's expectations could prove embarrassing to the mentor. During the relationship the mentor may experience stressful situations and risks having potentially embarrassing weaknesses revealed to others in the organization by the protégé. Finally, the mentor's reputation is partially dependent on the protégé and could be severely damaged if the protégé fails. Zey (1984, p. 40) describes the two-way exchange between mentor and protégé:

> In a mentor-protege relationship the benefits for the mentor can be just as striking as those enjoyed by the protege. Indeed, it is this mutuality that makes the relationship work in the first place. However this mutuality is often lost because the mentor-protege alliance is, by design, a relationship between unequals, and hence fraught with ambiguity.

Benefits to the Organization

The benefits of a mentoring relationship are enjoyed not only by the mentor and protégé, but by the organization as well. These benefits include smoothly functioning leadership teams and properly socialized and integrated members. One of the primary outcomes enjoyed by the organization is a clear line of leader succession that will ensure the continuation of organizational values and culture from one generation to another. In addition, the protégé will be more smoothly integrated into the organization, which, in turn, will ensure a continuance of the corporate culture. Myers and Humphreys' (1985) research indicates that many organizations use mentoring to reduce turnover among newly hired recruits and to build protégé loyalty. The relationship helps integrate protégés more smoothly into the organization, so that they do not get lost in the system. The skills that protégés learn from their mentors will ultimately assist in their productivity; as the protégé becomes more productive, so does the organization.

Apart from the benefits that mentoring brings to the organization, there are also risks and problems. Myers and Humphreys divide these problems into three categories. The first involves problems that arise in the selection process of mentors and protégés. Process problems that are encountered during the mentoring process fall into the second category, and the third comprises problems that arise as a result of an intense mentor relationship.

Selection problems include preselection, "old boy" networks, nepotism, and outright discrimination. People qualified to be protégés may be passed over because of race, sex, or lack of contacts within the organization. Some of the discrimination in the protégé selection process is undoubtedly unintentional; nevertheless, discrimination has adversely affected the careers of women and minorities.

Process problems occur when the mentor overburdens the protégé with work and vice versa. Protégés may also experience unwelcome or too much surveillance of their work by their mentors. When protégés make mistakes they may receive unduly harsh treatment or be publicly embarrassed by their mentors. Finally, some protégés feel as if they receive more criticism than is necessary. Process problems can be avoided if the mentor and protégé know what kind of relationship they are getting into beforehand and understand each other's goals.

Outcome problems in mentoring relationships arise when protégés experience guilt and embarrassment because they are associated with a failing mentor. If executives fail or fall out of favor with the organization, then their protégés also fall out of favor. This process, often referred to as the "black halo" effect, can block a protégé's promotion. Fairly or unfairly, the protégé becomes associated with the mentor. One-third of the people Reich (1985) studied reported that others identified them (protégés) too closely with their mentors. Blotnick observes that nearly half the protégés in his 25-year study end up being fired by their mentors. Levinson (1978) warns that mentoring relationships that last two or three years often end in rancor and bitterness. Although these reports appear to be negative, other evidence is more positive. In his book, *The Corporate Steeplechase*, Blotnick (1984) supports mentoring as a risk worth taking. In addition, although Reich's research recognizes some of the risks and problems associated with mentoring, his findings clearly show that the advantages outweigh the disadvantages.

Cross-Gender and Cross-Racial Mentoring

In *The Odyssey*, Athena, the Greek goddess of wisdom, disguised herself and stood in for Mentor to teach Ulysses' son. This fictionalized account of cross-gender mentoring has real-life counterparts. If it is necessary for a man to have a mentor to be successful, it may be even more essential for a woman (Ragins, 1989). Reich's 1986 research shows that, like men, women benefit from the mentoring relationship by gaining more leadership skills, joining winning teams, developing useful contacts, and being granted more autonomy in the workplace.

The greatest problem women face in the mentoring process is stereotypic perceptions by men. Women are socialized into performing traditional roles of parenting, whereas men are socialized to be successful in a career. Women continue to be conditioned in this manner despite the fact that childbearing is the only role that is uniquely gender-related (Schwartz, 1989). Women often must put their personal lives on hold or make trade-offs to seek leadership positions in an organization. They will put in long hours and make the most of opportunities to further their professional development. However, artificial barriers are often placed in their paths to the top of the organization. Mentoring can alter these barriers and allow women the same opportunities as men for upward mobility.

In addition to helping women acquire the same skills as men, mentoring relationships also help them with other problems. Zey (1984) observes that cross-gender mentoring helps in structural and attitudinal areas. Because mentoring represents the leader's public commitment to a junior member, the organization is brought closer to accepting a woman as a bonafide member of its leadership team. And as more women are given the unique opportunity to succeed that mentoring affords, these accomplishments will further establish their rightful place in leadership roles.

Because fewer women are in leadership positions than men, most mentors are male. Selection of a female protégé by a male mentor announces his commitment to the rest of the organization and eases the transition into the organizational power structure (Ragins, 1989; Dreher and Ash, 1990). Women are subject to mentor-protégé problems peculiar to the cross-gender mentoring process. Clawson and Kram (1984) categorize these problems into two sets: internal relationships and external relationships. Internal relationships are the levels of intimacy or interaction the cross-gender mentoring subjects experience and the way these levels affect the relationship. External relationships concern the amount of office gossip or innuendo that arises outside of the relationship. When a man and a woman interact in a close setting, they may be attracted to each other. Due to the closeness of the mentor-protégé relationship, it is easy for romance to develop. But romantic or sexual interests confound the mentor relationship and may create conflicts and power struggles. A woman may develop sexual feelings toward a male mentor and he toward her. Too often it is believed that the woman alone should be responsible for professional behavior. Fortunately, some male mentors feel that responsibility should be shared; although the potential for sexual attachment is always present, professional conduct by both people is essential. All things considered, the most common problem is the resentment of coworkers and spouses.

Another drawback to having a male mentor is that the successful women will be stereotyped as being masculine (Noe, 1988). This perception is difficult to avoid because the female is trying to pattern her behavior after that of the successful male mentor. Role modeling is essential for the success of the mentoring relationship. However, a woman can overcome this stereotype by developing a style uniquely hers, blending the best of her own style with that of her mentor. Such problems are also present for males who have female mentors.

Unique problems are also associated with cross-racial mentoring. Unfortunately, the little research conducted in this area indicates that the problems usually outmatch the benefits. The problems are particularly severe when the mentor-protégé relationship is both cross-racial and cross-gender. Most male-male mentoring relationships develop around shared male interests. Studies have shown that the typical shared male activities that normally occur after work usually do not exist with cross-racial mentoring (Thomas, 1989). Outside activities rarely facilitate the formation of close, cross-racial mentoring relationships for several reasons. Racism is the cause when the mentor or protégé considers it unacceptable to socialize with someone of a different race. Often intentions are misinterpreted because of cultural differences. In addition, minority protégés often have trouble finding a mentor if the mentoring process is informal (Murray and Owen, 1991).

In female-female cross-race mentoring, the same problems exist with additional complications because of historical relationships between minority and white women concerning domestic and child-care roles. Cross-gender and cross-racial relationships combine the problems of each with the addition of lack of acceptance of one of the individuals by friends and coworkers, particularly if emotional ties are perceived in the relationship (Thomas, 1989). The success of mentoring depends on a close, personal relationship that results in bonding, but the disapproval of associates puts the relationship and its outcome at risk. Once cross-gender and cross-racial mentoring become more common and a reasonable number of women have moved through the system, these problems will decrease. People will grow accustomed to the relationships. If they wish, women can mentor women, and the problems of cross-gender mentoring can be avoided altogether. Racism and sexism in the workplace will disappear as leaders learn to work in diverse teams and begin to view all members as friends and colleagues.

Formal Versus Informal Mentoring

Until recently, mentoring programs in most organizations have been informal. Some suggest that because of the importance of mentoring to organizations, formal systems should be developed. Formal systems may eliminate many of the problems and risks of the mentor-protégé relationship. Reich (1985) notes that one company used a formal system only for women and minorities. But he also found that 83 percent of respondents to his survey recommended against formal programs. Indeed, many feel that the mentoring process should never be made formal. Many argue that the relationship must be spontaneous to ensure the chemistry between the two individuals. Furthermore, others believe that if formal programs are implemented, protégés should not be allowed to choose their own mentors. Mentors chosen through formal programs seldom pull strings for the protégés, protect them, or become involved in the lasting and strong friendships that are characteristic in informal mentoring relationships. In fact, they appear to avoid such entanglements by specifying time limits and emphasizing task orientations.

Keele, Buckner, and Bushnell (1987) find three characteristics common to all successful formal mentoring programs. First, the mentoring activity is only a part of an overall development program for potential leaders; second, the programs emphasize coaching behaviors directed to job-related activities; and third, the mentoring programs are a part of an organizational culture that supports individual and organizational development and provides rewards for those who participate.

Although formal mentoring has not often been successful in the past, mentoring is such an integral part of human resource development that formal mentoring may eventually become an accepted mechanism for leadership development. Conditions or objectives for which a mentoring program may be desirable include a merger or major restructuring that results in a critical need to harmonize dissimilar cultures, promotion and advancement of equal opportunities for minority groups, development of the next generation of leaders, enrichment of the careers of mid-level managers, and stimulation of creativity and innovation (Collin, 1988; Clark, 1992). Before an organization implements a formal mentoring program, clear goals should be established and communicated to potential participants. The organization's ability to absorb individuals completing the program should be determined, and the cooperation of the entire organization should be encouraged through rewards. The selection process should be as autonomous as possible, and the mentors' commitment should be assured. Withdrawal from the program should be permitted, without prejudice. Finally, the program should be continually evaluated.

Conclusion

Strong leadership that motivates followers to perform beyond expectations is built upon personal identification with the leader, a shared vision of the future, and subordination of self-interests. This transformational form of leadership creates an organizational culture that values renewal and revitalization of the individual.

A culture of transformational leadership stimulates mentoring. Protégés are encouraged to believe in themselves and to achieve their leadership potential. Their success will ensure the continued influence, power, respect, and competitive advantage of the organization. Mentors affirm their self-confidence and view leader development as a part of their job. Mentoring is not appropriate for every individual or organization; it is an opportunity to share talent and prepare leaders. With a supportive environment and the right attitude, mentoring can be a powerful force to empower followers to be leaders.

Acknowledgments

The author wishes to thank Nancy Cahill-Helms, Edie Chudnow, Ron Crum, Leslie Garrett, George Kent, Larry Loosararian, Carla O'Connell, and Tom Peters, who assisted in the revision of this chapter.

References

Ball, A. "Mentors and Proteges: Portraits of Success." *Working Women*, October 1989, pp. 134–141.

Blotnick, S. *The Corporate Steeplechase: Predictable Crisis in a Business Career.* New York: Facts on File, 1984.

Borman, C., and S. Colson. "Mentoring: An Effective Career Guidance Technique." *The Vocational Guidance Journal*, Vol. 3, 1984, pp. 192–197.

Bowen, D. D. "The Role of Identification in Mentoring Female Proteges." *Group and Organization Studies,* March–June 1986, pp. 61–74.

Burke, R. J., and C. A. McKeen. "Developing Formal Mentoring Programs in Organizations." *Business Quarterly* 53(3), 1989, pp. 76–80.

Clark, F. A. *Total Career Management.* London: McGraw-Hill, 1992.

Clawson, J. G. "Is Mentoring Necessary?" *Training and Development Journal,* April 1985, pp. 36–39.

Clawson, J. G., and K. E. Kram. "Managing Cross Gender Mentoring." *Business Horizons,* May–June 1984, pp. 22–32.

Collin, A. "Mentoring." *Industrial and Commercial Training,* March–April 1988, pp. 23–27.

Cunningham, M. *Powerplay: What Really Happened at Bendix.* New York: Simon and Schuster, 1984.

Dreher, G. F., and R. A. Ash. "A Comparative Study of Mentoring Among Men and Women in Managerial, Professional and Technical Positions." *Journal of Applied Psychology* 75, 1990, pp. 539–546.

Farren, J.D. Gray, and B. Kaye. "Mentoring: A Boon to Career Development." *Personnel,* November–December 1984, pp. 20–24.

Fitt, L. W., and D. Newton. "When the Mentor Is a Man and the Protege a Woman." *Harvard Business Review,* March–April 1981, pp. 55–60.

Hennefrund, W. "Taking on the Measure of Mentoring." *Association Management,* January 1986, pp. 78–83.

Horgan, D. D., and R. J. Simeon. "Mentoring and Participation: An Application of the Vroom-Yetton Model." *Journal of Business Psychology* 5, 1990, pp. 63–84.

Jacoby, D. "Rewards Make the Mentor." *Personnel* 66 (12), 1989, pp. 10–14.

Johnston, W. B., and A. H. Packer. *Workforce 2000: Work and Workers for the 21st Century.* Indianapolis: Hudson Institute, 1987.

Jones, L. P. *Mentors and Proteges.* New York: Arbor House, 1982.

Keele, R., K. Buckner, and S. Bushnell. "Formal Mentoring Programs Are No Panacea." *Management Review,* February 1987, pp. 67–68.

Kram, K. E., and D. T. Hall. "Mentoring as an Antidote to Stress During Corporate Trauma." *Human Resource Management* 28, 1989, pp. 493–510.

Kram, K. E. "Improving the Mentoring Process." *Training and Development Journal,* April 1985, pp. 40–42.

Lasden, M. "A Mentor Can Be a Milestone." *Computer Decisions,* March 26, 1985, pp. 74–81.

Lean, E. "Cross-Gender Mentoring: Downright Upright and Good for Productivity." *Training and Development Journal,* May 1983, pp. 61–65.

Levinson, Daniel J. *The Seasons of a Man's Life.* New York: Alfred A. Knopf, 1978.

Megginson, D. "Instructor, Coach, Mentor: Three Ways of Helping for Managers." *Management Education and Development* 19 (1), 1991, pp. 33–46.

Murray, M., and M. A. Owen. *Beyond the Myths and Magic of Mentoring: How to Facilitate an Effective Mentoring Program.* San Francisco: Jossey-Bass, 1991.

Myers, D. W., and N. J. Humphreys. "The Caveats in Mentorship." *Business Horizon,* July–August 1985, pp. 9–14.

Noe, R. A. "Women and Mentoring: A Review and Research Agenda." *Academy of Management Review,* Vol. 13, No. 1, 1988, pp. 65–78.

Odiorne, G. S. "Mentoring—An American Management Innovation." *Personnel Administrator,* May, 1985, pp. 63–70.

Ragins, B. R. "Barriers to Mentoring: The Female Manager's Dilemma." *Human Relations* 42 (1), 1989, pp. 1–22.

Reich, M. H. "Executive Views from Both Sides of Mentoring." *Personnel,* March 1985, pp. 42–46.

_____. "The Mentor Connection." *Personnel,* February 1986, pp. 50–56.

Roche, G. R. "Much Ado About Mentors." *Harvard Business Review,* January–February 1979, pp. 14–28.

Schwartz, F. "Management Women and the New Facts of Life." *Harvard Business Review,* 647 (1), 1989, pp. 66–76.

Shea, G. "New Scripts for a Timeless Relationship." *Management Review: Human Resources Forum,* June 1991.

Sheeran, L. R., and O. Fenn. "Mentor System." *Inc.,* June 1987, pp. 138–142.

Thomas, D. A. "Mentoring and Irrationality: The Role of Racial Taboos." *Human Resource Management* 28, 1989, pp. 279–290.

Zey, M. G. *The Mentor Connection.* Homewood, IL: Dow-Jones-Irwin, 1984.

_____. "A Mentor for All Seasons." *Personnel Journal,* January 1988, pp. 46–51.

12

The Wheel
and the Light

W. CHAN KIM
RENÉE A. MAUBORGNE

Back in the third century B.C., the outbreak of fighting following the collapse of the Qin Dynasty had just ended. In its place now stood the Han Dynasty, whose emperor, Liu Bang, had consolidated China into a unified empire for the first time. To commemorate the event, Liu Bang had invited high-ranking military and political officials, poets, and teachers to a grand celebration. Among them was Chen Cen, the master to whom Liu Bang had often gone for enlightenment during his campaign to unify China.

The celebration was in full swing. A banquet grander than any ever seen was being held. At the center table sat Liu Bang with his three heads of staff: Xiao He, who administered the logistics of unification; Han Xin, who organized and led the fighting activity; and Chang Yang, who formulated the diplomatic and political strategies. At another table sat Chen Cen and his three disciples.

While food was served, speeches given, honors presented, and entertainment performed, all looked on with pride and exhilaration—all except Chen Cen's three disciples, who sat awestruck. Only midway through the festivities did they utter their first words. "Master," they remarked, "all is grand, all is befitting, but at the heart of the celebration lies one enigma." Sensing his disciples' hesitation, the master gently encouraged them to continue.

"At the central table sits Xiao He," they proceeded. "Xiao He's knowledge of logistics cannot be refuted. Under his administration, the soldiers have always been well fed and properly armed, whatever the terrain.

Next to him is Han Xin. Han Xin's military tactics are beyond reproach. He understands exactly where to ambush the enemy, when to advance, and when to retreat. He has won every battle he has led. Last is Chang Yang. Chang Yang sees the dynamics of political and diplomatic relations in his palm. He knows which states to form alliances with, how to gain political favors, and how to corner heads of states into surrendering without battle. This we understand well. What we cannot comprehend is the centerpiece of the table, the emperor himself. Liu Bang cannot claim noble birth, and his knowledge of logistics, fighting, and diplomacy does not equal that of his heads of staff. How is it, then, that he is emperor?"

The master smiled and asked his disciples to imagine the wheel of a chariot. "What determines the strength of a wheel in carrying a chariot forward?" he asked. After a moment of reflection, his disciples responded, "Is it not the sturdiness of the spokes, Master?" "But then, why is it," he rejoined, "that two wheels made of identical spokes differ in strength?" After a moment, the master continued, "See beyond what is seen. Never forget that a wheel is made not only of spokes but also of the space between the spokes. Sturdy spokes poorly placed make a weak wheel. Whether their full potential is realized depends on the harmony between them. The essence of wheelmaking lies in the craftsman's ability to conceive and create the space that holds and balances the spokes within the wheel. Think now, who is the craftsman here?"

A glimmer of moonlight was visible behind the door. Silence reigned until one disciple said, "But master, how does a craftsman secure the harmony between the spokes?" "Think of sunlight," replied the master. "The sun nurtures and vitalizes the trees and flowers. It does so by giving away its light. But in the end, in which direction do they all grow? So it is with a master craftsman like Liu Bang. After placing individuals in positions that fully realize their potential, he secures harmony among them by giving them all credit for their distinctive achievements. And in the end, as the trees and flowers grow toward the giver, the sun, individuals grow toward Liu Bang with devotion."

PART THREE

DIVERSITY: MANY PATHS TO LEADERSHIP EFFECTIVENESS

As we prepare to enter the twenty-first century, social changes will be evident in the work force. Many estimates suggest that the majority of people joining the work force in the next decade will not be native-born white males. Women have entered careers in large numbers over the past few decades; in the coming years, greater growth will come from people of color. Spanish-speaking people may well become the largest minority in the United States. Recent waves of immigration have landed large populations from Eastern Europe, Asia, and southern countries. Walk down the streets of many cities and you will hear several different languages spoken. Cosmopolitanism once reserved for foreign capitals is rapidly becoming commonplace in urban settings throughout the world.

Clearly, the global economy has an influence. Alliances, trade agreements, and the international marketplace are facts of life. Origins are no longer critical; what we find is a mix of peoples, ideas, and values. All of this diversity creates exciting possibilities, but it threatens the old order and suggests that leaders must rethink the environment in which they operate.

Diversity has become an organizational and ethical imperative, yet leaders have not been entirely successful in coping with the concept. In the pursuit of diversity, organizations educate people about national and cultural differences, employ and promote women and minorities, provide training in awareness of peoples and their sensitivities, and implement a host of other initiatives to foster tolerance of the many faces, values, behaviors, expectations, attitudes, professional disciplines, and cognitive styles one is likely to encounter.

Leadership research has not adequately addressed the challenges of diversity. We believe that recognition and appreciation of the heritage, characteristics, and values of different groups, and of the uniqueness of each individual, are critical for effective leadership. Historical studies uncover a predominantly "male" model of leadership; in the United States, it has been primarily white. Biographies of great leaders are most often about white males. Research studies, examinations of behaviors, and evaluations of effectiveness are predominantly focused on the white male model. Although inquiries into similarities and differences evoked by gender are appearing, there is an inevitable comparison ("Women tend to differ in that ...").

It is important to examine how women lead, but we believe that it is also important to avoid labeling certain traits "female" or "male." Instead, the focus should be on how committed leaders achieve their visions. This approach, we think, is more useful than pursuing the question of whether there are innately female or male leadership styles. The important question is why researchers and scholars have paid so little attention to female leaders and why collaborative styles of leadership are more effective than competitive styles in certain environments. The new paradigm of leadership, which embraces collaboration and empowerment, is often characterized as "female," but there is no need to describe the phenomenon in terms of gender. We know good leadership when we experience it, whether the leader is male or female, black or brown, native or foreign. We respond to leaders because of personal interrelationships that transcend any diversity. We respond as *individuals;* that is the key.

In the previous edition, we noted the construct of the "glass ceiling." This concept described women as systematically being denied access to top corporate jobs by their male counterparts. Since then, we have found fewer people talking about this subject. Many leaders seem to feel that where women want access, they can achieve it through performance. As men who have stereotypical views of working women change their views (or retire from the workplace), organizational opportunities are becoming open to both genders—especially as the need for talented leaders becomes more intense. There are feminists who will vehemently disagree with us, citing the growth of women's studies, support groups, and programs to address equal opportunity. Nonetheless, the leaders we've interviewed are firm in their conviction that the numbers of women in leadership positions have increased; they are "moving up the ladder," and that just as things have changed over the past twenty years, the future will bring even more change. Women will still differ from men, but they will compete equally and successfully for key leadership roles.

Regrettably, the same cannot be said for African-Americans. It seems the barrier of color prevails. Progress in getting jobs, promotions, and leadership roles remains slow for African-Americans in our society. There are new sources of blame: education and social structure. For whatever reasons, access still evades black Americans, and inequality is as dominant as ever.

All types of programs have been created to develop leadership among African-Americans. Businesses and corporations have provided mentoring and support to develop minority leadership within their organizations, yet there is little evidence that the number of African-Americans in leadership roles is increasing in the private sector. There appears to be more to praise in the public sector, as government has increased access for everyone. Perhaps we need to *listen* to African-Americans before encouraging them to fit into existing models—we may learn that there are other ways to lead.

But what about other minorities? There is not a great deal of literature about leadership among Hispanics, Asian-Americans, Jews, Native Americans, and so forth. The traditional sense of leadership is not important in many of these groups, and the setting apart of one individual from others can be quite dysfunctional. Perhaps it is more critical for members of minority groups to share power, responsibility, and tasks, creating a leadership of the whole. That might suggest yet another new paradigm.

For example, Hispanics maintain a strong sense of collective identity. The family is important; cooperation is more relevant than competence; and the group is more important than the individual. Native Americans have a rich history of leadership by tribal chiefs, with strong authority from tribal councils. Little is known about current leadership issues, as many Native Americans live on reservations apart from the rest of the population. Asian-Americans have yet another style of leadership, stressing form as much as substance, consensus more than assertiveness, and a strong respect for social position.

Researchers and scholars focus on the mainstream, so the development of followers and leaders in minority groups is not well recorded. It would appear, however, that the new paradigms of leadership are more compatible than the old ones with the collectivist nature of minority cultures. Perhaps access will be broadened once we take time to learn about and appreciate these cultures.

Leadership Perspectives

In "Leadership Diversity and Leadership Challenge" (Chapter 13), Ann M. Morrison examines a comprehensive research study by the Center for Creative Leadership. She notes that the level of challenge is considerably higher for nontraditional (i.e., non–white male) leaders. There are greater expectations placed on nontraditional leaders, to the extent that they often burn out, opt out, or fail. The key, she argues, is to provide support in a balanced way.

Malcolm Gladwell provides a unique biographical perspective with "The Changing Face of Science" (Chapter 14). Gladwell profiles the career of Bernadine Healy, highlighting the challenges and opportunities she faced on her way to becoming head of the National Institutes of Health. The piece raises interesting questions about whether Healy's gender affected her successes and failures. We suggest that the chronicle would have been just as interesting if its subject were male rather than female.

In Chapter 15, we present Ronald Dellums's "Black Leadership: For Change or for Status Quo?" Dellums challenges us to consider whether African-Americans have had leadership opportunities in terms of numbers *and* quality. The issue is systemic, he argues; we must change social institutions. Dellums supports revolutionary change and calls for a strategy that depends not on a great hero but rather on each individual.

Manning Marable follows in Chapter 16 with a brief essay, "Where Are Our Future Leaders?" He seeks men and women with vision, young people who can lead in the twenty-first century. Marable looks to education and social support to bridge the gaps between middle-class and poor African-Americans and provide a collective vision that will empower people to create their futures.

A truly collaborative, empowering brand of leadership must overcome race- and gender-based differences. The challenge to leaders of the future is to use diversity to the advantage of their organizations and define a unifying vision toward which men and women, whites and minorities can work with equal commitment.

13

Leadership Diversity and Leadership Challenge

ANN M. MORRISON

Diversity in the work force is rapidly becoming a fact of life in America. According to recent estimates, perhaps eighty-five percent of the net new workers entering the work force before the turn of the century will be from groups other than native-born white men (see *Workforce 2000*). Diversity in leadership, however, has been slow in coming. People of color and white women are, even after twenty years of affirmative action and some gains,[1] greatly underrepresented in management ranks, especially at the top levels.

This situation is likely to have a number of serious consequences, including labor unrest caused by the unequal opportunity of a two-tiered system, customer dissatisfaction because management is out of touch with growing markets made up of women and people of color, and a diminished competitiveness because a large pool of high-potential managers is not being tapped.

The Center for Creative Leadership conducted a study concerned with how this situation can be changed. Called Guidelines on Leadership Diversity, it involved extensive, confidential interviews with a diverse group of nearly two hundred managers from sixteen organizations (twelve in business, two in education, and two in government). These progressive, U.S.-based organizations are models in the sense that they all have made advances in promoting diversity within their management.

The 1992 book *The New Leaders* reports at length on the findings of this study. This chapter concentrates on one issue: understanding how one generally recognized aspect of leadership development-challenge relates to developing leadership diversity.

Challenge as a Key
to Leadership Development

It is now widely recognized that a good way to encourage the development of leadership in managers is to give them a series of challenging assignments. Witness, for instance, the practice of having managers who are identified as likely to become effective executives (so-called high-potential managers) rotate into new jobs every year or two. It is believed that this not only exposes people to the workings of an organization but also puts them into situations in which they must develop new skills or improve old ones.

Research (see Lindsey, Homes, and McCall, 1987; McCall, Lombardo, and Morrison, 1988) has given us a more specific understanding of this general development method. We identified the developmental assignments that typically figure in the success of white male managers (for example, promotions with dramatically increased responsibilities, transfers into staff functions at corporate headquarters, serving on task forces, troubleshooting stints, and start-up experiences that often involve time overseas), and we found eight sources of challenge shared by these assignments (McCall et al., 1988, pp. 124–131):

1. *Dealing with the boss.* Challenge arises when the boss is inexperienced or indifferent. The boss may also have a difficult style or even serious managerial flaws.
2. *Dealing with staff members.* Challenge arises when the staff is inexperienced, recalcitrant, or incompetent. Some staff members may hold a grudge against the manager for being promoted over them.
3. *Other significant relationships.* Challenge can come from having to present to senior executives, negotiate with outsiders, and collaborate with people from different backgrounds and functions or regions of the organization.
4. *High stakes.* Challenge comes from extreme visibility of certain assignments, especially with top management. Tight deadlines and financial risk add to the challenge.
5. *Adverse business conditions.* Often seen in overseas assignments, the challenge here is a result of physical hardships (because of a harsh climate or the lack of adequate living facilities), hostile governmen-

tal officials, or local business practices and values that differ from the manager's own.

6. *Scope and scale of the job.* Challenge comes from managing a large number of subordinates, including some who are geographically distant and some who have a superior technical knowledge.

7. *Missing trumps.* Challenge comes from the lack of traditionally required credential or background characteristics; the manager is required to establish credibility while learning a new job.

8. *Starkness of transition.* Challenge results from the suddenness or extent of change involved in the transition; sometimes the manager's personal life changes as the job changes.

These eight sources might be considered the standard model of challenge for traditional, white male managers. Elements of it are recognized in many organizations and have even sometimes been incorporated into their development programs and tools. It is thus being used to understand and plan for the development of many of today's managers. The question is, does this model work well for nontraditional managers—for people of color and white women?

There is evidence suggesting that despite some common ground, the development picture for nontraditional managers is distinct from that of white male managers. For instance, research on white female executives found that the group of developmental assignments they reported as being important overlapped with but was not the same as that reported by white male executives (see Morrison, White, & Van Velsor, 1992; Van Velsor & Hughes, 1990).

Findings indicate that, although these eight elements surely play some role in the development of nontraditional managers, the model does not adequately cover the challenge faced by them. It fails in two ways: First, there are important challenges that they typically encounter that are not included here; and, second, the model does not recognize that some of the challenges require more effort from them than from traditional managers. The additional and exaggerated challenges may not be taken into consideration when planning or assessing the developmental assignments given to nontraditional managers.

Additional and Exaggerated Challenges

Nontraditional managers often encounter major barriers—such as prejudice, isolation, and serious conflicts between career and personal life—that create additional challenges for them. It is not difficult to imagine, for example, the increased difficulty of dealing with a boss who not only lacks some skills and has a difficult style but who is also prejudiced (I define *prejudice* as the tendency on the part of many people to see differences as weaknesses). Similarly, there may be added difficulty in dealing with prejudiced subordinates, peers, and outsiders. The addition of prejudice to the first three sources of challenge complicates and deepens them in ways not encountered by many white men.

In addition, because of prejudice, the standards of performance may be higher for nontraditional than traditional managers. In our research on women in management, we discovered that nontraditional managers are often expected to perform at a higher level than white men who hold or who have held the same job. Having to do a job *better* than anyone else is likely to add to the challenge experienced by nontraditional managers.

Coping with adverse conditions is another ingredient that may increase the level of challenge for nontraditional managers. In describing the challenge of troubleshooting assignments, for example, white male managers sometimes mentioned the hostility of co-workers who resented their advice, their attempted interventions, and even their very presence. Also, their limited assignments in foreign countries sometimes entailed coping with capricious or unfriendly government officials. Such problems are typically confined to certain types of assignments or locations in the reports of traditional managers, but they appear to constitute the daily life of any nontraditional managers—even those in the progressive organizations included in our study.

Our findings indicate that there is still a great deal of resentment and hostility from subordinates who dislike reporting to anyone not white and male, and from co-workers who feel threatened when working side by side with a nontraditional manager. Some colleagues may not be hostile but merely skeptical. They may not be directly opposed to an integrated work force but they suspect that nontraditional managers are simply not up to the task; consequently they are cautious in the way they relate to, delegate to, and rely on a white woman or person of color. Such co-workers, consultants, suppliers, and customers may rationalize the presence of nontraditional managers as the outcome of a quota system. A Chinese manager in our study said that her boss has told her to "be as un-Asian as possible" and to have her Asian subordinates "be un-Asian" as well because the department "looks like an Asian connection." She has to be concerned on a daily basis with the effect of looking, acting, and seeming Asian as she performs her job.

There is also evidence from this study and other research that the pressure and visibility associated with their performance may also be greater for nontraditional managers, adding even more challenge to their work. All conscientious managers are likely to feel pressure to perform their jobs well, but our research indicated that a nontraditional manager is noticed, watched, and judged more than a traditional one, if only because the former stands out in the management ranks.

The added pressure of working under these circumstances is frustrating and draining. One Hispanic manager in our study explained, "Those minorities who are going up get excess scrutiny. They are put under the microscope, and there is pressure not to screw up." And the observers include not only the managers' bosses and colleagues—who may be curious, if not doubtful, about their competence—but also other nontraditional colleagues who desperately want them to succeed so that they, too, may be given a chance someday to show their worth.

The burden carried by many nontraditional managers to represent their demographic group while performing their job is one that can raise the level of challenge beyond that of white male managers in any assignment they have. Because they represent not only their ethnic or gender group (and sometimes even the concept of diversity in general), they are constantly called upon to promote the cause. The media want them for stories and profiles. Social scientists want them for research projects. Other members of their group, with ambitions of their own, want them as role models and regularly call them for advice or favors. Their bosses sometimes nudge them to serve on committees and task forces as the ranking woman or person of color to represent that point of view. Employee groups ask them to mentor other nontraditional managers. Top management may want their help to recruit nontraditional managers. The amount of necessary "volunteerism" within and outside the organization is higher for them, even though they must continue to do their jobs in a consistently outstanding fashion to stay in good stead with their bosses.

Although some nontraditional managers shun volunteerism, and some traditional managers elect to contribute considerable time to volunteer work, the reality seems to be that people of color and white women are generally under a great deal of pressure to do more of it. Those who don't support traditional activities run the risk of alienating their white male colleagues. Those who don't support their demographic colleagues risk being ostracized by them. Their visibility permits them no refuge from multiple, sometimes conflicting, obligations.

Another aspect of challenge for many nontraditional managers is balancing career demands with outside demands. The managers in our study generally agreed that women experience this more than men; the responsibilities of bearing and raising children, maintaining a household, and maintaining social relationships are still disproportionately borne by women. Women with the financial means to hire help may be freed from these duties personally, but that does not reduce their degree of responsibility. They still must hire and manage people to perform these jobs, intervene when sickness or problems occur, and account for the results. The continual challenge of juggling home and family with job demands creates conflict and stress that women in particular are expected to manage. Some men are also strained in seeking a balance between the two; Hispanic men may be especially vulnerable, as some managers noted, because their culture puts a high value on family life.

Overall, it appears that the level of challenge in a given assignment is considerably higher for nontraditional managers than for traditional managers. The former must combine the demands of meeting higher performance standards, regularly confronting adversity such as hostility or harassment, working under great scrutiny and contending with the expectations of both traditional and nontraditional groups, and struggling day after day with care-giving and social duties. Some executives may have concluded that if nontraditional managers have more difficulty performing an assignment, it must be because they are not as capable as their white male counterparts. But this view can be countered with the argument that nontraditional managers are facing greater challenges that are both within the assignment and surrounding it. The "same" assignment given to a traditional and nontraditional manager is not the same thing at all.

The Danger of Limiting Challenge

Because of the extraordinary challenge faced by nontraditional managers, some organizations may be tempted to provide some relief by assigning them to less consequential jobs. But this only blocks their advancement. Nontraditional managers are already more likely to be put into positions, often peripheral staff jobs, considered less important to the organization's performance. Then, when a higher-level opening comes up, they are not likely to get the job because of a lack of experience in strategic, central posts.

Instead of reducing the level of challenge by limiting nontraditional managers to assignments perceived to be less critical (and therefore less demanding), one alternative is to reduce demands from other sources: Use the same performance standards for all managers, traditional and nontraditional; reduce the impact of prejudice; promote a larger cadre of nontraditional managers so that the demands on any of these individuals to represent their demographic group are lessened; and provide benefit packages that allow managers to fulfill outside obligations while pursuing their careers. Such alternatives can provide relief from some of the additional sources of challenge without interfering with the advancement potential of the nontraditional manager.

Conclusion

Perhaps the biggest mistake that organizations make when attempting to increase leadership diversity is misusing challenge. Challenge is either heaped onto nontraditional managers until they burn out or opt out, or important challenges are withheld from them, causing them to plateau or derail.

Furthermore, organizations often rely on challenge alone to develop managers. This concept of leadership development is, in my view, too simplistic. Organizations must also provide managers with recognition and support.

What I mean by *recognition* is acknowledgment of, and rewards for, achievement. It can come in many different forms, including pay (salary and total cash compensation); promotion (advancement to positions of greater responsibility); perquisites (a company car, club membership, financial incentives and advice, and so on); participation (inclusion in decisionmaking); autonomy (freedom to act on one's own without supervision); resources (adequate staff, budget, and time to do the job); respect and credibility (one's priorities and opinions are taken into consideration and valued); and faith (the expectation that one's productivity will continue in increasingly responsible positions).

By *support,* I mean understanding and acceptance of each manager's individual situation, plus benefits that provide help in that situation. Common forms of support are collegiality (friendly association with co-workers); advocacy (backing and endorsement); permission to fail (the leeway to make mistakes that one can learn from); information (news about the business and the organization); feedback (data about one's abilities, prospects, and reputation); flexibility (the option to tailor a job to one's own strengths or circumstances); and stress relief (the reduction of anxiety and tension by accommodating family and other outside demands and by preventing on-the-job hostilities).

But merely seeing that these elements are present is not enough; they must be in balance. When challenge, recognition, and support are balanced, then leadership development, and leadership diversity, are more likely to occur. In fact, the balance of these elements could be seen as a new model for sustained leadership development.

Note

1. According to an Equal Employment Opportunity Commission report (cited by Bradsher, 1988), the number of women, blacks, and Hispanics in management has quadrupled since 1970, and the number of Asians has increased eightfold.

Bibliography

Bradsher, K. "Women Gain Numbers, Respect in Board Rooms." *The Los Angeles Times,* March 17, 1988, pp. 1, 6.

Lindsey, E. H., V. Homes, and M. W. McCall, Jr., *Key Events in Executives' Lives* (Technical Report No. 32). Greensboro, NC: Center for Creative Leadership, 1987.

McCall, M. W. Jr., M. M. Lombardo, and A. M. Morrison. *The Lessons of Experience: How Successful Executives Develop on the Job.* Lexington, MA: Lexington Books, 1988.

Morrison, A. M. *The New Leaders: Guidelines on Leadership Diversity in America.* San Francisco: Jossey-Bass, 1992.

Morrison, A. M., R. P. White, and E. Van Velsor. *Breaking the Glass Ceiling: Can Women Reach the Top of America's Largest Corporations?* (Updated ed.) Reading, MA: Addison-Wesley, 1992.

Van Velsor, E., and M. W. Hughes. *Gender Differences in the Development of Managers: How Women Managers Learn from Experience* (Technical Report No. 145). Greensboro, NC: Center for Creative Leadership, 1990.

Workforce 2000: Work and Workers for the 21st Century. Executive Summary. (Indianapolis, IN: Hudson Institute, 1987.

14

The Changing Face of Science

MALCOLM GLADWELL

There was—and still is—an all-male eating society at Johns Hopkins University medical school called the Pithotomy Club, which is famous for the comedy revue it stages every year lampooning the school's faculty.

The show dates back almost to the club's founding at the turn of the century, and in its heyday was hugely popular with the alumni. It was a bonding ritual for male students and faculty, a chance for the once and future elite of American medicine to gather for obscene songs and skits, get drunk, and then—because the club had only one toilet—urinate together in the alleyway next door. F. Scott Fitzgerald immortalized the "Pit" in a short story. H. L. Mencken said the only time he saw something cruder was in a show put on by sailors in London.

Bernadine Healy does not like to talk about the events that led her, ten years ago this spring, to do battle with the Pithotomy Club. To the woman who now holds the most powerful position in American science, the day the Pithotomy Club made her the subject of its annual show is a distant and traumatic memory, an episode so personally painful that over all of the intervening years she says she has tried to repress it.

But when Healy speaks of the plight of women in science, of her plans to redress the scientific establishment's neglect of women's issues, or when she confronts the establishment with her new and radical agenda—as she has over and over again in her first year as head of the National Institutes of Health—it is difficult not to call the Pithotomy episode to mind.

Healy was then one of the Hopkins medical school's brightest stars, an intense and ambitious young cardiologist who made an inviting target for the Pithotomy wags. She had recently been divorced from another member of the Hopkins faculty, Gregory Bulkley, and in the show's central skit he was portrayed as mad with jealousy, stalking physicians he suspected of sleeping with his ex-wife. Healy, played by a man dressed in a long blond wig, fish-net stockings and coconut-half brassiere, was depicted performing a variety of pornographic acts on other physicians until, at the end, she was discovered *in flagrante* by her ex-husband. The show closed with the man who played Bulkley singing "Cardiology Girl," a bawdy takeoff on the Playboy centerfold–inspired hit song "Calendar Girl."

"It would be one thing if a men's club got together and wrote degrading things about each other," Healy says, her voice rising with the memory. "But when they started to bring women into it, to bring women faculty into it, I thought it was offensive.

"I had just gone through a divorce. I was very vulnerable. I was a single mother trying to raise a child. This was the final straw. I let it be known that the club had to stop."

She tried to show that the show was sexual harassment. But this was 1982.

"I got no support when I brought it up. I was rebuffed repeatedly. I kept hearing, 'Bernadine, knock it off. Boys will be boys.'"

Still, she worried that the skit—including what the show's creators conceded was a groundless accusation of infidelity—might damage her reputation. She demanded a list of the participants in the show, and when she was refused, asked again. At staff meetings, she would not let the subject drop. Finally, after she threatened a lawsuit, she got a face-to-face meeting with the club's officers.

"I made every one of them answer how they would have felt if [the skit] was about their sister, their mother or their wife. I went around the table and questioned their integrity, their sensitivity, their character."

Only one friend at Hopkins, Healy remembers—a woman—ever came forward to tell her that what she was doing was right. Other faculty thought she had no sense of humor, no sense of perspective; that she was not playing the game. The dean told her he was worried about her career.

"I was one of the leaders of that institution," she says now. "But after that episode I would go in a room and there were different vibrations. It did not make me popular."

She was gone from Hopkins by the following year.

It's a cold day in February and Healy, now the chief of NIH, is at a science symposium at the University of Connecticut. To her right is a man, her host, the Independent governor of Connecticut, Lowell Weicker. To her left is another man, and to his left another man and another man and on and on down the lecture hall's long dais, 13 consecutive men, all but one white, all but two graying, the aristocracy of science.

In the audience there are more men. Rows of them in suits and ties. Biologists and chemists and clinicians here to listen to Healy's vision for the scientific future.

They do not like what they hear. She is new, and she wants to change things. She says she wants to restructure the American scientific enterprise, to make NIH, its $9-billion-a-year budget and the thousands of researchers it funds around the country, more responsive to the public. Borrowing metaphors and concepts from the world of industry, she talks of setting priorities, of bringing order to science, and these men—accustomed to the friendly anarchy of academia—shift uneasily on their seats.

Unlike the men who have come before her in this job, she does not soothe her audience or pause to attend to the hundreds of federally funded egos in the room. Instead, she talks powerfully and quickly; in complete, precise sentences separated by semicolons, not periods; in a cadence that leaves little room for contradiction or interruption.

Later, in a series of separate seminars around the building at which parts of Healy's plan are discussed, the scientists will stand up to cavil and complain. It is not that they do not respect her. Or that they doubt her intelligence or commitment. It seems something less intellectual than emotional. It is that she does not fit in.

This has been very much the story of Healy's first 12 months at the helm of NIH. At the peak of a career that has taken her from Johns Hopkins to the White House science policy staff in the mid-1980s to the presidency of the Cleveland Clinic, one of the country's most prestigious private medical research groups, the 47-year-old cardiologist came to Washington with an aggressive agenda to reform biomedical science. But she has not always been well received. She is a figure of controversy, intimidating to some and disparaged by others. Her efforts have often been viewed less as an attempt to help medical science regain its footing than as a blunt challenge to the accepted way of doing business.

This is partly the result of Healy's message, a tough-minded diagnosis of medicine's ills that calls for scientists to be more rigorous in setting priorities. It is more the result of the peculiar culture of medical science, which resists direction—and even more the result of the extraordinary, and sometimes overwhelming, character of Bernadine Healy herself.

She is, as head of NIH, one of the country's most important people. This may seem like an overstatement, because she is not a household name and does not draw a crowd when she goes shopping. But she is a person responsible for the hundreds of laboratories scattered around NIH's Bethesda, Md., campus as well as the thousands of basic and applied medical research facilities funded by NIH in universities and hospitals across the country, a vast enterprise without parallel anywhere in the world.

That enterprise is now in crisis. NIH has enough money only to fund about one-quarter of the very best research proposals it receives. Young scientists are becoming disillusioned and seeking careers elsewhere. Good ideas are being ignored. Many established scientists believe that what limited funds do exist are going to the wrong projects, to politically popular research areas like AIDS and the human genome effort—the multimillion-dollar attempt to map all the genes in the human body—rather than to smaller but crucial basic science projects. At the same time, American medical research is facing increasing scrutiny from Congress over the mismanagement of its resources and because of a perception that it cannot police itself adequately against scientific fraud.

If these challenges are met over the next few years, it will be because Healy met them; and if the crisis worsens, she, more than anyone else, will take the blame.

Healy has not shrunk from this responsibility. Upon taking office, she drafted a sweeping plan for the reorganization of NIH. To address the huge gaps in medicine's understanding of women's health, she proposed one of the largest and most expensive studies of human health in history. She has been straightforward about what she sees as the problems with the way science investigates misconduct and has proposed major changes in the investigative arm of NIH. She has spoken her mind. She has charged through the quiet halls of the institutes, raising more of a ruckus in her first few months than many of her predecessors did in a lifetime.

Along the way, Healy has won praise for her energy and her intelligence. But it has not been an easy year. At NIH, where every other director in the institute's history has been a man, where 12 of the 13 institute directors are men, and where 175 of the 203 top-level officials and 241 of the 294 senior managers are men, she remains something of an outsider. At meetings with the scientific community, her proposals for reform have drawn skepticism. She has fought with Democratic Rep. John Dingell of Michigan, the perennial NIH watchdog. Dingell staffers call her a "female John Sununu" because of what they say is her arrogance. She has fought with Nobel Prize–winning biologist James Watson, the longtime head of NIH's Human Genome Office. She has battled with her superiors in the Department of Health and Human Services.

At the University of Connecticut, she is focused and formidable. She looks a little like a younger Margaret Thatcher, with the same high-frosted blond hair, the same imperious cheekbones, the same iron gaze. She writes on a small notepad. She walks briskly from one seminar room to another, then sits in the back, alone, as the men complain in front of her.

"Maybe it's because I am a woman, but I have never felt like one of the boys," Healy says. "I have never really been in the inner circle. It doesn't matter that I was a professor. It doesn't matter that I was president of the

Cleveland Clinic. I have always been on the edge." She says this without rancor, as almost a point of pride: "It doesn't matter to me that the club is angry with me, because I've never been a member."

Healy is by profession a cardiologist, medicine's cowboy specialty. Cardiologists are to internal medicine what jet pilots are to the infantry. She is a feminist, a woman who has been outspoken and active on behalf of her sex from the very beginning of her career. And she is a New Yorker, with all the attendant moxie and brashness, who grew up with her three sisters above her parents' mom and pop perfume business in a working-class neighborhood in Queens.

Her parents were the children of poor Irish immigrants, her father, Michael Healy, an "independent character, a great American individualist," as she describes him, a man who quit school at 13 to take the ferry every day from Hoboken, N.J., to his first job as a messenger boy on Wall Street. He met her mother in a New York restaurant, where she waited on his table, and they moved to Long Island City, three blocks from the Queensboro Bridge, where he set up his own business in perfume oils in the family basement.

"My father had a strong sense of the world being a tough place," she says. "He lived through the Depression. He said you have to learn to take care of yourself. He was somewhat humorless when it came to frivolous things. My parents never went out to dinner. Everything was oriented toward improving yourself, toward education, the business, the family. It was very self-contained.

"When I was a little girl, I used to think I wanted to be a nun, and my father would say you can't be a nun—you'd always be taking orders from a priest. My father was a very old-fashioned conservative Irish Catholic, but he was also an unbelievable feminist. He had a strong sense that no doors should be closed to women, especially his daughters."

All four Healy girls would go on to bigger things. The eldest attended MIT on scholarship and then Columbia University for graduate school. The two youngest would follow Bernadine to Vassar College, also on scholarship, and one would go on to be a doctor and the other a lawyer. It was Bernadine, however, who was always the most academic, the most driven, the daughter most under the spell of Michael Healy.

"My father was fiercely devoted to the things that he thought were right. Our dinner table conversation was always about how he would solve the problems of the world from his perch in Long Island City. ... I am most like him. My mother always says that I'm his girl."

From Vassar, where friends say she was rarely spotted outside of the library, Healy went to Harvard Medical School and then for medical training and a full professorship at Johns Hopkins in Baltimore.

Her résumé glitters. She has been head of the American Federation for Clinical Research and the American Heart Association. She was a star in the Hopkins cardiology department, where she built a reputation as one of the school's most productive and creative researchers. In 1984, she went to the White House for a two-year stint in the Office of Science and Technology Policy and then was hired away by the Cleveland Clinic to head its research institute, which doubled in size during her five-year tenure.

She has two daughters, one from her first marriage to Bulkley and one from her second to Floyd Loop, a world-famous heart surgeon at the Cleveland Clinic. She and Loop met and married while she was at the White House, and then she joined him soon after she landed the Cleveland Clinic post. Theirs is a modern, high-powered marriage. Her husband and daughters stay in Cleveland and she flies home to be with them every weekend. They take fax machines with them on vacation.

Her friends are unremitting in their praise of her. "There are lots of smart people in medicine," says Stephen Achuff, who was a colleague of Healy's at Hopkins. "But what sets her apart is that she is so well organized. She solves a problem and then moves on. She's like Jack Nicklaus. She has this incredible ability to concentrate on something."

"She has these brilliant notions and ways of synthesizing information, which is why people in a room with her are spellbound. She knows how to sort out the baloney," says Myron Weisfeldt, chief of medicine at Columbia University Medical School. "One of the things I've always said about her is that she is never all wrong. It isn't that she never makes mistakes. It is that there is always an element of correctness in what she does."

"The one thing she has is true grit," says her husband. "You don't see that a lot in Washington. Lots of people are going along to get along. But she is not that way at all. She will study the facts and make a decision. She is very decisive."

She is also a formidable opponent, as Dingell found out when he called her before his oversight subcommittee last summer to testify about her handling of a case of scientific fraud while she was head of the Cleveland Clinic. It was a critical meeting—the first between Healy and NIH's most forbidding overseer, and the first on the subject of scientific misconduct, an issue with which Dingell has become almost obsessively involved over the past five years.

But though Dingell routinely turns the most senior of government officials into quivering and compliant witnesses, he had no such power over Healy. She came out blazing, by turns combative, sarcastic and brusque.

"I cannot handle this witness," one of Dingell's colleagues on the committee, Republican Rep. Norman Lent of New York, said at one point. At another, after Dingell sarcastically told Healy that "I am just a poor foolish lawyer from Detroit and I get a little befuddled in some of these questions," she shot back: "And I'm just a poor girl from New York."

Her most memorable moment, however, was a wisecrack, impeccably delivered, that punctured Dingell's heavy-handed interrogation. At issue was why Healy signed off on a grant application alleged to have been fraudulent before the accused researcher did. Dingell thought it odd. Healy couldn't see how it made any difference. It was an arcane point. But much to Healy's obvious exasperation, Dingell dragged it out.

Healy: "The actual sequences of the signatures, I think, is being blown out of proportion. If he had signed first and then I had signed, you could argue how could he have signed before I gave my institutional assurances that we were going to give him the space. Somebody had to sign first."

Dingell: "That is an indisputable point. The question, though, is why was it you that had to sign first?"

Healy: "I didn't have to sign first. This is the way it was brought to me."

Dingell: "He signed second and you signed first."

Healy (with a comic's timing): "Who's on third?"

The room erupted into gales of laughter.

Healy works on the fringe of the NIH campus in a red brick building that looks like a college dormitory.

Visitors enter through a plain brown door to the left of the front entrance, on the first floor, just past an unmanned guard's desk, and sit on a chair jammed between two secretaries' desks. Healy's office is adjoining, a long spare room, an unprepossessing arrangement for the head of a multibillion-dollar-a-year enterprise.

This is not a traditional Washington agency, with clean, vertical lines of authority and a corner office for the chief. The men who built NIH purposefully located all the constituent institutes—the Cancer Institute, the Heart, Lung, and Blood Institute, the Infectious Disease Institute among others—in separate buildings scattered across 300 rolling acres. They wanted to send a not-so-subtle message about the role the director would play: He was not to lead so much as cheerlead, to be a statesman for science, a bookkeeper, someone to lobby Congress for more money but otherwise stay on the periphery. It was a reflection of what the scientific community believed and continues to believe is critical for the most creative and productive research: that science be as unstructured and scientists be as unfettered as possible, that the best minds be left free to follow the idiosyncratic and unpredictable course of scientific discovery.

It is this idea, this catechism, that Healy has chosen to confront. In speeches to scientists around the country over the past few months, she has been saying that it is no longer acceptable for an agency as large as NIH to be without some kind of coherent, central strategy that governs how it distributes its research money. In the 1950s, she says, when NIH was a sleepy research group, the ad hoc way in which the agency and its member institutes organize themselves might have been acceptable. But biochemical science is now a huge enterprise, she argues. The field of biology is exploding. There are suddenly more ideas to pursue than there are resources to pursue them. Congress, once friendly, has grown wary of the scientific community. Huge areas of medical research, such as women's health, cry out for more attention. Borrowing a line from the popular Oldsmobile commercial, she says, "This is no longer your father's NIH."

In her first six months in office, Healy gathered all the top NIH officials together and prepared a strategic plan for the future of the agency, a meticulously detailed document that in its draft form ran to hundreds of pages. One by one, research areas of special interest such as vaccines or biotechnology were identified, and specific research initiatives to expand critical areas of knowledge in each field were drawn up, complete with individual budgets.

It was an enormous undertaking, unprecedented in NIH history. But the response from scientists has been less than overwhelming. Asked to review the draft document, the big biomedical research groups wrote back long rebuttals. It was attacked when Healy presented the plan at a major scientific conference in San Antonio in January and again when she presented it at the University of Connecticut in February.

"The negative feeling that prevails is a feeling that this is corporate mentality of management from the top down," says William Brinkley, dean of the graduate school at Baylor College of Medicine in Houston. "Science in this country is great because of just the opposite philosophy, of ideas coming from the bottom up. The notion is that scientists identify what is important, and that is often quite unexpected and serendipitous. Now it seems that we are being asked to focus our research on what someone at the top thinks is important."

It is not clear how much of this fear is real and how much is imagined. Healy argues that the idea that American biochemical research is currently unfettered is something of a myth. Some of NIH's constituent institutes, she says, do this kind of "top down" research planning already. But they do it behind closed doors. Her plan is also, on a larger scale, similar to what Congress did twenty years ago when it gave NIH a big chunk of money with special instructions to look for a cure for cancer. The war was not won, but it produced some of the most stunning advances in biology in the past century, which may some day lead to a cure.

Healy says her plan will not confine the creativity of researchers but simply give the biochemical establishment a loose but necessary structure. A science policy without central direction can sometimes miss hugely important subjects, she says, like the health of women and minorities. She also sees a straight plan as the best way to get money out of Congress. Why would anyone vote science an extra two or three billion dollars if scientists can't demonstrate convincingly how they would put that money to good use?

"I don't think we will inspire substantial investment unless we have a compelling vision, a compelling statement," she says. "We have so often portrayed ourselves as an agency that only worries about the number of grants. I don't think that is an idea that inspires people."

But the antagonism of the science community can't be defused with logic alone; it's partly about something more subtle. It seems as much a difference of language and style as it is of substance, the culture shock caused by introducing an active and powerful leader to a world that never really wanted one. At the conclusion of the San Antonio meeting, for example, the assembled scientists presented Healy with a manifesto. It wasn't so much that the idea of planning was dead wrong, they said, but that she was moving too quickly, moving without consulting the scientists themselves.

At the Connecticut meeting, the men in the audience flinch when she uses the phrase "strategic plan" over and over again. It is the language of MBAs. They are MDs and PhDs. For people accustomed to the gentle rhythms of laboratory work, there is an unseemly insistence about Healy's manner. "She thinks like a cardiologist," is how one prominent scientist puts it, not meaning the phrase as a compliment.

Within NIH, the unease with Healy seems just as marked.

"There is a lot of waiting in our system, so we learn not to shoot from the hip," says one NIH official. "We have to wait on Congress. We have to wait on our researchers. We have to wait for ideas to come in. We have to wait for paperwork to be done. ... We're never quick to say something is good or bad."

Healy, by contrast, likes argument and open discussion. "I don't mind when people disagree with me," she says. "I love it when people disagree with me." But she says that sometimes when she is seeking frank opinion, she doesn't get it. This puzzles her, and she worries that her colleagues disagree with her behind her back.

At NIH, it also matters that she is a woman in what is still very much a man's world, a fraternity with its own private code. The hallway leading to Healy's office is lined with the solemn-faced portraits of her predecessors, every one a white man. Healy herself is something of an accident: The Bush administration's first six choices, all male, turned down the $143,800-a-year job. "Many men I've seen have a group around them. They have a large body of people with whom they interact, and they make a decision by the group method," says Florence Haseltine, director of the Center for Population Research at NIH. "But I've never known a woman who has gotten to the top who makes a decision that way. We've always been isolated. There aren't enough of us. We make decisions independently. It's not that we don't consult. It's that we don't have a lot of people we can talk to.

"I suspect that a lot of the old-time men are nervous because they don't know how to access her," Haseltine adds. "Many of them never knew her before she came here, and men feel uncomfortable if they don't know how to have a handle on a person in power. Everyone knew [Healy's predecessor James B.] Wyngaarden because he was in the gel, in the matrix. But she doesn't owe her success to anyone. She made it on her own."

Healy's most audacious act as director of NIH has been the Women's Health Initiative. The idea came from Congress, from the Congressional Caucus for Women's Issues, which had been pressuring NIH for some time to pay more attention to women's health. When Healy came aboard, she listened.

"I was faced with a choice," she says. "Do I become an apologist for NIH, or do I look at it and say, 'Let's fix it.' We had all been apologizing for years, and now was the time to fix it."

It is an issue about which she has always been outspoken. She comes from a profession, cardiology, that decided to explore heart disease risk factors by studying 15,000 men—and zero women; that looked at aspirin as a preventative therapy for coronary disease in 22,000 men—and zero women; and that tried to answer the question of whether estrogen was protective against heart disease in women by conducting a study of the role of estrogen in preventing heart disease in men.

She successfully pushed for an initiative on women and heart disease while active in the American Heart Association in the 1980s, fighting the indifference of her colleagues, she says, and the perception in the field that "women's complaints about chest pain were emotional or inconsequential."

At NIH she saw an opportunity to push the same goal on a much larger scale, and within months of taking office proposed one of the largest and most expensive clinical studies in history, a $500 million, 10-year trial involving 140,000 American women. The idea is ambitious: to measure, in a single study, the effectiveness of hormone replacement, dietary modification, and vitamin supplements to combat heart disease, breast and colon cancer, and bone loss in post-menopausal women, simultaneously overcoming the huge knowledge deficits about both the health of women and the health of the elderly.

The idea is not without critics. In a letter to Healy last summer, a group of epidemiologists complained that the design of the trial seemed rushed, that the premises on which it was based were suspect. Part of the study involves a comparison of women on a modified low-fat diet with those on a normal diet. But how do you keep a large group on a low-fat diet for 10 years? And won't the control group naturally decrease its fat intake over time, as has been the general dietary pattern of the past decade? After a decade how can anyone be sure there will be any difference in the diets of the two groups? Another question is age. What if there is a major connection between diet and illness, but it makes a difference only in younger women? Aren't there risks in limiting the trial to post-menopausal women? Does it make sense to gamble on one big study?

"It is a massively expensive study, and it seems rather risky to put so many eggs in one basket," says Lynn Rosenberg, professor of epidemiology at Boston University. "It might be a surer bet to do a larger number of smaller studies so that it wouldn't matter much if one turned out to be a dead end. Whereas if one of the larger studies turned out to be infeasible, it would all have been a huge loss."

Some of these criticisms have been heeded by NIH, and the study design continues to go through refinement. But it is clear that on the big issue of how large the trial should be and how quickly it should proceed, Healy's mind is made up. The boldness that seems to scare off some epidemiologists is precisely what she finds compelling about the idea.

A large trial allows you to include a very diverse population, she says. It allows you to draw conclusions about the lives and experiences of ordinary people. It gets away from the limits of white male populations usually picked for study by medicine.

She is passionate on the subject. She calls it "one of the most exciting clinical trials ever done." It represents everything she has worked for, everything she's been trying to accomplish by asserting herself among men. "Women's issues have been ignored because women have not been a force in our society," she says. "Women have not been listened to; even women of professional standing have not been taken seriously."

She remembers when she fought at the American Heart Association for a new focus on women's health, a campaign to educate patients and doctors about the threat of heart disease.

"Initially my efforts were not well received; it wasn't viewed as important." But, she says, she kept pushing anyway, year in, year out, until she got her way.

"It just goes to show that you should never get discouraged if you think you are right." She pauses and reconsiders. "You should never get discouraged if you *are* right."

Each Friday afternoon, Healy flies to Cleveland to be with her husband and two daughters. She gets home in time for dinner and leaves Monday morning after she has kissed her children goodbye. In a year at NIH, she has never missed a weekend home. She has turned down five honorary degrees because they were given out on weekends. She has passed up the

White House correspondents' dinner and the vice president's Christmas party. She has skipped or rescheduled important meetings. During the week, she talks with her husband or daughters at least three times a day, more if there is a difficult homework assignment or an appointment to be arranged.

"Everyone sort of looks at Bernadine," says her husband, "and says, 'How do you manage?' But the family has been very supportive. We haven't had any problems. The children have been fine. If anything, they are closer to their busy father than they have ever been. And on weekends we spend a lot of time together. ... Call me up in five years and ask me how it is, though, and I might say something else."

In Washington, things have been a little harder. There is Dingell's office, which has never quite forgiven Healy for her performance at last summer's hearing. Dingell staffers write or call, demanding information, sometimes daily. The men on Dingell's staff gossip about her with reporters, seeming to delight in the slightest innuendo. It is a constant annoyance for Healy, leading some to conclude she made a tactical error in confronting him so boldly last summer.

This spring there was a much-reported flap with James Watson, the Nobel laureate biologist who ran NIH's effort to decode the human genome. He does not like Healy. Years ago, when Healy was at the White House, he blasted her in a speech, saying that the person setting science policy was "either unimportant or a woman." When she came aboard, he publicly criticized her decision to consider patenting human genes isolated by NIH, saying it would stifle research. Later when officials of the Department of Health and Human Services raised conflict of interest concerns about his stock ownership and directorship in biotechnology firms that were interested in those same patents, he noisily quit, saying that Healy didn't like him and wanted him out.

Then there are Healy's relations with her superiors at HHS. They did not like her original strategic plan. "The only 'strategy' ... seems to be the acquisition of additional funds," wrote one top official in an internal memo, after estimating that Healy's proposed initiatives would double the NIH budget. Department insiders whisper maliciously that she is campaigning for the job of HHS secretary.

Her press notices have not always been good. In one *New York Times* profile, she was called impulsive, which rankled.

"I'm many things, but I am not impulsive," she says. "I make up my mind and I'm fierce about pursuing it, and I'm relentless and tenacious. But I'm very rational. I'm very nonemotional in the way I do my business and the way I conduct myself. I bend over backwards to make sure I'm not allowing my emotions to influence my decisions."

Still, the theme has been picked up in one account of Healy after another. *Science* magazine, reporting on the Watson affair, said that she "lost her cool." The influential *Science and Government Report* called her the "short-tempered diva of biomedical research." And on and on.

"A woman is bitchy, and a man knows what he wants. A woman is aggressive and harsh, and a man is direct and goal-oriented," says Pam Douglas, a cardiologist at Harvard Medical School. "These things are kind of cliches now, but they are still very true. If we expect women to be emotional and warm and fuzzy, then a woman who knows what she wants and gets it is going to be a real shock."

At the University of Connecticut, there is frustration of a different kind. Healy would like to draw up a list of research topics that deserve to be priorities. She has assembled a sample list to work from. But the scientists all have their own special interests and quiver at the thought of excluding anything.

A man from the Pfizer pharmaceutical company says he is upset because fermentation technology was excluded. "There is no mention of chemistry," says another. "You have structural biology but not developmental biology." A man from Pittsburgh asks why the document is "unnecessarily defensive about computing." A man from the University of Connecticut worries about the absence of software systems, a man from Brown about biomaterials, another from Brandeis about conventional electron microscopy, and yet another about "parasitic diseases" and the "excess of stress on applied immunology."

They do not like the idea of listing priorities.

"This is not what the scientific community wants to see," says one distinguished-looking gray-haired man. "What we need is the same kind of science-driven process we have always seen. We ought to get back to the basic question of 'Is it good or bad science?'"

There is applause.

At midday, Healy leaves to go back to Washington. On the plane she reexplains her position carefully. She is philosophical about the reception she has received. It is not the first time she has walked into a room and felt the vibrations changing.

"You can't be NIH director if you want to be loved," Healy says. "You find your love somewhere else. From your husband, your kids, your dog."

She laughs and brightens. Later, she tells a story about taking her troubles home to her daughters. Someone had written an article making fun of the way she talks, about her fondness for quoting Saint Augustine, and it bothered her. In many ways she is honest about still being the bookish Catholic schoolgirl. She peppers her speeches with references to everyone from Confucius to Cotton Mather, and she says one of the first things she did after getting the NIH job was read the Constitution. But on the particular day she read the critical news article, after dodging all the other arrows at NIH, it hit her the wrong way.

"I read it to my 12-year-old, saying this is what I have to put up with. But she said, 'Mommy, that's not bad. He's saying you're not a wannabe.'" Girls of my daughter's age, Healy explains, do not want to be wannabes—people whose ambition is to be like someone else.

Healy's features soften. Then her voice rises an octave as she imitates her little girl. "What he's saying is that you're not a wannabe. You're an original."

15

Black Leadership: For Change or for Status Quo?

RONALD V. DELLUMS

The challenge to black leadership is extraordinary, in that it causes us to address fundamental questions that relate not only to the qualities of that leadership, but also to the role of leadership generally in effecting change within the society.

When a group of people who have long been rejected and removed from all positions of influence comes to challenge the system, a difficult dilemma presents itself: Do we merely want members of our group to attain high positions within the system, or do we want to change the system as a whole, to remove those factors that lead to the oppression of the whole group?

It might be said that black leaders do not face this dilemma. After all, black leaders were not tempted to join the Watergate conspiracy—they weren't asked. Nonetheless, while we have avoided the strain of the short-sighted views on the nature and need for freedom that have enshrined the name "Watergate" in our national archives, I do not think we ought to rely on this kind of exclusion for safeguarding our political virtue. It is preeminently clear that as the times progress, blacks will move more and more toward a central leadership position throughout the towns, cities and states of the nation, and in the national administration as well. It is important that we address the leadership question very early—not in terms of numbers, which will come inevitably, but in terms of quality. Hence, this important question blacks might ask about Watergate is not why we were not there, but what would we have done had we been

Reprinted by permission from *The Black Scholar* (January–February 1977), pp. 2–5.

given the opportunity? In other words, are we prepared to change the nature of the public morality, or is our object merely to change the color of the perpetrator of the immorality? The point is that if we are not prepared to change the nature of that immorality we have in fact shied away from the leadership role that history has given us.

Blacks are now getting elected to very important high political offices. Unfortunately all too often this election is not used as an opportunity to change the nature of oppression, but it is taken as an opportunity to change the color of oppression.

The growing number of black-elected officials around the country and the growing power of many of the Congressional Black Caucus members within the House of Representatives have given us new and different tools to work with. It is time for black America to demand more than just black faces in politics, it is time for black people to demand some "black politics." My definition of "black politics" is a set of commitments to the eradication of all oppression—of all people, for all time. My definition is based upon an assumption that black people will never experience freedom in a vacuum. As long as anyone who walks among us is not free, we are all to that extent enslaved. The injustices we fight are rooted in the system—the status quo. If we simply change the color of the situation, without changing the situation, we have done nothing to justify the claim to leadership.

"The system" we all speak of is one that does not even guarantee the full participation of all whites in this society. How then can it guarantee the full participation of all blacks and other victims of oppression in this society? Thus, our politics must be the politics of change—not the politics of status quo. We must not simply demand black faces in politics; we must demand politicians who will end oppression. The hope of freedom is rooted in the politics of change.

We must not only dedicate ourselves to this position—we must convince the black community of its necessity. The natural tendency of any community is to see its own needs in isolation. This comes most naturally to blacks, who have not had a very good experience in working with other groups and relying on their loyalty. Yet this is exactly what the defenders of the system want! They want to see all the separate groups who have been victimized by the workings of the system fighting among themselves instead of fighting the system. And they have a thousand ways of obtaining this result, from throwing out crumbs for minorities to fight over to devising policies where one poor person's gain is another poor person's loss. We must be careful not to be taken in by this strategy.

More importantly, we need to devise concrete politics that unite victims of all races, of all sexes, of all ages. I am convinced that if we show each victimized group that the same basic factors in the system are responsible for the oppression of all of them, we can get the working unity that is necessary for basic reform. This is the special task of the *leadership*, because we are the link between the black community and other groups.

I believe it is imperative that we dedicate ourselves to a higher morality than we presently witness, and that we come to believe in ourselves as a people with such strength that we can lead the movement toward a higher public morality and a recognition of new rights.

The mediocre and corrupt administrations of the past eight years make it graphically clear that unless the leadership toward a new morality springs from the living rooms of America, the passivity of self-interested leadership will allow the moral drift to continue and worsen, and make the fight for freedom, justice, and equality even more difficult, and success even more remote. If we believe in ourselves to the extent that we should believe in ourselves, we can set aside arguments that isolate us in the struggle, and dedicate ourselves to participate in and help lead any movement that speaks to enlarging the measure of freedom that any human being presently enslaved to any degree should have. As Dr. King once said, "It is not a question of what is popular, what is safe, or what is expedient. The ultimate question that conscientious leadership must always raise is, 'is it right?'"

Every single one of our people knows what our problems are. They know there is misery in this country. While on the national level we carry on the insane football mentality debate over who is No. 1 in the business of producing the means to world annihilation, it is known at the street level that we are a third-rate power in many of the areas that speak to the human misery of the people, for we do not face the reality that democracy must be meaningful for people in this country, and that the greatest tyranny on earth is the multifarious manifestations of economic and spiritual poverty.

One of the greatest challenges to black leadership in America inheres in the fact that many of us have already lost the will to fight back. However, leaders must personally have faith in the fact that we have the ability to change the world and the courage to struggle with respect to issues that are critical in this country.

I have often reflected that the beautiful thing about freedom is that we cannot compromise it. We cannot be content with half freedom or three-quarters freedom. Once we start walking down the road to freedom, we have to continue until everybody is free. The reality is that until we deal with the millions of Americans dying of hunger and the one-third in America who are illiterate, we have not done the job.

The challenge to domestic leadership is to realize that we are still in the process of developing and evolving freedom in this country. What the Bicentennial ought to have been about is not the sitting on our laurels of the past 200 years, but rather, making certain that if we endure through the last quarter of the 20th Century that we will make democracy mean more than ever before, so that the people of this country can have their interest in real democracy quickened and their generally positive feelings about their government restored. Today they are cynical, having lost faith in their leadership, having seen them over the past eight years pontificate and attack each other rather than addressing the problems that are meaningful to their everyday lives.

We must understand that the history in this country has been to resist and to oppose necessary alternatives. Basic to much of what I have said to the people in my district and around the country, is that if we want real freedom, justice, and democracy in America, there must come together a coalition of groups and individuals, blacks, browns, reds, yellows, women, senior citizens and other deprived groups who have experienced the nature of oppression and who are determined to subordinate the prejudices of the past in order to cooperate with one another. Only by coming together can we challenge the institutions of the country and by rearranging and reorganizing its politics can we make of this country a place that is worthy of us as human beings. We must lead a movement that will make the world a place that respects human life, and where the various forms of human degradation—poverty, hunger, sickness, polluted environments, and war, will no longer be tolerated.

This is why we must realize our potential, not simply as an aggrieved group seeking redress, but as an oppressed group seeking revolutionary changes. Black people have known the pain of injustice and oppression and it is only right that we assume the burden of leadership in this campaign and in the struggle to better society. Blacks should take leadership roles and bring about the unity of focus of all oppressed peoples and individuals so that we can address with courage the issues that face us.

In order to have a set of politics, we must have a set of values, a set of common perceptions, goals and objectives. We must then formulate and agree upon a strategy by which we move to achieve those goals.

As we reflect on almost every aspect of American life, it appears that we have moved into a period when the great hero is dead. We no longer expect a savior outside ourselves. More and more the fate of America appears to be in the hands of all of us who can muster the moral courage, tenacity and faith to work aggressively to turn freedom and justice into a reality; to take this country on a trip—from madness to humanity, from exploitation to equality, from racism to freedom and from war to peace.

There is a history of great people who blazed the trail of greatness at a time in our national life when blacks were subject to unthinkable oppression. I have to reflect on what they must have thought of their personal capabilities in order to allow them to continue against the odds. People such as Frederick Douglass, James Weldon Johnson, Sojourner Truth, W.E.B. DuBois, Dr. Martin Luther King, Jr., and others. It would appear, reflecting on the qualities that they personally brought to the situation, that they found themselves to be human beings of extraordinary capability, and went from there to succeed in their individual life struggles in a way that led to a better world for all people, of all races for all times.

With these examples in front of us, it is difficult to see how we can fail in the responsibilities we have toward our community and toward the whole American people.

16

Where Are
Our Future Leaders?

MANNING MARABLE

Who will lead us into the twenty-first century? It is time for us to decide. A generation ago the objective of African-American activists was to destroy racial segregation and integrate mainstream political and economic institutions. Many of us accomplished these goals. But despite examples of individual success, there remains a simmering leadership crisis that can split our community apart.

Historically the social classes in the Black community were bound together by Jim Crow segregation laws. Blacks on welfare and Black Ph.D.'s alike were ordered to the back of the bus or denied work because of their race. This common experience of racial oppression gave us a sense of solidarity and interdependence. Black physicians depended on Black patients; Black lawyers and accountants served Black clients.

With desegregation, many affluent African-Americans moved from the ghetto into integrated suburbs. Graduates of Howard and Spelman now send their children to Harvard and Swarthmore. In the cities, our sense of community has gradually deteriorated. Millions of our young people are trapped in a destructive web of inferior schools, violence, drugs and unemployment.

We can't depend on the political system—the Democrats or Republicans—or the corporate world to solve our problems; all too often their policies have contributed to them. Instead we must recognize that one of the root causes of our divisions and social unrest is an absence of creative, dynamic leadership.

Oppressed people need leaders to liberate them. These leaders must be women and men with vision who have the capacity to articulate the common grievances and goals of the community. Such leaders as Ida B. Wells, W.E.B. Du Bois, Malcolm X, Fannie Lou Hamer and Martin Luther King, Jr., came from different walks of life but shared a willingness to set aside their personal interests and advance the objectives of our people.

Leaders are not born but made. Our struggle for freedom now requires that we identify creative young people in our cities who will lead us into the next century. Black professionals have the moral and political obligation to provide the resources necessary to develop leadership abilities in our young. Along with technological and research skills, our future leaders need a sound foundation in our culture and history.

We should establish "freedom schools," with curricula that provide a social and political consciousness, which children can attend after school and on Saturdays. Black professionals in corporations should promote partnership programs between their firms and public schools that enrich school curricula and encourage young African-Americans to seek careers in business. Black religious institutions should open credit unions, food cooperatives and other programs designed to provide capital, food and necessary resources to the community. Through such activities, young people can learn skills that directly benefit their neighbors.

Our fraternities and sororities should provide special training opportunities for young African-Americans interested in civil rights and social justice by sponsoring internships with Black public-policy groups and with elected officials. Our focus must be to strengthen the bridge of understanding between the next generation of middle-class youngsters and poor and working-class Black people.

If we fail to strengthen this bridge, we will increasingly have Black leaders who are "Black" by race only and who have no connection to or compassion for the plight of the majority of our people. With the expansion of prisons, the escalation of the death penalty for people of color and the increased use of drugs in our communities, the fragmentation and social destruction of the vast majority of African-Americans will continue. Without leaders who possess collective vision for the empowerment of our people, we will continue to be oppressed.

PART FOUR

OPPORTUNITY: THE ESSENCE OF LEADERSHIP

The student of leadership is confronted with a variety of ideas, approaches, and conclusions. Interest in leadership has consumed us over the past few decades, and there is still no consensus. Where power was once a key element of leadership, we now talk about vision, intuition, commitment, action, and even humor as necessary attributes. Global communications bring us world events at an ever-increasing pace; "rational" is viewed differently by a maze of cultures; and people are overloaded with data yet starved for information. It is harder than ever for leaders and followers to develop a clear sense of purpose and direction.

Power is still important, but the concept has changed. Leaders once focused on accumulating resources to make things happen, but the reality is that no one person or group can easily or quickly accumulate what is needed to change. The magnitude of change has grown larger, and the amount of resources required has increased: More money, materials, people, and information are necessary. Only by forging alliances and creating a cooperative agenda can leaders get results. The many replace the few, consensus is favored over authority, and leaders must share power if they are to achieve the goal.

We have tried to describe the new realities with the term "empowerment." Rife with misuse, it is regarded as a meaningless term by many. However, we believe that it still best describes the need for leaders to allocate the resources and decisionmaking authority to those who are closest to the action and give them the freedom to fail. In most organizations, the leader is furthest from the action, has the least valid information, and must entrust decisions and actions to others. Everyone must "own" the goal in the future and share in a common understanding of what is to be done.

Vision remains the hallmark of effective leadership, the element that creates opportunity. What separates leaders from others is that leaders see the future. But only by "telling the story" and getting others involved can the leader find a common direction for the organization. With the creation of symbols and a constant retelling of the story, the leader soon has people modifying, embellishing, and creating a shared understanding. Ultimately, visionary leadership becomes independent of the leader. Should anything happen to the leader, the others forge ahead because it is *their* vision. New leaders may be recruited and empowered, but they must accept the existing vision. The vision is the group's, not the leader's.

Because people see (and act in) the world differently, leaders will have to develop a path that allows each individual to contribute. Where we have expected the leader to "tell us the way," the opportunity for leaders in the future is more complex. The values of the leader—and often the organization—can be in conflict with the values of the followers. Finding common ground so that followers can achieve personal goals and objectives by accomplishing organizational goals is a new challenge. Leaders can no longer demand that others simply adhere to a single set of values. They must negotiate and compromise, whether by altering the rules or using technology to replace the unacceptable tasks of organizational life. "Taking action" will not entail the bold, relentless pursuit of the vision. Leaders will provide advice, stimulate others to act, and be content with giving support and encouragement. This leadership style is more difficult to master than merely giving orders or wielding rewards and punishments.

As we look to the future of leadership, a sense of timing looms large. Many people lament the rapid pace of our lives and the increasing amount of change—all too often, we need to make important decisions "yesterday." Yet the impact of each decision seems to have everlasting consequences: Whatever we do today has a significant impact on the future. Considering the long-term effects is complex and often time-consuming. Where we once encouraged leaders to make decisions *now*, we shall soon ask them to confer, involve as many followers as possible, and develop a consensus that may not be optimal for the present but addresses the future with caring and confidence.

Our expectations of leaders continue to grow. We look for leaders who can help us cope with change and uncertainty and inspire the self-confidence we need to meet the future with hope. Thus, the opportunity for leadership has never been greater. Whether or not to accept the challenges of leadership is our choice to make. How and why we make it may be different than in the past.

Leadership Perspectives

We conclude this study of leadership with some perspectives on the new realities. Our intent is to describe what is changing and why. At the same time, we want to elaborate on the elements of leadership that will be critical in the future.

John W. Gardner's essay from 1965, "The Antileadership Vaccine" (Chapter 17), concerns the dispersion of power and our failure to cope with the "big question." In his opinion, the antileadership vaccine is administered by our educational system and by the structure of our society, causing people to lose the confidence they need to assume a leadership role. In training people for leadership, we have neglected the broader moral view of shared values, thus inhibiting vision, creativity, and risk-taking. We appear to be approaching a point, he argues, at which everyone will value the technical expert who advises the leader or the intellectual who stands off and criticizes the leader, but no one will be concerned with the development of leadership itself.

Marshall Sashkin and Molly Goltman Sashkin apply some of the new ideas to the field of education in Chapter 18, "Leadership and Culture Building in Schools." Effective leaders must rebuild organizational cultures to include values of excellence. Culture building is easier when the leader helps people adapt to change while achieving individual and organizational goals and coordinating the tasks necessary for success. The authors note that leaders carry out the vision with their behaviors: They lead by example, not by words.

No anthology on leadership would be complete without the thoughts of Warren Bennis. In "Managing the Dream: Leadership in the 21st Century" (Chapter 19), Bennis clearly differentiates the leader from the manager. He notes that leaders have a confidence in their dream (vision) and a strength to persist even in the event of failure—*this* is commitment. Modern leaders communicate the vision with symbols and stories in ways that reflect new international alliances and a global view. Sharing a vision among cultures is a new challenge for the leader of today and tomorrow.

In Chapter 20, we present an excerpt from the 1991 annual report of General Electric Company. Signed by John F. Welch, Jr., and Edward E. Hood, Jr., this statement reflects some very powerful realities. Welch's dominant style of the 1970s and 1980s has been transformed into a new philosophy: He now sees leadership everywhere in the company. He and Hood characterize leaders as having two attributes: The ability to deliver on commitments and the willingness to share common values. There must be a balance between the "numbers" and values. The future has created a new opportunity for understanding and executing effective leadership.

In Chapter 21, Joseph C. Rost discusses "Leadership in the Future," challenging us to understand a paradigm shift. Rost notes the change from an "industrial" model of management and leadership to a more collaborative model. All kinds of futures are possible, he says, and we must work together to make the relevant choices. Transforming leadership will require scholars, practitioners, and leaders themselves to think about the world in more creative ways.

17

The Antileadership Vaccine

JOHN W. GARDNER

It is generally believed that we need enlightened and responsible leaders—at every level and in every phase of our national life. Everyone says so. But the nature of leadership in our society is very imperfectly understood, and many of the public statements about it are utter nonsense.

This is unfortunate because there are serious issues of leadership facing this society, and we had better understand them.

The Dispersion of Power

The most fundamental thing to be said about leadership in the United States is also the most obvious. We have gone as far as any known society in creating a leadership system that is *not* based on caste or class, nor even on wealth. There is not yet equal access to leadership (witness the remaining barriers facing women and Negroes), but we have come a long, long way from the family- or class-based leadership group. Even with its present defects, ours is a relatively open system.

The next important thing to be said is that leadership is dispersed among a great many groups in our society. The President, of course, has a unique, and uniquely important, leadership role, but beneath him, fragmentation is the rule. This idea is directly at odds with the notion that the society is run by a coherent power group—the Power Elite, as C. Wright Mills called it, or the Establishment, as later writers have named it. It is hard not to believe that such a group exists. Foreigners find it particularly difficult to believe in the reality of the fluid, scattered, shifting leadership that is visible to the naked eye. The real leadership, they imagine, must be behind the scenes. But at a national level this simply isn't so.

President's essay reprinted from Carnegie Corporation of New York 1965 annual report.

In many local communities and even in some states there *is* a coherent power group, sometimes behind the scenes, sometimes out in the open. In communities where such an "establishment," that is, a coherent ruling group, exists, the leading citizen can be thought of as having power in a generalized sense: he can bring about a change in zoning ordinances, influence the location of a new factory, and determine whether the local museum will buy contemporary paintings. But in the dispersed and fragmented power system that prevails in the nation as a whole one cannot say "So-and-so is powerful," without further elaboration. Those who know how our system works always want to know, "Powerful in what way? Powerful to accomplish what?" We have leaders in business and leaders in government, military leaders and educational leaders, leaders in labor and in agriculture, leaders in science, in the world of art, and in many other special fields. As a rule, leaders in any one of these fields do not recognize the authority of leaders from a neighboring field. Often they don't even know one another, nor do they particularly want to. Mutual suspicion is just about as common as mutual respect—and a lot more common than mutual cooperation in manipulating society's levers.

Most of the significant issues in our society are settled by a balancing of forces. A lot of people and groups are involved and the most powerful do not always win. Sometimes a coalition of the less powerful wins. Sometimes an individual of very limited power gets himself into the position of casting the deciding ballot.

Not only are there apt to be many groups involved in any critical issue, but their relative strength varies with each issue that comes up. A group that is powerful today may not be powerful next year. A group that can cast a decisive vote on question A may not even be listened to when question B comes up.

The Nature of Leadership

People who have never exercised power have all kinds of curious ideas about it. The popular notion of top leadership is a fantasy of capricious power: the top man presses a button and something remarkable happens; he gives an order as the whim strikes him, and it is obeyed.

Actually, the capricious use of power is relatively rare except in some large dictatorships and some small family firms. Most leaders are hedged around by constraints—tradition, constitutional limitations, the realities of the external situation, rights and privileges of followers, the requirements of teamwork, and most of all the inexorable demands of large-scale organization, which does not operate on capriciousness. In short, most power is wielded circumspectly.

There are many different ways of leading, many kinds of leaders. Consider, for example, the marked contrasts between the politician and the intellectual leader, the large-scale manager and the spiritual leader. One sees solemn descriptions of the qualities needed for leadership without any reference at all to the fact that the necessary attributes depend on the kind of leadership under discussion. Even in a single field there may be different kinds of leadership with different required attributes. Think of the difference between the military hero and the military manager.

If social action is to occur certain functions must be performed. The problems facing the group or organization must be clarified, and ideas necessary to their solution formulated. Objectives must be defined. There must be widespread awareness of those objectives, and the will to achieve them. Often those on whom action depends must develop new attitudes and habits. Social machinery must be set in motion. The consequences of social effort must be evaluated and criticized, and new goals set.

A particular leader may contribute at only one point to this process. He may be gifted in analysis of the problem, but limited in his capacity to communicate. He may be superb in communicating, but incapable of managing. He may, in short, be an outstanding leader without being good at every aspect of leadership.

If anything significant is to be accomplished, leaders must understand the social institutions and processes through which action is carried out. And in a society as complex as ours, that is no mean achievement. A leader, whether corporation president, university dean, or labor official, knows his organization, understands what makes it move, comprehends its limitations. Every social system or institution has a logic and dynamic of its own that cannot be ignored.

We have all seen men with lots of bright ideas but no patience with the machinery by which ideas are translated into action. As a rule, the machinery defeats them. It is a pity, because the professional and academic man can play a useful role in practical affairs. But too often he is a dilettante. He dips in here or there; he gives bits of advice on a dozen fronts; he never gets his hands dirty working with one piece of the social machinery until he knows it well. He will not take the time to understand the social institutions and processes by which change is accomplished.

Although our decentralized system of leadership has served us well, we must not be so complacent as to imagine that it has no weaknesses, that it faces no new challenges, or that we have nothing to learn. There are grave questions to be answered concerning the leadership of our society. Are we living up to standards of leadership that we have achieved in our own past? Do the conditions of modern life introduce new complications into the task of leadership? Are we failing to prepare leaders for tomorrow?

Here are some of our salient difficulties.

Failure to Cope with the Big Questions

Nothing should be allowed to impair the effectiveness and independence of our specialized leadership groups. But such fragmented leadership does create certain problems. One of them is that it isn't anybody's business to think about the big questions that cut across specialties—the largest questions facing our society. Where are we headed? Where do we *want* to head? What are the major trends determining our future? Should we do anything about them? Our fragmented leadership fails to deal effectively with these transcendent questions.

Very few of our most prominent people take a really large view of the leadership assignment. Most of them are simply tending the machinery of that part of society to which they belong. The machinery may be a great corporation or a great government agency or a great law practice or a great university. These people may tend it very well indeed, but they are not pursuing a vision of what the total society needs. They have not developed a strategy as to how it can be achieved, and they are not moving to accomplish it.

One does not blame them, of course. They do not see themselves as leaders of the society at large, and they have plenty to do handling their own specialized role.

Yet is is doubtful that we can any longer afford such widespread inattention to the largest questions facing us. We achieved greatness in an era when changes came more slowly than now. The problems facing the society took shape at a stately pace. We could afford to be slow in recognizing them, slow in coping with them. Today, problems of enormous import hit us swiftly. Great social changes emerge with frightening speed. We can no longer afford to respond in a leisurely fashion.

Our inability to cope with the largest questions tends to weaken the private sector. Any question that cannot be dealt with by one of the special leadership groups—that is, any question that cuts across special fields—tends to end up being dealt with by government. Most Americans value the role played by nongovernmental leadership in this country and would wish it to continue. In my judgment it will not continue under the present conditions.

The cure is not to work against the fragmentation of leadership, which is a vital element in our pluralism, but to create better channels of communication among significant leadership groups, especially in connection with the great issues that transcend any particular group.

Failure of Confidence

Another of the maladies of leadership today is a failure of confidence. Anyone who accomplishes anything of significance has more confidence than the facts would justify. It is something that outstanding executives have in common with gifted military commanders, brilliant political leaders, and great artists. It is true of societies as well as of individuals. Every great civilization has been characterized by confidence in itself.

Lacking such confidence, too many leaders add ingenious new twists to the modern art which I call "How to reach a decision without really deciding." They require that the question be put through a series of clearances within the organization and let the clearance process settle it. Or take a public opinion poll and let the poll settle it. Or devise elaborate statistical systems, cost-accounting systems, information-processing systems, hoping that out of them will come unassailable support for one course of action rather than another.

This is not to say that leadership cannot profit enormously from good information. If the modern leader doesn't know the facts he is in grave trouble, but rarely do the facts provide unqualified guidance. After the facts are in, the leader must in some measure emulate the little girl who told the teacher she was going to draw a picture of God. The teacher said, "But, Mary, no one knows what God looks like"; and Mary said, "They will when I get through."

The confidence required of leaders poses a delicate problem for a free society. We don't want to be led by Men of Destiny who think they know all the answers. Neither do we wish to be led by Nervous Nellies. It is a matter of balance. We are no longer in much danger, in this society, from Men of Destiny. But we *are* in danger of falling under the leadership of men who lack the confidence to lead. And we are in danger of destroying the effectiveness of those who have a natural gift for leadership.

Of all our deficiencies with respect to leadership, one of the gravest is that we are not doing what we should to encourage potential leaders. In the late eighteenth century we produced out of a small population a truly extraordinary group of leaders—Washington, Adams, Jefferson, Franklin, Madison, Monroe, and others. Why is it so difficult today, out of a vastly greater population, to produce men of that caliber? It is a question that most reflective people ask themselves sooner or later. There is no reason to doubt that the human material is still there, but there is excellent reason to believe that we are failing to develop it—or that we are diverting it into nonleadership activities.

The Antileadership Vaccine

Indeed, it is my belief that we are immunizing a high proportion of our most gifted young people against any tendencies to leadership. It will be worth our time to examine how the antileadership vaccine is administered.

The process is initiated by the society itself. The conditions of life in a modern, complex society are not conducive to the emergence of leaders. The young person today is acutely aware of the fact that he is an anonymous member of a mass society, an individual lost among millions of others. The processes by which leadership is exercised are not visible to him, and he is bound to believe that they are exceedingly intricate. Very little in his experience encourages him to think that he might some day exercise a role of leadership.

This unfocused discouragement is of little consequence compared with the expert dissuasion the young person will encounter if he is sufficiently bright to attend a college or university. In those institutions today, the best students are carefully schooled to avoid leadership responsibilities.

Most of our intellectually gifted young people go from college directly into graduate school or into one of the older and more prestigious professional schools. There they are introduced to—or, more correctly, powerfully indoctrinated in—a set of attitudes appropriate to scholars, scientists, and professional men. This is all to the good. The students learn to identify themselves strongly with their calling and its ideals. They acquire a conception of what a good scholar, scientist, or professional man is like.

As things stand now, however, that conception leaves little room for leadership in the normal sense; the only kind of leadership encouraged is that which follows from the performing of purely professional tasks in a superior manner. Entry into what most of us would regard as the leadership roles in the society at large is discouraged.

In the early stages of a career, there is a good reason for this: becoming a first-class scholar, scientist, or professional requires single-minded dedication. Unfortunately, by the time the individual is sufficiently far along in his career to afford a broadening of interests, he often finds himself irrevocably set in a narrow mold.

The antileadership vaccine has other more subtle and powerful ingredients. The image of the corporation president, politician, or college president that is current among most intellectuals and professionals today has some decidedly unattractive features. It is said that such men compromise their convictions almost daily, if not hourly. It is said that they have tasted the corrupting experience of power. They must be status seekers, the argument goes, or they would not be where they are.

Needless to say, the student picks up such attitudes. It is not that professors propound these views and students learn them. Rather, they are in the air and students absorb them. The resulting unfavorable image contrasts dramatically with the image these young people are given of the professional who is almost by definition dedicated to his field, pure in his motives, and unencumbered by worldly ambition.

My own extensive acquaintance with scholars and professionals on the one hand and administrators and managers on the other does not confirm this contrast in character. In my experience, each category has its share of opportunists. Nevertheless, the negative attitudes persist.

As a result the academic world appears to be approaching a point at which everyone will want to educate the technical expert who advises the leader, or the intellectual who stands off and criticizes the leader, but no one will want to educate the leader himself.

Are Leaders Necessary?

For a good many academic and other professional people, negative attitudes toward leadership go deeper than skepticism concerning the leader's integrity. Many have real doubts, not always explicitly formulated, about the necessity for leadership.

The doubts are of two kinds. First, many scientific and professional people are accustomed to the kinds of problems that can be solved by expert technical advice or action. It is easy for them to imagine that any social enterprise could be managed in the same way. They envisage a world that does not need leaders, only experts. The notion is based, of course, upon a false conception of the leader's function. The supplying of technically correct solutions is the least of his responsibilities.

There is another kind of question that some academic or professional people raise concerning leadership: Is the very notion of leadership somehow at odds with the ideals of a free society? Is it a throwback to earlier notions of social organization?

These are not foolish questions. We have in fact outgrown or rejected several varieties of leadership that have loomed large in the history of mankind. We do not want autocratic leaders who treat us like inferior beings. We do not want leaders, no matter how wise or kind, who treat us like children.

But at the same time that we were rejecting those forms of leadership, we were evolving forms more suitable to our values. As a result our best leaders today are *not* out of place in a free society—on the contrary, they strengthen our free society.

We can have the kinds of leaders we want, but we cannot choose to do without them. It is in the nature of social organization that we must have them at all levels of our national life, in and out of government—in business, labor, politics, education, science, the arts, and every other field. Since we must have them, it helps considerably if they are gifted in the performance of their appointed task. The sad truth is that a great many of our organizations are badly managed or badly led. And because of that, people within those organizations are frustrated when they need not be frustrated. They are not helped when they could be helped. They are not given the opportunities to fulfill themselves that are clearly possible.

In the minds of some, leadership is associated with goals that are dis-
tasteful—power, profit, efficiency, and the like. But leadership, properly
conceived, also serves the individual human goals that our society values
so highly, and we shall not achieve those goals without it.

Leaders worthy of the name, whether they are university presidents or
senators, corporation executives or newspaper editors, school superintendents or governors, contribute to the continuing definition and articulation of the most cherished values of our society. They offer, in short, moral
leadership.

So much of our energy has been devoted to tending the machinery of
our complex society that we have neglected this element in leadership. I
am using the word "moral" to refer to the shared values that must under-
gird any functioning society. The thing that makes a number of individuals a society rather than a population or a crowd is the presence of shared
attitudes, habits and values, a shared conception of the enterprise of
which they are all a part, shared views of why it is worthwhile for the enterprise to continue and to flourish. Leaders can help in bringing that
about. In fact, it is required that they do so. When leaders lose their credibility or their moral authority, then the society begins to disintegrate.

Leaders have a significant role in creating the state of mind that is the
society. They can serve as symbols of the moral unity of the society. They
can express the values that hold the society together. Most important,
they can conceive and articulate goals that lift people out of their petty
preoccupations, carry them above the conflicts that tear a society apart,
and unite them in the pursuit of objectives worthy of their best efforts.

18

Leadership and Culture Building in Schools

MARSHALL SASHKIN
MOLLY GOLTMAN SASHKIN

Only in the past decade have researchers begun to study leadership in schools as opposed to "administration." It was not so long ago that Ralph Stogdill (1973) wrote that the only leadership in schools was laissez-faire leadership. This situation was largely a consequence of training educational administrators to be good bureaucrats and nothing more. That image of school leadership has been changing and will change still more.

That successful schools have effective leaders has become an axiom of what has come to be called the "effective schools literature" (Edmonds, 1979; Purkey and Smith, 1983). Summarizing this literature, Bossert (1985) observed that studies of effective elementary schools consistently show that such schools have "a school principal who is a strong programmatic leader. ..." (p. 39). Since then much has been written about the leadership role of principals (Sheive and Schoenheit, 1987; Sashkin, 1988a; Sergiovanni, 1987). There has even been some progress in selecting effective school leaders (U. S. Department of Education, 1987) based on the current concept of "transformational" leadership (Burns, 1978; Schein, 1985). A recent Illinois law suggests that practitioners and state policymakers have started to engage this issue. This law requires all school principals to spend at least 51 percent of their time as "instructional leaders" (although it is not exactly clear just what that means in practice).

An earlier version of this paper was prepared for and presented at the annual meeting of the American Educational Research Association, Boston, April 20, 1990, as part of the refereed symposium, "Leadership and Culture: Qualitative and Quantitative Research Approaches and Results" (Division A).

It has become more and more common to read and hear that the essential factor underlying effective schools is an "ethos" or "culture" of excellence and that effective school leaders are "culture builders." This idea originated in the more general treatment of "corporate cultures" developed by Deal and Kennedy (1982) and translated by Deal (1987) into the school context. Deal speaks, for example, of telling stories about heroes, establishing ceremonies, and engaging in culture-building rituals. These are all examples of actions effective school leaders take to create cultures of excellence.

This chapter explores the way school leaders build cultures, using qualitative methods to explore and understand such work. The arguments presented derive in part from the work of Deal and Peterson (1990) on the culture-building role of the school principal and partly from Sashkin's research on school leadership (Sashkin, 1987, 1988a; Sashkin and Burke, 1990). We will extend this work by showing how, through both strategic leadership approaches and concrete behaviors, school principals construct effective cultures.

Examining School Leadership

Deal and Peterson analyzed case studies of effective culture building by principals. In their report they draw on the work of Schein (1985) and others to provide a framework in which to understand culture building. They focused on five specific action strategies school leaders use to create effective cultures. Our chapter builds on these five themes, but it differs in three important ways from the analysis of Deal and Peterson. First, we make certain assumptions about how the five strategies fit together, with some taking a primary and others a secondary role. Second, our argument differs in its explication of the underlying problems and challenges involved in applying the five strategies. Finally, our approach attempts to place the principal's culture building role in a broader context of school leadership.

The five themes identified and described in detail by Deal and Peterson involve (1) staffing, (2) conflict, (3) modeling, (4) telling stories, and (5) creating traditions, ceremonies, and rituals. For each strategy, we will look at two levels of tactical action. At the first level we see relatively obvious activities. At the second level we offer some insights on the subtleties of using each strategy.

Strategy I: Value-Based Staffing

The headmaster of an old, successful private school was asked what his first actions were when he stepped into the role five years earlier. He said, "Well, I guess I picked as my key staff people who shared my own philosophy, who had beliefs about education similar to mine." Selecting (or re-moving) staff based on the fit between their educational values and those of the principal is a critical strategy for effective school leadership and cul-ture building. Each of the five school leaders reviewed by Deal and Peterson had selected (or in some cases removed) staff based on their un-derlying values and beliefs. They had done so even where they lacked for-mal authority to hire or fire.

One principal (Dwyer et al., 1984) who had no such power was none-theless able to let "the right people"—individuals she had come to know well during her twenty years in the district—know about forthcoming openings. Of course, it was a more difficult process without formal staff-ing authority, and it took some time—three years—to build a cadre of deeply committed staff who shared and supported the principal's vision and values. Still, this effective principal was able to do so, in part because of her long-term vision (Sashkin, 1988a).

A principal needs a core group of like-minded individuals who can identify with and support his or her values. Only then can the principal successfully instill those values within the school's culture, building a foundation for excellence. At least some members of that core group will probably have to be brought into the school. Selecting key staff may sound difficult, but this is not the sole or even the most significant challenge. The real difficulty is in knowing how to identify the underlying educational values and beliefs of potential staff members and having the skill to apply that knowledge.

To sum up, there are two aspects to value-based staffing. On an obvious level, ways must be found to select staff members who share the princi-pal's values (or to remove those who hold opposing values). But on a deeper and more subtle level, principals must identify individuals' values and decide whether those values will strengthen or weaken the desired culture.

Strategy II: Using Conflict Constructively

Confronting conflict is generally the best and often the only way to re-solve disagreements constructively (Thomas, 1976; Sashkin, 1989). Yet how often does one hear about principals who hide from disputes in their offices or who use written rules and rigid procedures as "fair" ways to deal with differences? Withdrawal is never a solution, and although rule- or third-party based compromises may not be *un*fair, neither are such approaches seen as fair by the parties involved. Fairness is in the eye of the beholder, and it results only if that beholder is a party to the resolution (Maier, 1963).

An obvious prerequisite for dealing constructively with conflict is to confront it rather than ignore or avoid it. But a less-recognized factor concerns the development of shared values to resolve conflicts. Common values can anchor whatever resolution the conflicting parties come up with, both ensuring the success of the solution and strengthening the shared culture. Without a framework of superordinate values, it is not likely that the parties can work out the conflict in a "win-win" manner that eradicates the problem. At best, the parties might arrive at a reasonable compromise or bargain; however, bargaining and compromise, though not necessarily destructive, are almost never *constructive*. Dealing with conflict constructively (Sashkin, 1989) means developing a creative, integrative resolution that meets the desires of all parties.

One of the cases reviewed by Deal and Peterson, that of Frances Hedges (originally examined by Dwyer et al., 1984) shows clearly the effective use of conflict as a culture-building strategy. Hedges confronted faculty who disapproved of her installation of a reading specialist (reading was a key priority of basic and unquestionable value to her). She called a weekend retreat to work on the issue and to develop procedures that involved the reading specialist as well as teachers. Hedges made sure that the retreat did not simply open up professional turf wars between teachers and the reading specialist. Instead, she focused everyone on how to support the overarching value of strong reading skills.

Using conflict constructively to build culture calls for the active involvement of all parties. But even more important is the use of the conflict-resolution process to tie issues back to—and to reinforce—shared beliefs and values. There are, then, two important tactical issues in managing conflict constructively. On a somewhat superficial level, conflict must be openly examined and dealt with, never denied or avoided. But on a deeper level, resolution of conflict must begin by explicitly identifying shared values, which can then serve as the basis for a solution.

Strategy III: Modeling Values in Action

By their behavior, effective school leaders actively model the values on which they strive to build school cultures. As the saying goes, "Actions speak louder than words." Words can clarify, interpret, draw attention to, and reinforce values and thus help build and strengthen cultures. But directly observable action—preferably involving interaction with others—is more effective than speech for instilling values that guide subsequent actions. The challenge is not just in doing but also in designing and in doing over time. That is, to strengthen cultural values, one's behavior must be persistent, consistent, and in a sense planned. Only repeated action ensures that others will clearly see the values one models. Only when actions consistently illustrate the same values will those values be seen as operative (and not just espoused) aspects of the school's culture (Argyris and Schon, 1974).

These two requirements are unlikely to be met without some degree of forethought about one's aims (which may involve formal planning or may be based more on instinct and intuition). This is one reason people say that effective leaders have vision. Such leaders think in terms of the future, not just for the moment. D. Quinn Mills, a management scholar at the Harvard Business School, has said, "Leaders live in the future, and planning is their language."

Deal and Peterson review the case of Ray Murdock, principal of an elementary school in a poor rural area of a southwestern state (a case initially developed by Dwyer et al., 1984). Murdock's overriding objective during the sixteen years he had been principal was to create an environment in which children felt personally cared for. This value of *caring* was primary for Murdock and pervaded all his actions. For example, he met with each student on his or her birthday to talk about achievements and plans. When Murdock had cafeteria duty, he would serve food to children in the line, and as they passed he would make personal contact with each one. These are but two specific examples of a large set of behavioral actions that served to model the value of personal care.

On the superficial level, then, the specific actions of the principal count more than the words the principal uses to espouse values. However, on a deeper level, values must be "designed" into actions, with constancy and consistency.

Strategy IV: Telling Stories about Heroes and Heroines

We often think of storytelling as a way of entertaining children. But storytelling is also a very powerful way of acculturating children to the norms and values of a society. Thus, it is important to discard the implicit "for kids only" label often attached to storytelling.

As in other types of organizations (Deal and Kennedy, 1982), successful school leaders typically use stories that illustrate the values embodied in the school's culture. This approach both reinforces those values and strengthens the culture. Most leaders seem to identify archetypes and create metaphors, then use them to define and clarify values through inspiring stories. For example, in *The Headmaster,* John McPhee (1966) writes about Frank Boyden, headmaster of a private school during the first part of this century. Perhaps the value Boyden saw as most central to the culture he was building was that of commitment to the school and its students. Boyden often told of a faculty member whose commitment was so great that he rejected an offer from another school that would have increased both his prestige and his income. "He's not in it for the money," Boyden would say.

It is important to note that the stories are not simply made up or manufactured to illustrate a point. Stories used to define and reinforce basic values *must* be true. Of course, the storytelling principal may interpret the raw facts of the story in terms of certain values and beliefs, but this is different from inventing a tale.

Some principals probably avoid storytelling simply because they don't see themselves as good storytellers or don't feel they have the required communication skills. This is a real but shallow reason. The effective use of stories requires more than an interesting tale and good storytelling ability. It also requires a deep appreciation of the importance of stories as vehicles for defining and reinforcing values. The principal as storyteller must identify archetypes and metaphors that, in an inspiring way, illustrate the values he or she promotes. This can be a difficult conceptual task, calling for skill in the manipulation of symbols.

Thus, we have noted two aspects of how stories clarify and reinforce cultural values. The more superficial involves applying sound interpersonal communication (storytelling) skills. At a far deeper level, stories must be constructed so that they clearly connect to specific values, applying archetypes and metaphors to a concrete example.

Strategy V: Creating Traditions, Ceremonies, and Rituals

Formal and semiformal customs, some typically large scale (ceremonies) and some usually small scale (rituals), recognize and "celebrate" the values that define the school's culture. Traditions and ceremonies accomplish this end in highly visible, formalized ways, whereas rituals usually do so through somewhat less grand but much more frequent patterns of action.

Frances Hedges, of whom we spoke earlier, did not use ceremonies but relied on routines that became almost ritualized. For example, she made sure to be highly visible as she visited classes and monitored the hallways. Often she would just happen to "drop in on" teachers, who had grown accustomed to having her ask about exceptional student work at such times. Hedges thus gave teachers an opportunity to tell her about some outstanding student paper or achievement. Through this ritual Hedges showed her concern for the value of increasing self-esteem. Not only did the student look good, but the teacher gained recognition, too. Also reinforced was the value Hedges placed on reading and language skills. The ritualized situation that Hedges created led to enhanced positive feelings for all those involved.

There is an obvious problem with ceremonies, traditions, and rituals: They take time to establish and to carry out. Time is no insignificant issue for most principals, whose days are typically fragmented and filled with "buzzing, blooming confusion," but it is not the most important problem. The real difficulty is in building into the event the values to be illustrated and reinforced. This must be done in ways that create a strong positive effect, leading teachers and students to internalize the values. Constructing inspiring traditions, rituals, and ceremonies is difficult. Ray Murdock, mentioned earlier, was exceptionally creative in doing so. For example, he started an annual student art auction, at which students' drawings were sold to the highest bidder. Murdock ritually purchased the first item himself. In this way he demonstrated by his action the deeply held value of caring for students.

The more superficial aspect of this strategy requires good time management, planning (implicit and explicit), and the effective use of scarce personal and organizational time. The more subtle and deeper level involves creating traditions, ceremonies, and rituals that connect clearly to cultural values and involve participants in a positive emotional manner (and that may also uproot and replace negative traditions and dysfunctional beliefs).

Primary and Secondary Strategies and Tactics

The first three strategies define and construct culture by embedding values in the day-to-day action patterns of people in the school. The latter two strategies clarify and reinforce those values but do not usually by themselves construct culture or instill values. Principals build values into the school's culture—or, perhaps more properly, school cultures are constructed of values—only through value-based actions. These actions must involve the actual business of the school: teaching, learning, and administration. This is not to suggest that storytelling and traditions are of little consequence; they can be powerful tools for expanding people's understanding of values and reinforcing the values on which the culture is built. There is, however, a far more important distinction to be made, one involving the tactics used to implement the five strategies.

For each of the approaches described above, we identified two levels of difficulty in applying the strategy to the task of culture building. At one level the difficulty was fairly obvious and, although perhaps not easy to deal with, was unlikely to be a crucial problem. Thus, a principal may have inadequate communication skills for effective storytelling, but such skills can be developed by almost anyone, certainly by someone with the ability to attain the position of school principal. The *real* problem is how to construct a story that gets at a particular value in a way that is both concrete and metaphorical. Doing so is much harder than just telling a story. Constructing a story that interprets the school's history and reinforces certain cultural values is a difficult tactic for school leaders to apply. Similarly, finding time for major ceremonies or minor rituals is an obvious but not crucial problem in using traditions. Effective time management can overcome this obstacle fairly easily. The deeper, more subtle, and far trickier problem involves the value-linked design of such activities.

In summary, for each strategy we found one relatively superficial factor: taking actions that illustrate values, in the case of the modeling strategy; recognizing and confronting conflicts to deal with them, in the case of conflict management; and, finding ways to get like-minded key staff, in the case of value-based staffing. And in each case we identified a much more important, deeper, and more subtle tactical issue: designing one's actions as part of a coherent value-based culture-building strategy; using conflicts to identify and internalize common superordinate values among the parties involved; and developing the skills and methods needed to identify the values of potential staff members and determine whether those values will support or undermine the culture the principal is building. This line of thought, contrasting the two aspects of each strategy, the superficial and the deep, leads to a greater understanding of the nature of leadership.

Levels of Leadership

Firestone and Wilson (1985) make it strikingly clear that school leadership has two essential categories of activity. One set is called "building bureaucratic linkages," which means doing the required administrative chores that keep things running smoothly: filing reports, scheduling meetings, making sure students get on the busses on time (and that the busses are there for them to board), and so on. Firestone and Wilson go on to describe a very different but no less important category of activity they call "building cultural linkages," which is very much what we have been talking about: the creation of strong cultures built on values that link action to excellent outcomes. It has become common to think of the first set of activities as management and the second as leadership. Two of the foremost management and leadership scholars of our time, Peter Drucker and Warren Bennis, have observed, "Managers do things right; leaders do the right things" (Bennis and Nanus, 1985). But it is not quite that simple.

As part of their program of research at the National Center for Research on School Leadership, Martin Maehr and his associates arranged for a group of about fifty principals in the greater Chicago area to participate in what he calls "the beeper study." Each principal agreed to carry a paging device, and the beepers were programmed to go off at random (all at once) during the school day. Each time, every principal was to write down on a card what he or she was doing; at the end of the day this data was to be entered into a logbook and elaborated upon as necessary.

As you might imagine, after a few days of this the principals were close to revolting; but what makes this study so interesting are the specific action vignettes recorded by the researchers. One of the best involved two principals whose actions were compared when the beepers went off at about 3:15 P.M. What are most principals doing at that time? It is a good bet that they are dealing with school busses. One wrote, "3:15—Supervising school bus loading" on his card. Another wrote "3:15—Working with kids to encourage and raise expectations of success as they board the busses."

Could anything be more striking? One was attending to bureaucratic linkages, dealing—effectively, one assumes—with the usual administrative problems of scheduling and loading school busses. The other was also doing this but at the same time and through some of the same behaviors was building cultural linkages, too. The first principal is the sort who might carefully schedule a minimum of 51 percent of his time for "instructional leadership activities." The second is already spending 100 percent of her time as a school leader. We can now see more clearly just why the Illinois law cited at the beginning of this article is off base: Principals should be instructional leaders not 51 percent of the time but 100 percent of the time, *all* the time.

All too many principals spend most or all their time building bureaucratic linkages. They are operating at "level one," or management. Varying from bureaucratic ritual at worst to effective management at best, it is never the sort of leadership needed for effective—let alone excellent— schools. Level one meets the needs of schools that don't exist today, if they ever did. Some call it the "egg crate" theory of school organization—that is, the notion that each class is a wholly independent and autonomous entity and that the only reason classes meet in one building is for economy of scale in heating, hiring, and so forth. Level one management is necessary, but it is not enough. The five strategic issues must be attended to not just in a superficial manner but at a deeper level of action as well.

To the extent that a principal tackles the difficult problems in strategic culture building—the more subtle of the two levels identified— that principal is at "level two," instructional leadership. At this level, one must do the right things—or, at least, many of them—while doing them right. It is a matter of degree; an individual might use one or two of the strategies, doing most things right and some right things as well. Unlike level one management, level two is a form of leadership. It is, however, leadership best suited to a "factory/production line" theory of school organization. In earlier times, this sort of simple linear planning model made sense for schools as well as for factories. It is grossly inadequate for both schools and factories in today's society.

Consider, finally, the principal who does things right, who does the *right* things right, and who expresses and embeds in the school's culture his or her own values and vision. Doing so would almost certainly require use of all five of the culture-building strategies, not just in their superficial first-level aspects but in their more subtle and difficult second-level manner as well. This is just the sort of leadership needed to manage change, deal with the unpredictable, and operate on the basis of real teamwork and collaboration. This is "level three," school leadership. Recall Ray Murdock, who expressed caring for the children while doing cafeteria duty and who, in myriad other ways, exhibited level-three school leadership. Remember Frances Hedges, who created an opportunity for teachers to participate in a ritual that reinforced the importance of student reading achievement. Level-three leadership is appropriate for a *culture-driven* theory of school organization.

One way to think about these three levels of leadership is to imagine that level-one leadership represents the overt textual material of leadership, the concrete fabric of which culture is made. Level two is the "subtext," the messages woven into the fabric. Not always easy to discern, these nonetheless constitute the "stuff" of which meaning is made. Finally, level-three represents the integrative, interpretive analysis that tells us about the larger picture, pulling together the various messages and meanings, helping people to perceive not a crazy quilt but a complete and coherent tapestry.

School Leadership and Culture:
Some Conclusions

Used consistently and fully (that is, in both obvious and subtle manifestations), the five strategies are major tools of school leaders. It is through their skillful application that effective school cultures are built. There is no easy or simple way; in fact, there is still more to the nature and task of leadership than has been described here. We are beginning, through careful observational research, to understand both the nature of successful school leadership and, just as important, how it can be applied. Qualitative analyses such as that of Deal and Peterson are crucial. Through such analyses we can understand in a practical way just how school leaders go about using the behaviors that produce effective school cultures, as assessed in quantitative terms by instruments such as Sashkin's Leader Behavior Questionnaire (see Sashkin and Rosenbach, Chapter 6, as well as Sashkin, 1988b, and Sashkin and Burke, 1990, for details on the LBQ). The next step is to develop better methods for teaching principals how to think about and how to construct school cultures of excellence.

Note

The views expressed here are those of the authors and do not necessarily represent the positions or policies of the Office of Educational Research and Improvement or the U.S. Department of Education.

References

Argyris, C., and Schon, D. A. (1974). *Theory in Practice: Increasing Professional Effectiveness.* San Francisco: Jossey-Bass.

Bennis, Warren, and Nanus, Bert. (1985). *Leaders.* New York: Harper & Row.

Bossert, Steven T. (1985). "Effective Elementary Schools." In R.M.J. Kyle (Ed.), *Reaching for Excellence.* Washington: U. S. Government Printing Office.

Burns, J. M. (1978). *Leadership.* New York: Harper and Row.

Deal, Terrence E. (1987). "The Culture of Schools." In L. T. Sheive and M. B. Schoenheit (Eds.), *Leadership: Examining the Elusive* (1987 Yearbook of the Association for Supervision and Curriculum Development). Arlington, VA: Association for Supervision and Curriculum Development.

Deal, Terrence E., and Alan Kennedy. (1982). *Corporate Cultures.* Reading, MA: Addison-Wesley.

Deal, Terrence E., and Kent D. Peterson. (1990). *The Principal's Role in Shaping School Culture.* Washington: U.S. Government Printing Office.

Dwyer, David C., Ginny V. Lee, Bruce G. Barnett, Nikola N. Filby, and Bryan Rowan. (1984, November). "Frances Hedges and Orchard Park Elementary School: Instructional Leadership in a Stable Urban Setting." San Francisco: Far West Laboratory for Educational Research and Development.

Dwyer, David C., Ginny V. Lee, Bruce G. Barnett, Nikola N. Filby, and Bryan Rowan. (1984, November). "Ray Murdock and Jefferson Elementary School: Instructional Leadership in a Rural Setting." San Francisco: Far West Laboratory for Educational Research and Development.

Edmonds, Ron. (1979). "Some Schools Work and More Can." *Social Policy* 9.

Firestone, William A., and Bruce Wilson. (1985). "Using Bureaucratic and Cultural Linkages to Improve Instruction: The Principal's Contribution." *Educational Administration Quarterly* 21, 17–30.

Maier, Norman R.F. (1963). *Problem-solving Discussions and Conferences.* New York: McGraw-Hill.

McPhee, John. (1966). *The Headmaster.* New York: Farrar, Straus & Giroux.

Purkey, Stuart C., and Marshall S. Smith. (1983). "Effective Schools: A Review." *Elementary School Journal* 83, 427–452.

Sashkin, Marshall. (1987). "Explaining Excellence in Leadership in Light of Parsonian Theory." Paper presented at the annual meeting of the American Educational Research Association, Washington, D.C., April 24.

_____. (1988a). "The Visionary Principal: School Leadership for the Next Century." *Education and Urban Society* 20, 239–249.

_____. (1988b). *The Leader Behavior Questionnaire: The Visionary Leader* (3rd ed.) King of Prussia, PA: Organization Design and Development.

_____. (1989). *Managing Conflict Constructively.* King of Prussia, PA: Organization Design and Development.

Sashkin, Marshall, and W. Warner Burke. (1990). "Understanding and Assessing Organizational Leadership." In Kenneth E. Clark and Miriam B. Clark (Eds.), *Measures of Leadership.* West Orange, NJ: Leadership Library of America.

Schein, Edgar H. (1985). *Organizational Culture and Leadership.* San Francisco: Jossey-Bass.

Sergiovanni, Thomas. (1987). *The Principalship.* Newton, MA: Allyn & Bacon.

Sheive, Linda T., and Marian B. Schoenheit. (1987). *Leadership: Examining the Elusive.* Washington, D.C.: Association for Supervision and Curriculum Development.

Stogdill, Ralph M. (1973). "The Trait Approach to the Study of Educational Leadership." In L. L. Cunningham and W. J. Gephart (Eds.), *Leadership: The Science and the Art Today.* Itasca, IL: Peacock.

Thomas, Kenneth. (1976). "Conflict and Conflict Management." In Marvin D. Dunnette (Ed.), *Handbook of Industrial and Organizational Psychology.* Chicago: Rand McNally.

United States Department of Education. (1987). *Principal Selection Guide.* Washington, D.C.: Government Printing Office.

19

Managing the Dream: Leadership in the 21st Century

WARREN BENNIS

Pick up any business magazine or newspaper and you'll find the same story: pessimism about America's capacity to compete successfully in the new, spirited global economy. *The Wall Street Journal* laments, "The sudden emergence of America as the world's largest debtor, Japan as the globe's richest creditor, and the Soviet Union as its most ardent preacher of pacifism seems, to many Americans, to have turned the world upside down, raising doubts about whether America can or should lead." The *Washington Post* kicks in with "Kiss Number One Goodbye, Folks." A headline in the *International Herald Tribune* warns, "America, Europe Is Coming."

If there is reason to despair and join the handwringing and head shaking of doomsayers, it's because traditional American managers were brought up in a different time, when all they had to do was build the greatest mousetraps, and the world beat a path to their doors. "Leadership in a traditional U.S. company," says R. B. Horton, CEO of BP America, "consisted of creating a management able to cope with competitors who all played with basically the same deck of economic cards." And it was an American game. The competition was fierce but knowable. If you played your cards right, you could win.

But the game has changed and strange new rules have appeared. The deck has been shuffled and jokers have been added. Never before has American business faced so many challenges, and never before have there been so many choices about how to face those challenges. Uncertainties and complexities abound. The only thing truly predictable is unpredictability. The new chic is chaos chic. As Yogi Berra put it, "The future ain't what it used to be."

Constant change disturbs some managers—it always has, and it always will. Machiavelli said, "Change has no constituency." Well, it better have one—and soon. Forget about regaining global leadership. With only a single, short decade remaining before the 21st century, we must look now at what it's going to take simply to remain a player in the game. We can do that because the 21st century is with us now. Cultures don't turn sharply with the pages of the calendar—they evolve. By paying attention to what is changing today, we know what we must do better tomorrow.

Leaders, Not Managers

Given the nature and constancy of change and the transnational challenges facing American business leadership, the key to making the right choices will come from understanding and embodying the leadership qualities necessary to succeed in a mercurial global economy. To survive in the 21st century, we're going to need a new generation of leaders—leaders, not managers.

The distinction is an important one. Leaders conquer the context—the volatile, turbulent, ambiguous surroundings that sometimes seem to conspire against us and will surely suffocate us if we let them—while managers surrender to it. There are other differences, as well, and they are crucial:

- The manager administers; the leader innovates.
- The manager is a copy; the leader is an original.
- The manager maintains; the leader develops.
- The manager focuses on systems and structure; the leader focuses on people.
- The manager relies on control; the leader inspires trust.
- The manager has a short-range view; the leader has a long-range perspective.
- The manager asks how and when; the leader asks what and why.
- The manager has his eye on the bottom line; the leader has his eye on the horizon.
- The manager accepts the status quo; the leader challenges it.
- The manager is the classic good soldier; the leader is his own person.
- The manager does things right; the leader does the right thing.

Field Marshal Sir William Slim led the 14th British Army from 1943 to 1945 in the reconquest of Burma from the Japanese—one of the epic campaigns of World War II. He recognized the distinction between leaders and managers when he said: "Managers are necessary; leaders are essential. ... Leadership is of the spirit, compounded of personality and vision. ... Management is of the mind, more a matter of accurate calculation, statistics, methods, timetables and routine."

I've spent the last 10 years talking with leaders, including Jim Burke at Johnson & Johnson, John Scully at Apple, television producer Norman Lear, and close to 100 other men and women, some famous and some not. In the course of my research, I've learned something about the current crop of leaders and something about the kind of leadership that will be necessary to forge the future. While leaders come in every size, shape and disposition—short, tall, neat, sloppy, young, old, male and female—every leader I talked with shared at least one characteristic: a concern with a guiding purpose, an overarching vision. They were more than goal-directed. As Karl Wallenda said, "Walking the tightwire is living; everything else is waiting."

Leaders have a clear idea of what they want to do—personally and professionally—and the strength to persist in the face of setbacks, even failures. They know where they are going and why. Senator Howard Baker said of President Reagan, whom he served as Chief of Staff, "He knew who he was, what he believed in and where he wanted to go."

Managing the Dream

Many leaders find a metaphor that embodies and implements their vision. For Charles Darwin, the fecund metaphor was a branching tree of evolution on which he could trace the rise and fate of various species. William James viewed mental processes as a stream or river. John Locke focused on the falconer, whose release of a bird symbolized his "own emerging view of the creative process"—that is, the quest for human knowledge.

I think of it this way: *Leaders manage the dream.* All leaders have the capacity to create a compelling vision, one that takes people to a new place, and the ability to translate that vision into reality. Peter Drucker said that the first task of the leader is to define the mission. Max De Pree, former CEO of Herman Miller Inc., the Zeeland, MI, office furniture maker, put it another way in *Leadership Is an Art:* "The first responsibility of a leader is to define reality. The last is to say thank you. In between, the leader is a servant."

Managing the dream can be broken down into five parts. The first part is communicating the vision. Jung said: "A dream that is not understood remains a mere occurrence. Understood, it becomes a living experience."

Jim Burke spends 40 percent of his time communicating the Johnson & Johnson credo. More than 800 managers have attended J&J challenge meetings, where they go through the credo line by line to see what changes need to be made. Over the years some of those changes have been fundamental. But like the U.S. Constitution, the credo itself endures.

The other basic parts of managing the dream are recruiting meticulously, rewarding, retraining and reorganizing. Jan Carlzon, CEO of Scandinavian Air System (SAS), is a leader who embraces all five parts.

Carlzon's vision was to make SAS one of the five or six remaining international carriers by the year 1995. (He thinks that only five or six will be left by that time, and I think he's probably right.) To accomplish this, he developed two goals. The first was to make SAS 1 percent better in 100 different ways than its competitors. The second was to create a market niche.

Carlzon chose the business traveler—rather than college students, travel agent deals or any of a host of other possibilities—because he believed that this would be the most profitable niche. In order to attract business travelers, Carlzon had to make sure that every interaction they had with every SAS employee was rewarding. He had to endow every interaction with purpose, relevance, courtesy and caring. He estimated that there were 63,000 of these interactions each day between SAS employees and current or potential customers. He called these interactions "moments of truth."

Carlzon developed a marvelous cartoon book, *The Little Red Book*, to communicate the new SAS vision to employees. And he set up a corporate college in Copenhagen to train them. Just as important, he has "debureaucratized" the whole organization. The organization chart no longer looks like a pyramid; it looks like a set of circles, a galaxy. In fact, Carlzon's book, which is called *Moments of Truth* in English, is titled *Destroying the Pyramids* in its original Swedish.

One of those circles, one organizational segment, is the Copenhagen–New York route. All the pilots, the navigators, the engineers, the flight attendants, the baggage handlers, the reservations agents—everybody who has anything to do with the Copenhagen–New York route—are involved in a self-managed, autonomous work group with a gain-sharing plan so that they all participate in whatever profits that particular route brings in. There's also a Copenhagen-Frankfurt organizational segment, and so on. The whole corporation is structured in terms of these small, egalitarian groups.

General Electric CEO Jack Welch said: "Yesterday's idea of the boss, who became the boss because he or she knew one more fact than the person working for them, is yesterday's manager. Tomorrow's person leads through a vision, a shared set of values, a shared objective." The single defining quality of leaders is the capacity to create and realize a vision. Yeats said, "In dreams begins responsibility." Vision is a waking dream. For leaders, the responsibility is to transform the vision into reality. By doing so, they transform their dominion, whether an airline, a motion picture, the computer industry or America itself.

Thoreau put it this way: "If one advances confidently in the direction of his dreams, and endeavors to live the life he has imagined, he will meet with a success in common hours. ... If you have built castles in the air, your work need not be lost. It is where they should be. Now put the foundation under them."

The New Global Alliances

Jan Carlzon also illustrates one element that I believe will distinguish the vision of 21st-century leaders from the current model. His is a global vision; he is fully aware of the need for transnational networking and alliances.

Carlzon is not alone. A recent United Research Co./Harris survey of 150 CEOs of *Forbes 500* companies found that they saw the greatest opportunity and challenge for the future in the global market. In the same vein, senior-level managers polled in a Carnegie-Mellon University survey of business school alumni named competing effectively on a global basis as the most difficult management issue for the next decade. Global interdependence is one of six pivotal forces working on the world today. (The others are technology, mergers and acquisitions, deregulation and reregulation, demographics and values, and the environment. Leadership is necessary for coping with each of these forces, but those are subjects for another time.) One of the first things the astute businessperson checks daily now is the yen-dollar ratio. Fifty percent of the property in downtown Los Angeles is owned by the Japanese.

Foreign investment in America—in real estate, finance and business—continues to escalate. But the changes aren't simply on our shores. In 1992, when Europe becomes a true Common Market, it will contain 330 million consumers, compared with 240 million in this country.

American leaders who want to be a part of that new market are planning now. Michael Eisner of Disney has sent Robert Fitzpatrick to France to head up the new EuroDisney project. CalFed, which already has a bank in England, is preparing for the future with plans for banks in Brussels, Barcelona, Paris and Vienna. In Spain, AT&T has spent $220 million for a semiconductor plant, and General Electric has budgeted $1.7 billion for a plastics facility. Ford, Nissan, Sony and Matsushita have opened factories in or near Barcelona in the last two years.

In most cases, however, buying into Europe is prohibitively expensive. The shrewd leaders of the future are recognizing the wisdom of creating alliances with other organizations whose fates are correlated with their own. The Norwegian counterpart of Federal Express—which has 3,500 employees, one of the largest companies in Norway—is setting up a partnership with Federal Express. First Boston has linked up with Credit Suisse, forming FBCS. GE has recently set up a number of joint ventures with GE of Great Britain, meshing four product divisions. Despite the names, the companies hadn't been related. GE had considered buying its British namesake, but ultimately chose alliance rather than acquisition.

Buying in is not the choice of the Europeans themselves: Glaxco, a British pharmaceutical firm, made a deal with Hoffman-LaRoche for the distribution of Zantac, a stomach tranquilizer, and knocked SmithKline Beecham's Tagamet out of the game. Kabi Virtum, a Swedish pharmaceutical company, is looking for a partner in Japan to build a joint laboratory, in exchange for which the Japanese would get help in licensing drugs in Sweden.

And as for Jan Carlzon, when he tried and failed to buy Sabena, a rival airline, he established an alliance instead. SAS also works with an Argentine airline and with Eastern Airlines, sharing gates and connecting routes.

The global strategy is firmly rooted in Carlzon's vision for SAS. All leaders' guiding visions provide clearly marked road maps for their organizations; every member can see which direction the corporation is going. The communication of the vision generates excitement about the trip. The plans for the journey create order out of chaos, instill confidence and trust, and offer criteria for success. The group knows when it has arrived.

The critical factor for success in global joint ventures is a shared vision between the two companies. If you're not sure of your company's vision, how can you tell what the advantages of an alliance would be? You must be certain you have the right map before embarking on the journey. If you think your company's vision lacks definition, here are some questions that may help give it color and dimension:

- What is unique about us?
- What values are true priorities for the next year?
- What would make me professionally commit my mind and heart to this vision over the next five to 10 years?
- What does the world really need that our company can and should provide?
- What do I want our company to accomplish so that I will be committed, aligned and proud of my association with the institution?

Ask yourself those questions today. Your answers will be the fire that heats the forge of your company's future.

20

Leadership

JOHN F. WELCH, JR., & EDWARD E. HOOD, JR.

In our view, leaders, whether on the shop floor or at the tops of our businesses, can be characterized in at least four ways.

The first is one who delivers on commitments—financial or otherwise—and shares the values of our Company. His or her future is an easy call. Onward and upward.

The second type of leader is one who does not meet commitments and does not share our values. Not as pleasant a call, but equally easy.

The third is one who misses commitments but shares the values. He or she usually gets a second chance, preferably in a different environment.

Then there's the fourth type—the most difficult for many of us to deal with. That leader delivers on commitments, makes all the numbers, but doesn't share the values we must have. This is the individual who typically forces performance out of people rather than inspires it: the autocrat, the big shot, the tyrant. Too often all of us have looked the other way—tolerated these "Type 4" managers because "they always deliver"—at least in the short term.

And perhaps this type was more acceptable in easier times, but in an environment where we must have every good idea from every man and woman in the organization, we cannot afford management styles that suppress and intimidate. Whether we can convince and help these managers to change—recognizing how difficult that can be—or part company with them if they cannot—will be the ultimate test of our commitment to the transformation of this Company and will determine the future of the mutual trust and respect we are building. In 1991, we continued to improve our personnel management to achieve much better balance between values and "numbers." That balance will change further in '92 and beyond, because we know that without leaders who "walk the talk," all of our plans, promises and dreams for the future are just that—talk.

Reprinted by permission from the 1991 annual report of General Electric Company.

21

Leadership
in the Future

JOSEPH C. ROST

"Leadership," Chester Barnard wrote in 1948, "has been the subject of an extraordinary amount of dogmatically stated nonsense" (p. 80). If he could say that in 1948, when the leadership literature, if piled together, would amount to only a small hill, what would he say in 1990, when the leadership literature approaches the size of a small mountain?

In one way, I agree with Barnard's assessment. A large number of works on leadership cannot be taken seriously when the authors of those works either do not define what leadership is or provide a definition that does not distinguish leadership from numerous other relationships, or social processes which some human beings use to coordinate, direct, control, and govern other human beings. That assessment includes roughly 450 of the almost 600 books, chapters, and journal articles reviewed in this study. This literature, in essence, sees leadership as being all things to all people, and that view is literally nonsensical, as Barnard said. When leadership is anything anyone wants to say it is, the concept of leadership is meaningless, hence nonsense.

A different assessment is, perhaps, necessary for approximately 150 of the works reviewed for this study. In these books, chapters, and journal articles, which are about one-fourth of the total number of works, the authors struggled with a definition of leadership, and they were more or less successful in trying to understand the phenomena they called leadership. They tried to put boundaries around the phenomena of leadership, but they were only partially successful. Many of these scholars established that leadership relationships are substantially different from other human relationships, but they were hard pressed to articulate that difference clearly. Many of these scholars understood leadership as an influence process that human beings use to give direction to their organizational and societal lives, but only a few of them were able to consistently explain how and why the leadership process is distinct from other processes that human beings use to order their existence.

In the end, many commentators, including myself, have roundly criticized these scholars for not coming to grips with the nature of leadership in order to develop a school of leadership that clearly and consistently articulates an understanding of what leadership is. Instead, these authors have tended to confuse their readers with contradictory conceptual frameworks, their theories and models have not added up to any meaningful conclusion about the nature of leadership, and they have been accused of emphasizing the peripheral elements of leadership: traits, styles, preferred behaviors, contingencies and situations, and effectiveness. In other words, though practitioners read the leadership definitions of these scholars and study their models of leadership, they find it almost impossible to integrate and synthesize a clear, consistent picture of what leadership is and how leaders and followers actually engage in leadership. They find only contradictory and confusing understandings of the nature of leadership and almost no explanation of how leaders and followers really do leadership.

At a deeper level of analysis, however, I have suggested that what does not make sense when a first-cut analysis is done may make sense when a second or third cut penetrates the background assumptions embedded in the definitions and looks behind the words in the theories and models. When that kind of analysis is done, a consistent picture of the nature of leadership appears and begins to make sense. In short, the picture paints what should have been obvious all along: Leadership is good management. In a more detailed, bigger picture, the painted surface reveals this: Leadership is great men and women with certain preferred traits influencing followers to do what the leaders wish in order to achieve group/organizational goals that reflect excellence defined as some kind of higher-level effectiveness.

This understanding of leadership, I have argued, is pervasive in the leadership literature, both the serious works and those which could be evaluated as nonsense. And it permeates the works in all of the major academic disciplines that address the subject of leadership. This understanding is what I have called the industrial leadership paradigm. It is industrial because it accepts almost all of the major characteristics of the industrial paradigm: (1) a structural-functionalist view of organizations, (2) a view of management as the preeminent profession, (3) a personalistic focus on the leader, (4) a dominant objective of goal achievement, (5) a self-interested and individualistic outlook, (6) a male model of life, (7) a utilitarian and materialistic ethical perspective, and (8) a rational, techno-cratic, linear, quantitative, and scientific language and methodology.

The problem with the industrial leadership paradigm is that it increas-ingly ill serves the needs of a world rapidly being transformed by a mas-sive paradigm shift in societal values. There is more and more evidence to conclude that the industrial paradigm is losing its hold on the culture of Western societies (and perhaps all societies in the world—but that is an-other issue) and that some kind of postindustrial paradigm will dominate these societies in the twenty-first century. In this view of paradigmatic change, the 1980s and 1990s are seen as a transition period wherein the dominant values and cultural norms shift from an industrial to a postin-dustrial frame. While no one knows with certainty when the postindus-trial paradigm will achieve dominance, many analysts assume it will be sometime in the early twenty-first century. No one knows with certainty, either, what values will form the core of the postindustrial paradigm; but if the shift is going to have any significance of note, the values will have to be quite different from, and even opposed to, the core values of the indus-trial paradigm. In trying to develop a way out of the problems that the in-dustrial era has produced in the world, many commentators have pointed to the importance of such values as collaboration, common good, global concern, diversity and pluralism in structures and participation, client ori-entation, civic virtues, freedom of expression in all organizations, critical dialogue, qualitative language and methodologies, substantive justice, and consensus-oriented policy-making process.

If these values and others like them are going to achieve dominance in the future, they must be embedded in a new understanding of what lead-ership is, in a postindustrial school of leadership. Such a school of leader-ship is not possible without a paradigm shift in leadership studies as an academic discipline, in the definition of leadership, in the theories and models that flow from a new definition of leadership, and in the practice of leadership in our organizations and societies. While Burns made a seri-ous attempt in 1978 to initiate such a paradigm shift in the nature and practice of leadership and to begin to construct a new school of leadership, the overwhelming evidence indicates that, contrary to early, more opti-mistic assessments, not much has changed in leadership studies. The in-dustrial paradigm of leadership continues to dominate the study and practice of leadership as we begin the 1990s. This important work remains ahead of us.

I think it is time to attack the problem head-on. Building on what Burns accomplished but differing in significant ways from his conceptual frame-work, I shall present a definition of leadership that does not accept the values of the industrial paradigm. Rather, the predicted values of the postindustrial paradigm are built into the definition of leadership, and in developing such a definition, I have deliberately set out to construct a postindustrial school of leadership. Such a school is crucial to the development of leadership theory and practice and to the transition from an industrial to a postindustrial society. By its very nature, leadership understood as intending change should be one of the primary social processes that people use to make paradigmatic changes. On the contrary and by its very nature, leadership understood as good management would be one of the primary social processes people use to maintain the old order, the industrial paradigm. Thus, only a new paradigm of leadership will help the people in the Western world transform their societies according to postindustrial frames.

I do not want to be misunderstood. I am not suggesting that a new postindustrial paradigm of leadership will save the world or Western societies, or will solve the problems left over from the industrial era—pollution, population explosion, poverty and hunger, warming of the atmosphere, atomic destruction, garbage, self-interested politics, greed, individualism, racial injustice, expressive therapeutic life-styles, economic inequities, and so on. The larger, societal paradigm shift to a postindustrial era will be an effort to resolve some of those issues by coming to grips with many of the problems that the industrial era was unwilling and unable to solve. A new paradigm of leadership is not the solution to those problems. Rather, a postindustrial school of leadership will help people change the dominant paradigm governing their society, thereby empowering them to transform their society and, one hopes, solve some of these outstanding problems. There are no guarantees that any of this paradigmatic change will be successful. We are not sure that the postindustrial era will be any better than the industrial era. All we know with certainty is that the industrial paradigm has not had a very good record in solving certain intractable problems that stem from the industrial era. Thus many people say, "Let's give a new paradigm a chance." The new paradigm of leadership might help make that chance work.

The Study and Practice
of Leadership in the Future

Leadership studies as an academic discipline needs to come out of the woodwork of management science in all of its guises (business, education, health, public, nonprofit) and out of such disciplines as social psychology, political science, and sociology wherein academics have developed an interest in leadership as a subspecialty. Leadership scholars need to develop an academic presence as an interdisciplinary area of studies serving both undergraduate and graduate students in specialized programs that deal with the study and practice of leadership in organizations and in societies.

Looking at leadership through the lens of a single discipline has not worked well in the past, and it 'will not work any better in the future. Indeed, a case could be made that organizations and societies in the future, with their collaborative, community, and global orientations, may not be hospitable to a concept of leadership that is grounded in only one academic discipline.

Universities are institutions that have been molded and shaped by the industrial paradigm. They have not been particularly hospitable to professors and students engaging in interdisciplinary programs of study; thus the recommendation given above may be difficult to operationalize. Universities themselves may have to go through their own paradigm shift in order to promote and develop such programs and make them work successfully.

In the meantime there are some prototypes that can serve as models. There are multidisciplinary leadership programs (some may actually be interdisciplinary) at perhaps fifty colleges and universities serving undergraduate and graduate students who major and minor in leadership studies or take graduate degrees in leadership. I expect that these programs will increase in size and number in the 1990s. Most of these programs, I suspect, are wedded to the industrial paradigm of leadership as good management, but many of them will be transformed and move to a postindustrial concept of leadership in the near future. Some of these programs have established centers on leadership to reach out into the community. Several business persons have recently endowed centers, and it will be interesting to see what impact these centers will have on the study and practice of leadership.

Leadership scholars in the future are going to have to think new thoughts about leadership, using postindustrial assumptions about human beings, organizations, societies, and the planet Earth. With that kind of thinking, scholars must settle on a definition of leadership, conduct research based on that definition, and construct new theories and models of leadership that will address the wants and needs of the people in a postindustrial society. With that kind of thinking, leadership scholars must experiment with different research designs and methodologies. They must invent new research strategies that enable them to explain what leadership is and how it operates at all levels of organizations and societies.

With this new kind of thinking, leadership scholars must develop a new school of leadership that is grounded in what is real, what actually happens when leaders and followers do engage in leadership. With this new kind of thinking, leadership scholars must critically analyze one another's theories and models and engage in dialogic conversations about those conceptual frameworks. Leadership studies would be vastly improved with a large dose of critical thought and methodology.

As evidence of this kind of new thinking, I can point to several dissertations by leadership doctoral candidates at the University of San Diego. Shay Sayre (1986) studied a nonmale model of leadership that transformed a business organization. Kevin Freiberg (1987) did a study of transformational leadership in an airline corporation. Alex Kodiath (1987) researched the commonalities and differences of male and female spiritual leaders. Rita King (1988) researched how mentor teachers changed schools and a school district by working from the bottom up and using a collaborative notion of leadership. Stuart Grauer (1989) developed an interactive model of leadership in studying educators' attempts to internationalize schools. Richard Henrickson (1989) developed a cultural model of leadership from his studies of anthropology. James Kelly, Jr., (1989) did a historical study of leadership in the transformation of a mature organization. Bertha Pendleton (1989) investigated the impact of leadership among various members of a Schools of the Future Commission in a large, urban school district. Kathleen Allen (1990) interviewed alternative (nonstandard) types of reputed leaders to see if they voiced different models of leadership. Dallas Boggs (1990) studied several literary classics in each of four eras in an effort to understand how leadership was understood in those eras. Robert Fink (1990) completed a study of a national professional association using an interactive model of transformational leadership. James Ford (1990) researched nonordained pastors and religious education coordinators in the Roman Catholic Church and analyzed their concepts of leadership according to a postindustrial model of leadership. Rita Marinoble (1990) studied the connection between spirituality and leadership. And there are more exciting research projects in the works for 1991 and 1992.

While not all these research projects were entirely successful, they were all serious attempts to study leadership from a postindustrial perspective and had a clearly articulated definition of leadership at work in the analysis. Some of the studies were exploratory in design and methodology; most of them were exploratory in the leadership they described and in the conclusions they developed. These authors were not afraid of studying leadership from the perspective of alternative frameworks because they did not see the traditional framework as providing answers to the fundamental questions they wanted to ask about leadership. When hundreds of people all over the country complete research studies such as these, we will begin to get some answers about the nature of leadership and how leaders and followers do leadership in organizations and societies.

But scholars cannot do it alone. In fact, what it means to be a scholar may change radically in the postindustrial paradigm. Scholars may include training and development experts who translate theories into action through professional development and practitioners who put new theories of leadership to work and then reflect critically on those experiences. Leadership studies as an academic discipline needs both of these types of scholars as well as academics based in universities and think tanks.

How do we translate a new paradigm of leadership to leaders and followers who are actually engaged in leadership? Centers on leadership are one obvious way, but such centers have not been particularly good at doing that in the past. Most, if not all, of these centers are solidly entrenched in the industrial paradigm of leadership. Consultants, training and development specialists, professional development packages, and electronic media software are other methods that have been used to inculcate newer aspects of the old paradigm with some success. But these vehicles would themselves have to be transformed before they could begin to translate a new paradigm of leadership so that others could use it. Indeed, vast numbers of people throughout our society, including many professional people in our organizations, would have to rethink their commitment to professional development and take it more seriously.

While consultants, trainers, packagers, and software designers who are dedicated to the application of postindustrial leadership models will be of enormous help in achieving some praxis of leadership theory and practice, it is becoming more apparent that leaders and followers in the future will need new and different relationships with these translations experts. The usual short-term consulting contracts, inservice workshops, convention speeches, one-day seminars, simulations, and organizational development tricks of the trade will not do the job.

These specialists may, first of all, have to see themselves as scholars who are doing grounded research on the nature and practice of leadership in organizations, and they should view their scholarship as being as important as that done by academics in universities and think tanks. They may have to see their relationships with clients as leadership relationships wherein they and the clients influence one another concerning intended real changes that reflect their mutual purposes. They may have to develop long-term contracts that allow for the possibility of transformation rather than incremental change. They may have to insist on week-long professional development sessions and follow-up peer coaching or collaborative mentoring strategies. They may have to create computer simulations that teach consensus policy-making processes and interactive decision-making strategies among diverse populations. If not by computer simulations, they will somehow have to learn, and then teach others, how to build consensus from diverse points of view without compromising end-values. They may have to model the kinds of influence behaviors that the postindustrial leadership paradigm calls for and engage in the kind of critical, honest, dialectical analysis that the new leadership models require of leaders and followers. They may have to create a new moral language that will help leaders and followers to practice civic virtues rather than self-interest politics, that will help them serve the common good rather than individualistic goods, that will help them move to substantive justice instead of being satisfied with procedural justice.

Practitioners are also going to have to think new thoughts if leadership studies is going to be taken seriously in the future. My guess is that practitioners are going to have to become leadership scholars as well. I don't mean the kind of scholars who conduct formal research on leadership and publish the results in books and journal articles, although that is possible in some instances. There are practitioners who do that now. Rather, these practitioners are going to have to be the kind of scholars who do critical thinking as they do leadership.

The kind of scholars I have in mind are those thinking women and men who understand that leadership is more complex than the mythology of leadership would have us believe. They are those thinking men and women who will surely be dissatisfied with one-minute leadership, quick and simple leadership models that can be mastered in a three-hour seminar, slick presentations on leadership at conventions, and the kind of nonsense that pervades the leadership literature from about 1930 up to and including 1990. These scholars know that such minimalist efforts will not give them what they need to know about the new paradigm of leadership to meet the wants and needs of the people, organizations, and societies of the twenty-first century.

These scholars are reflective practitioners (Schon, 1984), thinking women and men who reflect on their reflections-in-actions (the more or less automatic actions that result from countless previous experiences upon which they have reflected). They do research about leadership in context, leadership in this organization, this community, this society. They see themselves as doing action research because they are at the center of where the action is, because they are involved in the paradigm shift, because they are agents of transformational change. They understand that there are quite literally no other people who have the perspective on leadership that they have because they are the ones who have been doing postindustrial leadership.

These practitioners think of themselves as educators, scholars who have the expertise to help other women and men understand what leadership is all about and inform their practice of leadership in their organizations and societies. In this sense, these thinking men and women share their leadership expertise in order to generate other leaders and followers who have a deep understanding of postindustrial leadership and the practical experience to put that understanding to work.

In the end, leadership studies as an academic discipline would be significantly improved if practitioners, translation specialists, and academic scholars would collaborate in research projects on postindustrial leadership. In fact, such collaborative efforts may be the only way to find out and document how leadership actually occurs in organizations and societies. With that kind of documentation, leadership scholars would have a much better chance of developing grounded conceptual frameworks that make sense and inform the practice of leadership in the future.

References

Allen, K. E. (1990). *Leadership in a different voice: Different rhythms and emerging harmonies.* Doctoral dissertation, University of San Diego.

Barnard, C. I. (1948). *Organizations and management.* Cambridge, MA: Harvard University Press.

Boggs, D. B. (1990). *Literary perceptions of leadership.* Doctoral dissertation, University of San Diego.

Burns, J. M. (1978). *Leadership.* New York: Harper & Row.

Fink, R. A. (1990). *Vision: An essential component of transformational leadership.* Doctoral dissertation, University of San Diego.

Ford, J. F. (1990). *Education for Christian leadership.* Doctoral dissertation, University of San Diego.

Freiberg, K. L. (1987). *The heart and spirit of transformational leadership: A qualitative case study of Herb Kelleher's passion for Southwest Airlines.* Doctoral dissertation, University of San Diego.

Grauer, S. R. (1989). *Think globally, act locally: A Dephi study of educational leadership through the development of international resources in the local community.* Doctoral dissertation, University of San Diego.

Henrickson, R. L. (1989). *Leadership and culture.* Doctoral dissertation, University of San Diego.

Kelly, J. F., Jr. (1989). *The transformation of a corporate culture in a mature organization.* Doctoral dissertation, University of San Diego.

King, R. M. (1988). *A study of shared instructional leadership by mentor teachers in Southern California.* Doctoral dissertation, University of San Diego.

Kodiath, A. (1987). *A study of the commonalities and differences of male and female spiritual leaders.* Doctoral dissertation, University of San Diego.

Marinoble, R. M. (1990). *Faith and leadership: The spiritual journeys of transformational leaders.* Doctoral dissertation, University of San Diego.

Sayre, S. (1986). *Leadership communication and organizational culture: A field study.* Doctoral dissertation, University of San Diego.

Schon, D. A. (1984). Leadership as reflection in action. In T. J. Sergiovanni & J. E. Corbally (Eds.), *Leadership and organizational culture* (pp. 36–63). Urbana: University of Illinois Press.

About the Book

Leadership—and leadership studies—are in flux. This new edition of *Contemporary Issues in Leadership* speaks directly to the central points of change: leadership versus management; leadership and followership; and especially, the diversity of leadership styles and pathways. Tapping the wisdom of more than fifteen new readings, Rosenbach and Taylor present a renewed framework for understanding leaders and leadership from a contemporary perspective. Opportunity, vision, empowerment, action, values, and timing are essential ingredients in the new paradigm of leadership outlined here.

About the Editors
and Contributors

Editors

William E. Rosenbach is the Evans Professor of Eisenhower Leadership Studies in the Department of Management at Gettysburg College. Formerly professor and head of the Department of Behavioral Sciences and Leadership at the U.S. Air Force Academy, he is the author or coauthor of numerous articles and books on leadership topics. He is especially interested in leadership development of young men and women and is an active consultant to organizations in North America, Europe, and Australia on executive leadership development.

Robert L. Taylor is dean of the College of Business and Public Administration and professor of management at the University of Louisville. He also served as the Carl N. Jacobs Professor of Business at the University of Wisconsin–Stevens Point and professor and head of the Department of Management at the USAF Academy. A speaker, consultant, researcher, and writer, his interest in leadership spans more than twenty years.

Contributors

Warren Bennis is the Joseph DeBell Professor of Management at the University of Southern California. Formerly he held professorships at MIT's Sloan School of Management and Harvard and was president of the University of Cincinnati. His books include *The Unconscious Conspiracy: Why Leaders Can't Lead, Leaders, On Becoming a Leader,* and *Why Leaders Can't Lead: The Unconscious Conspiracy Continues.*

Thomas E. Cronin is president of Whitman College. Formerly he was McHugh Professor of American Institutions and Leadership at The Colorado College. He is the author, editor, or coauthor of numerous publications, including *The State of the Presidency, The Government by the People,* and *Direct Democracy: The Politics of Initiative, Referendum and Recall.* He is working on a book about leadership theories and strategies.

Ronald V. Dellums has served as a member of the U.S. Congress from the eighth congressional district of California since 1970. He is described as bringing dignity and devotion to duty to his work on congressional subcommittees.

Max De Pree is chairman of the board of Herman Miller, Inc., the primary innovator in the furniture business for sixty years and regularly included among the top twenty-five firms on *Fortune*'s list of the most admired companies in the United States. He is the author of the bestseller *Leadership Is an Art.* Max De Pree was recently elected by *Fortune* magazine to the National Business Hall of Fame.

John W. Gardner has served six presidents of the United States in various leadership capacities. He was secretary of Health, Education and Welfare, chairman of the National Coalition, founding chairman of Common Cause, cofounder of Independent Sector, and president of the Carnegie Corporation and the Carnegie Foundation for the Advancement of Teaching. He has served as director of several major U.S. corporations. The author of *Excellence, Self-Renewal,* and *On Leadership,* he is currently Miriam and Peter Haas Centennial Professor at Stanford Business School.

Malcolm Gladwell is a 1984 graduate of Trinity College, University of Toronto, Canada. He has worked for the *Washington Post* since 1987, first as a business reporter, then as a science writer, and now as the New York Bureau chief.

Edwin P. Hollander is University Distinguished Professor of Psychology in the CUNY Industrial Organizational Psychology Doctoral Subprogram at Baruch College and the University Graduate Center. He is the author of *Leaders, Groups, and Influence; Leadership Dynamics;* and *Principles and Methods of Social Psychology.*

Edward E. Hood, Jr., is vice chairman of the board and executive officer of General Electric Company.

Robert Kelley is an adjunct professor of business at the Graduate School of Industrial Management at Carnegie Mellon University in Pittsburgh. He is the author of *The Gold Collar Worker* and *The Power of Followership.*

W. Chan Kim is associate professor of strategy and international management at the European Institute of Business Administration (INSEAD), Fontainebleau, France.

John P. Kotter is professor of organizational behavior at the Harvard Business School and the author of *The General Managers, Power and Influence, The Leadership Factor,* and *A Force for Change: How Leadership Differs from Management.*

James M. Kouzes is president of TPG/Learning Systems, a company in the Tom Peters Group, and former director of the Executive Development Center at Santa Clara University. He is coauthor of *The Leadership Challenge.*

Chris Lee has been the managing editor of *Training* magazine since 1984. Her experience includes training director for a university newspaper, high school English teacher, freelance writer, and managing editor for a construction industry magazine.

Manning Marable is professor of political science and history and an adjunct professor of sociology at the University of Colorado–Boulder. He is affiliated with the Center for Studies of Ethnicity and Race in America and is also cochair of the Critical Studies of the Americas Committee.

Renée A. Mauborgne is research associate of management and international business at The European Institute of Business Administration (INSEAD), Fontainebleau, France.

Ann M. Morrison is president of New Leaders Institute and former director of research on leadership diversity at the Center for Creative Research, La Jolla, California. Her books include *Breaking the Glass Ceiling: Can Women Reach the Top of America's Largest Corporations, The Lessons of Experience: How Successful Executives Develop on the Job,* and *The New Leaders.*

Lynn R. Offermann is an associate professor of psychology at George Washington University.

Barry Z. Posner is professor of management and former director of graduate education and customer service, Leavey School of Business and Administration, Santa Clara University. He is the coauthor of *The Leadership Challenge* and author of numerous articles on leadership.

Joseph C. Rost is professor of leadership and administration in the School of Education at the University of San Diego, where he assisted in inaugurating a doctoral program in leadership and a leadership minor for undergraduate students. He is the author of *Leadership for the 21st Century.*

Marshall Sashkin holds a doctorate in organizational psychology from the University of Michigan and teaches as adjunct professor at George Washington University. For several years his primary assignment has been in the U.S. Department of Education's Office of Educational Research and Improvement, where he developed and guided applied research aimed at improving leadership and organization in schools. More than fifty of his research papers on leadership, participation, and organizational change have been published in academic journals, and he is the author or coauthor of more than a dozen books. His most recent book is *Putting Total Quality Management to Work* (with Kenneth Kiser).

Molly Goltman Sashkin holds two master's degrees, the first in secondary education and the second in guidance and personnel services. She has teaching experience at every level of the educational system, from preschool through elementary, secondary, and college levels. She is a partner in Marshall Sashkin & Associates, a management and organizational consulting firm, where she is responsible for the development, publication, and distribution of materials for management and organizational development.

John F. Welch, Jr., is chairman of the board and chief executive officer of General Electric Company.

Abraham Zaleznik is the Konosuke Matsushita Professor of Leadership Emeritus at the Harvard Business School. He is the author of numerous articles and fourteen books, including *The Managerial Mystique: Restoring Leadership in Business* and *Learning Leadership.*